Fine Margins

HOW ECONOMICS EXPLAINS SPORTS BETTING

Karl Whelan

Contents

ISBN: 978-1-0676213-1-5

Edition Note: This is the International edition of the book. A separate US edition is also available.

To Martina, for her love, encouragement, patience and understanding.

Introduction

You're interested in sports betting. You want to know more about how it really works: how bookmakers set odds, which types of bets tend to be badly priced, whether it's worth trying a betting exchange instead of bookmakers. Why on earth would you read a book by an economics professor?

Here's why. Bookmakers are firms. And firms set prices to maximise profits. That's economics. People are more likely to accept a bet if the odds are higher. That's also economics. And bookmakers use the logic of economics when designing their products. Economics is the perfect tool to understand the world of betting. Think of it as a pair of X-ray specs – once you've put them on, you can't unsee how betting markets really work.

Why *Fine Margins*? Every odds quote from a bookmaker combines two things: its assessment of a bet's chance of winning and a built-in profit margin. The lower the chance of winning, the higher the odds you will get. The higher the built-in profit margin, the less generous the odds will be.

This means that if you want to do better at betting, there are two things you can focus on. Get better at figuring out when the bookmaker's probabilities are wrong. And get better at avoiding bets where the bookmaker has a high built-in profit margin (fine for them, not for you). Economics doesn't have much to teach you about the first one – economists aren't any better at picking winners. But it can teach you plenty about the second one: how profit margins are built into the odds, and where they're highest.

Importantly, this book is not just an academic view of betting. Much of the research underlying it was done in collaboration with someone who has spent many years working as a bookmaker. Over the past few years, we've built comprehensive datasets on modern betting markets: millions of individual odds and results from bookmakers and exchanges across many sports and seasons. This means the book can show you patterns that bookmakers would prefer you didn't see – from where margins are highest to how odds deteriorate once play starts, from the big losses on special bets like whether an NFL player will score a touchdown to the horrendous average returns from betting on late in-play longshots.

Most of this evidence has either only appeared in scattered academic articles or has never been published at all. This book is the first to pull it all together to provide a level of transparency that hasn't been available before about how bookmakers price bets.

The Professor and the Bookmaker

I'm an economics professor at University College Dublin (UCD). I got my PhD from MIT and spent eleven years working in central banks, first at the Federal Reserve Board in Washington DC and then at the Central Bank of Ireland, before becoming a professor in 2007. My research has generally focused on macroeconomics: I've published over fifty peer-reviewed journal articles and spent fifteen years advising the European Parliament on monetary policy.

But I'm also a lifelong sports fan, spending far too much time following Liverpool, Leinster, the Boston Red Sox and the multi-Super-Bowl-winning New England Patriots (sorry, not sorry). That mix of economics and sport is how I ended up thinking seriously about betting markets.

One of our PhD students at UCD was Tadgh Hegarty (pronounced like Tiger without the er). He has a degree in physics and years of experience working as a bookmaker. We began working together on a sports-related project and I started asking him how sports betting really worked. How do bookmakers actually set odds? What is an overround? What the hell is the Asian Handicap? That kind of thing. Tadgh has now earned his PhD and I am grateful to him for teaching me so much about the business.

The result has been a series of research projects, some with Tadgh and some on my own. So far, I've published 13 peer-reviewed papers on betting markets, with others in the pipeline. The more I worked on this topic, the more I kept asking "is there a book that explains it all?" Well, four years later, this is that book: an economist's take on sports betting, informed by someone who has been on the bookmaker's side of the business.

Three Ideas from Economics

This book uses a few simple ideas from economics — and tests them against large datasets of real odds and results — to show what bookmakers are actually doing and the implications this has for bettors.

1. Normal Economics in an Unusual Setting

The first idea is that standard economic principles apply to betting markets just as they do to any other market. Previous research by economists often treated bettors as risk chasers with strange preferences. But once you look at the data, bettors largely behave like price-sensitive customers who back the side they think offers better value. Bookmakers, in turn, behave like any profit-maximising firm: they vary margins across different products and push the bets that make them the most money. Once you apply this standard economic lens, a lot of familiar myths start to fall away — including the idea that bookmakers focus on eliminating risk by balancing their books.

2. Differences in Beliefs Drive Betting Markets

The second idea is that betting markets are driven by people having differing beliefs about probabilities. Two sensible people can look at the same match and genuinely differ about how likely each outcome is. If they sat down to discuss it, they'd probably just agree to disagree. This is the reason betting exists. We will see how bookmakers integrate this disagreement into their pricing, and I'll explain how to spot its impact on the odds.

If differing beliefs is what drives betting, it raises two interesting questions. Do the resulting odds reflect the average view of the crowd? And do they converge on the "true" probabilities? The answer to both questions is typically No. Betting markets don't automatically aggregate beliefs in the tidy "wisdom of crowds" way people imagine.

The mechanisms matter: whether the bet is placed with a bookmaker, at the track, or on an exchange, changes how the public's beliefs translate into odds. So even if bettors are on average reasonably well informed, the odds can still be systematically distorted - and recognising those distortions is key to understanding betting markets.

3. Complexity and the Limits to Rationality

The third idea is that rational decision-making has its limits, and those limits become most important when betting becomes fast or complex. Behavioural economists have uncovered a long list of ways people can go wrong when taking decisions — misjudging small probabilities, using "mental accounting", making poorly-informed snap judgements — and these aren't just academic curiosities. They have a considerable influence on how the odds are set.

Bookmakers understand where decision-making is hardest, and they adjust products and margins accordingly. In particular, once a game goes in-play, prices typically deteriorate and some late-game bets deliver terrible returns. I will show where margins are largest, how they change over time, and what that means for how different kinds of bets perform.

Will This Book Help You Make Money?

Short answer: No, this book won't make you rich.
Longer answer: It will help you understand how betting markets work - and how to bet in a way that at least gives you a fighting chance.

Let's start putting the ideas of economics to work. Economists argue that people generally act in their own self-interest. If I had a magic recipe for winning bets, would I be sharing it with everyone in a book? It's more likely I'd be relaxing in my villa in the south of France than writing this from rainy Dublin.

So don't expect sure-fire tips for making money. But we will explain how not all sports bets are made equal: some types of bets have much higher profit margins for bookmakers than others. Bookmakers have strategies to part you with your money - you need to understand them if any betting strategy of your own is going to work. Success in betting, like sports, can be a matter of fine margins and small adjustments can make a big difference to your performance over time.

In practice, the biggest improvement most people can get is simply learning where the hidden "taxes" of high margins on bettors are applied. I will show you plenty of these, perhaps annoying a few bookmakers along the way. And sometimes they even hand out little gifts such as free bets or boosted odds. I'll show you the best way to turn these into small amounts of guaranteed profit – and why you really don't need to pay subscription services to do it.

Beyond that, making money in sports betting also requires having an edge of some sort in predicting outcomes. Getting that edge is hard and I won't have much to say about it but a good way to maximise any edge you might have is to take positions where, even without an edge, you wouldn't lose much on average. This requires avoiding the most popular ways of betting.

Some bettors do consistently have an edge, usually based on running complex statistical models to identify value in the odds. We are not going to cover those models, but I can tell you that these bettors typically place bets in very specific ways. For example, they tend to place Asian Handicap bets on football with "sharp" bookmakers like Pinnacle. Not sure what that's all about? Then read on.

A Roadmap

Part I covers the history of sports betting, from the industry's early years to how the internet turned bookmakers from corner shop operations into data-driven technology firms. It also shows how economics explains the structure of global betting markets today.

Part II builds the essential toolkit: going from odds to how often you need to win to break even, calculating margins and understanding why accumulator bets multiply bookmaker profits far beyond what most bettors realise.

Part III introduces our core framework: betting markets are driven by people differing in their beliefs about probabilities. It shows this simple assumption solves a decades-old puzzle about horse racing odds that stumped economists for years.

Part IV reveals how bookmakers operate. Contrary to a popular myth, they don't set odds to balance their books. They set them to maximise profits. We describe how typical bettors maintain only two bookmaker accounts, giving operators far more pricing power than you might imagine. Crucially, we see how this allows bookmakers to vary their pricing in ways that make some bets systematically worse than others.

Part V assesses these ideas using data. Lots of data. Millions of historical quotes from bookmakers. In fact, combined together, this is the most comprehensive collection of data ever publicly analysed on how bookmakers set odds and the outcomes from placing bets with them. There are many interesting findings. Betting on favourites in the Premier League costs you about 4% on average; betting on longshots costs you 15%. We see why draws are decent bets in balanced matches but terrible ones in mismatches, analyse the Asian Handicap market that is dominated by sharp money, debunk the academic literature on insider trading and corruption, and document how margins rise systematically as the number of competitors increases.

Part VI examines the products bookmakers push hardest. Bettors lose about 30% on average placing bets like whether a player will score a Premier League goal or an NFL touchdown. We show you how bookmakers exploit biases in beliefs and people's willingness to back a favoured team or player. For NFL rushing player prop bets, "over" loses 11%, "under" loses 1%. Official US state data shows that accumulators and multi-leg "bet builders" which combine different specials together, have profit margins for bookmakers four times higher than regular bets. We also discuss the best strategies for using free bets and odds boosts and why bookmakers offer these promotions.

Part VII documents in-play betting, showing how the odds get about 1.5% worse as soon as the match starts and how late-game NBA longshots deliver 95% average losses – possibly the worst returns in all of sports betting. We show why taking cash-out offers reduces your returns despite feeling like sensible risk management.

Part VIII explains betting exchanges and presents evidence from

200,000 football matches showing the average odds on exchanges predict outcomes with near-perfect accuracy. We show that some strategies on exchanges do better than others – making offers gives higher payoffs than accepting them and you are much better off to be on the other side of late-game longshot bets.

Part IX addresses where edges in betting come from and why they're elusive. It covers optimal bet sizing for the rare bettor with a genuine edge and explains why you shouldn't bet on accumulators even when you have an edge on each of the component legs.

Part X discusses policy issues, such as how betting should be taxed and regulated, and offers final advice for bettors.

I should also note that I have never done any paid or unpaid work for bookmakers, betting platforms, prediction markets, gambling companies or anti-gambling organisations.

I. A Brief History of Sports Betting

I'm not a historian but there's plenty to learn about the economics of sports betting from its backstory. Here, we'll look at how betting on sports has evolved, constantly changing to adapt to the times: outlawed by Roman emperors, hijacked by mobsters, and then supercharged by the internet. That journey – from smoke-filled backrooms to global platforms taking orders from millions of smartphones – sets the stage for the economics that follows.

Chapter 1

Sports Betting Before the Internet

An Ancient Pastime

Before there were bookmakers or even organised sports, people gambled on games of chance with dice. The earliest known dice – simple knucklebones carved into cubes – date from Mesopotamia around 3000 BC.

Today, many still play games of chance like this, gambling at casinos, risking money on games that are openly designed for the house to win. I must admit that I don't get the appeal. Sure, you might win this time but play long enough and you will definitely lose. In contrast, betting on sports feels different. Unlike roulette or slot machines, which involve no skill, betting on sports requires assessing the relative merits of the various options and deciding whether it makes sense to take bets at the odds offered. This sense that you might turn a profit via skill rather than random chance perhaps explains why betting on sports has always been so popular.

The evidence shows people were betting on organised sports from the very beginning. The ancient Greeks were holding Olympic Games from 776 BC, and where there were games, there were gamblers. In Rome, chariot races thundered around the Circus Maximus and gladiators fought in the Colosseum while, away from the spectacle, huge sums were exchanged on the outcomes.

Some of the problems that have plagued sports betting over the years could already be seen in ancient times. The boxer Eupolus of

Thessaly was caught paying off opponents to throw Olympic bouts in 388 BC. Roman emperor, Augustus Caesar (63 BC – 14 AD), reportedly a heavy gambler himself, worried that excessive gambling was leading to moral decay and tried to restrict it to the week-long Saturnalia festival. Needless to say, Romans (including Augustus) kept gambling. Betting scandals and half-hearted regulation go back as far as betting itself. One lesson from economics that Augustus might have taken to heart is that it's often easier to announce regulations than to enforce them.

The Sport of Kings (and Fraudsters)

For most of the past few centuries, betting on sport largely meant betting on horses. The first racecourse opened in Chester in 1539 and the first track in North America opened on Long Island in 1665. Charles II was a regular at Newmarket, leading to racing being known as the "sport of kings."

During these times, betting mainly meant agreeing a wager directly with another person (or a small syndicate of them). Modern-style bookmaking is usually dated to the 1790s, when Harry Ogden began operating at Newmarket and, according to later accounts, started quoting a full set of odds across the field based on his knowledge of the horses.

History doesn't record much else about Harry but there are plenty of reports that his fellow bookmakers were often not respectable businessmen. Bookmakers had a tendency to disappear when a race didn't work out in their favour. There were no licences and no regulatory safeguards. If you backed a winner and the bookmaker disappeared, you were just out of luck.

Joseph Oller and Pari-Mutuel Pools

Enter Joseph Oller, a Spanish entrepreneur best known for co-founding the famous Moulin Rouge nightclub in Paris. In the betting world, he's remembered for something that lacked the glamour of velvet curtains and can-can dancers but that left a lasting mark of its own.

In 1867, Oller introduced a new way to bet – the pari-mutuel system. Instead of betting against a bookmaker, bettors placed money into a pool. The house took a fixed percentage, and the rest went to the winners, split proportionally based on how much each of them had staked on the winning horse. The more popular the horse, the more other bettors you had to share the winnings with and the lower your percentage return would be if it won.

For bettors, this was revolutionary. You knew the pari-mutuel operator had the money to pay out and they were going to make a profit, so there was a substantially reduced risk of them skipping town.

Initially, Oller's invention was viewed with suspicion by the French authorities, and he was arrested multiple times for violating anti-gambling laws. But Oller had the last word. Eventually deciding that pari-mutuel pools were the lesser of two evils, France ended up banning bookmakers altogether and made pari-mutuel the only legal way to bet. Pari-mutuel betting also caught on at racetracks in the rest of the world. To help manage these pools, operators began using a machine known as the "totaliser" to keep track of how much had been placed on each horse and to inform the public of the likely odds. Today, pari-mutuel betting operations at racetracks are often known as "the Tote."

The Fun Police

Just as betting was becoming more organised, it became a target for moral crusaders. The late 19th and early 20th centuries saw the rise of "progressive movements." Not to be confused with today's "progressives", these were largely religious groups whose idea of progress was banning alcohol, gambling and other things that involved having fun.

Another element that sparked a backlash against betting was the evidence that it was undermining the integrity of sports. In the early years of professional sport, poorly paid players were easy prey for big-money bettors who wanted to rig the outcome. As any economist will tell you, people respond to incentives. And when those incentives reward match-fixing, it's no surprise if that's what you get.

A turning point came in 1919 when Shoeless Joe Jackson and other players on the Chicago White Sox were bribed to throw the World Series. The scandal shocked the American public – the plaintive cry from a youngster of "say it ain't so, Joe" went down in history. Gambling became associated with corruption, and lawmakers and sports leagues worked to outlaw it.

The resulting restrictions on sports betting were severe. In the US, all off-course betting was outlawed by the 1920s, and even on-course pari-mutuel betting was only allowed in a limited number of venues, most notably in Kentucky and Maryland. In the UK, the Street Betting Act of 1906 had already criminalised all off-course betting, pushing legal gambling to the margins in both countries.

Backstreet Betting

As with the prohibition of alcohol, making betting illegal didn't stop it. It just changed who ran it. In the US, that generally meant organised crime. Already strengthened by the alcohol-prohibition era, sports betting was a lucrative part of the mob's portfolio of businesses.

With telecommunications advancing in the 20th century and underground betting becoming a national industry, the organised crime groups "took a interest" in the wire services that transmitted results to bookmakers around the country. Sometimes this meant mobsters knew the outcome of races while other punters were still placing bets.

The mob seems to have had plenty of reasons for ordering the famous Hollywood Hills hit on the glamorous underworld icon Bugsy Siegel, now remembered as a key founder of the Las Vegas casino business. But among them was his refusal to share money from his California wire service, which involved bribing or intimidating Western Union employees to provide phone lines to bookmakers who paid up – and to delay or cut off those who didn't.

The rest of the world also restricted betting for much of the 20th century. In the UK, most bets were placed via off-course "runners" who collected bets in pubs or on the street. Technically, this was illegal. But in the absence of the large-scale organised crime outfits seen in the US, it seems to have been largely ignored by the police. [1]

Legalisation in the UK

The UK was the first country to legalise retail bookmaking, with the first betting shops opening in 1961. However, the government didn't really want people to use them, so many restrictions were put in place. Betting shops were not allowed to have chairs, carpets or even televisions for watching the races. Windows had to be blacked out, and the exteriors could not feature advertising. Shops could not serve drinks to customers, so you couldn't even have a cup of tea.

During this period, there were also strict limits on how you could place bets. At first, betting shops could not display odds inside the shop - you had to go up to the counter and request them - and the odds they offered had to match the on-course Tote. Bets on individual football matches were banned; the football authorities were concerned that bets on single games would encourage corruption, so punters had to place a three-match multiple bet. To further discourage betting, it was also heavily taxed. There was a betting duty of 10% - placing a £10 bet required you to put up £11, with the extra pound going to the government.

Despite all this, legalised betting proved hugely popular. A year after legalisation, over 13,000 betting shops were licensed across the UK. Many people really like betting, and they will preferably do it legally if that's possible. Over time, some of the draconian restrictions were lifted. By 1986, betting shops could display their own odds, show events on TVs in the shops and transmit race commentaries. You could even sit in a chair. But the industry remained heavily taxed and regulated (you still couldn't get a cup of tea ...) and, overall, not much changed.

Until, well, everything changed.

CHAPTER 2

The Internet Changes Everything

The biggest economic event during my time working for the Fed was the dot-com crash of 2000. The internet had been hyped as a force that would transform the economy, with online firms set to take over from traditional bricks-and-mortar outlets – until people started to wonder whether those online companies would ever make profits. But in time, many did. And no sector was more disrupted than sports betting.

Victor Goes to Gibraltar

British bookies were quick to see the opportunities the internet presented. Punters wouldn't need to go to a shop to place a bet anymore and so bookies could take in bets from anywhere.[2] In 1999, one of Britain's smartest bookmakers, Victor Chandler, moved his operation to Gibraltar, which had no betting tax, so punters could bet with Victor without paying the betting duty. Others soon set up shop in the Isle of Man, Malta and other places with no taxes on betting.

Faced with losing lots of tax revenue, the UK scrapped its betting duty, replacing it with a tax on the profits bookmakers made on bets. The new regime approximately halved the amount of money taken in tax for each pound placed with bookmakers. The response was remarkable. Economists David Paton, Donald Siegel and Leighton Vaughan Williams showed that after the change in the tax regime in October 2001, the amounts placed with off-course bookmakers doubled almost immediately.[3]

There is an important lesson here about the economics of betting.

Some people are so keen on gambling that they are willing to place bets even with taxes that make it almost impossible to break even over time. But most of us are not so foolish with our money. The potential to make a profit matters and getting rid of the betting duty made it significantly easier to do so. And in this case, the demand for bets was so sensitive to the terms being offered that the tax raised stayed about the same, despite the effective tax rate being cut in half.

Faced with bookmakers credibly threatening to relocate abroad, the UK government also began lifting all the old restrictions. Finally, you could bet on individual football matches and, as a result, betting on football exploded; today the amount placed on football is well above betting on horse racing, which had previously dominated the industry. The Gambling Act of 2005 lifted most of the restrictions on betting shops including allowing them to provide various one-armed bandit machines for punters who wanted to take a break from perhaps losing money while betting on sports to instead losing for sure.

Crucially, the Act legalised advertising by bookmakers. This hugely promoted the industry's profile. Today, it is impossible to watch a sporting event in the UK (or pretty much anywhere else) without being bombarded with advertising from betting companies. This partly stems from the explosion of the industry that accompanied the introduction of the smartphone.

Thanks to Steve Jobs, suddenly you could bet at any time of day or night from a touch of a screen. With millions of new customers ready and willing to bet in this easy manner, bookmakers found all sorts of new ways to offer bets - accumulators; bet builders (e.g. Arsenal to win by 2 and Saka to score in the second half); in-play betting on anything that could possibly happen (penalties, yellow cards - you name it). Online sports betting surged in the UK, from about £1 billion per year in 2005 to over £40 billion today. Online accounts for over 90% of bets placed in the UK today, with many retail shops closing and those still open largely catering for an older clientele.

Football, as the most popular sport in the UK, now has a financially symbiotic relationship with betting companies. Many teams have had shirt sponsorship deals with bookmakers and pitch-side ads for betting companies are ubiquitous. Some of these bookmakers don't even operate in the UK: Being visible on a Premier League TV feed is a great way to get publicity in China, where betting is technically illegal. Beyond the sponsorship deals, the revenue from the relentless advertising of sports betting has increased the value of the TV contracts the Premier League sells all around the world.

Today, sports betting is a huge global industry. Other countries have followed the UK approach of lifting restrictions and the world's biggest bookmakers are now sizeable multi-national conglomerates.

Asymmetric Information

The internet presented bookmakers with new opportunities to make profits: suddenly, anyone in the world could be a customer. But it also introduced new threats: literally anyone in the world could be a customer. Local betting shops usually knew their punters and recognised that most of them posed no danger to profitability. Online, though, customers could come from anywhere in the world - and some of them might know more about sports than you did.

Even before the internet, computers were changing the face of sports betting. Bookies everywhere knew the story of how Bill Benter and Alan Woods used computers to build statistical models that made them tens of millions of dollars betting at Hong Kong racetracks - a story to make bookmakers shudder with fear. Because Hong Kong used a pari-mutuel system, there were no bookmakers being fleeced - and the Jockey Club, which ran the tracks, welcomed their bets because they added to total profits.[4] But traditional bookies were rightly concerned about the prospect of being ripped off by a bunch of internet nerds.

The Benter-Woods story was an example of what economists call *asymmetric information,* where one side of a transaction knows more than the other - in this case, sharp bettors having better information than bookmakers. Economists, George Akerlof, Michael Spence and Joe Stiglitz were awarded the Nobel Prize in 2001 for their research explaining how asymmetric information can cause markets to work badly or even collapse.

Among Stiglitz's many contributions, he showed how asymmetric information impacts health insurance markets. People buying the insurance know more about their lifestyle and health prognosis than the insurance company. This problem can cause the market to collapse, with nobody willing to provide health insurance because of the risk of losing money.[5]

Akerlof's famous paper "*The Market for Lemons*" described why the market for used cars worked so badly: Some of the cars are perfectly good but others are lemons and it is hard to tell which is which, so the market doesn't work well. Even selling a car in great condition to a dealer won't get you the price it is really worth. Again, if the problem is bad enough, the whole market can collapse.[6]

Sharps and Softs

But online betting markets didn't collapse. Instead, they produced an outcome that the third Nobel amigo, Michael Spence, had explained could happen.[7] Economists call this a *separating equilibrium;* an outcome where different types of people separate themselves into different choices, and these choices reveal their type. Spence gave an example involving education and the job market. He described how high-ability workers could signal their value by getting more education, even if education itself wasn't what made them productive. The result was an economy where people got separated into highly paid well-educated workers and less-educated workers who were paid badly.

In online betting, the separating equilibrium involves different types of customers who bet with different kinds of bookmakers, known in the business as *sharp* and *soft* bookmakers.

Soft bookmakers are the brands most people know. They target casual punters with advertising and marketing promotions like free bets. Their strategy is based on discouraging well-informed bettors. They set odds with a high built-in profit margin, which discourages those who are price sensitive. More directly, customers who build up a track record of winning will find their stakes limited and could eventually have their accounts closed. Big losers often get VIP treatment – like free tickets to sporting events – so long as they keep losing.[8] These perks are marketed as rewards for loyalty, but they're really just a way to keep valuable "profit centres" from switching to the competition.

Sharp bookmakers have the opposite strategy. They attract the most-informed bettors by setting odds with a small built-in profit margin. Their strategy focuses on taking a large volume of bets and turning a small per-bet profit margin into a big overall profit. Because their target customers are highly price sensitive, sharp bookmakers often locate in countries without taxes on betting, allowing them to turn a profit while offering more generous odds. This means these bookmakers are not easily accessible to retail customers in many countries, so most of the money placed with them comes from international betting syndicates, professional gamblers, high rollers with offshore bank accounts or brokers.

The evolution of online betting shows markets don't always unravel under asymmetric information - sometimes they just sort people into different markets. In Spence's original model, education served as a signal of hidden ability, triggering the separating equilibrium. In betting, the willingness to take bad odds, a preference for convenience over profitability, and a track record of success (or lack of it) all serve as signals that help separate casual punters from more professional gamblers.

The Wild West: Sports Betting in the US

At the same time as the UK was legalising betting on sports in the 1960s, the US authorities became even more determined to outlaw it, with the exceptions of racetracks and, of course, Nevada. This reflected a greater concern about organised crime and sporting integrity, partly due to the lingering memories of the 1919 World Series.

Attorney general, Robert F. Kennedy, launched a major clampdown on organised crime and made dismantling their sports betting operations a key priority. The Wire Act of 1961 made it illegal to *"...transmit bets or wagers or information assisting in the placing of bets or wagers on any sporting event or contest"* across state lines. Other anti-mafia legislation followed over the next few decades, including further efforts to prevent organised betting on sports.

Of course, betting continued unabated. The FBI regularly admitted they could not enforce the federal anti-gambling laws, and the state and local police had higher priorities than enforcing their own betting prohibitions. Indeed, American police officers, district attorneys and politicians of this era were often bribed to turn a blind eye to illegal gambling.

Since betting was still happening, there remained concerns about the effects it could have on the integrity of sports. College sports being so popular in the US provided a particular weak point, with unpaid college athletes an obvious target for criminals looking to rig an event. Corruption scandals involving basketball teams at Boston College (1978) and Tulane (1985) were feared to be the tip of the iceberg.

By the early 1990s, some other states had become envious of the tax revenues that Nevada earned on sports betting and were considering legalising it in their own jurisdictions. Enter Bill Bradley, US Senator for New Jersey and former NBA player. Encouraged by the National Collegiate Athletic Association (NCAA) and the professional sports leagues, Bradley declared "*We must draw a line. We must put the interests of sports and young people ahead of gambling interests*" and he proposed a legislative solution.

Up to this point, bans on gambling had only been state-level laws. Sponsored by Bradley, the Professional and Amateur Sports Protection Act (PASPA) passed in 1992, prohibiting any more states from legalising betting on sports. As the world of sports betting started to be transformed by the internet, the US remained frozen in time.

Ironically, it was Bradley's own state, New Jersey, that brought down PASPA. Atlantic City had casinos, but they were not allowed to offer sports betting, thus losing customers to their competitors in Las Vegas. The state of New Jersey challenged PASPA all the way to the Supreme Court and won. The Court ruled PASPA unconstitutional, finding it violated states' rights. Many states immediately moved to allow sports betting. As of 2026, it is legal in 39 US states.

Despite previously having been against legalised sports betting when PASPA had passed, by the time it was repealed, the US professional sports leagues had seen how much money European clubs made from betting-related revenues. The leagues looked into their souls and decided their wallets were more important than their concerns about integrity. Today, they are gorging on many different sources of revenue from sports betting, ranging from official sponsorships ("official sports betting partner of the NBA"), to data-provision deals and team sponsorships while also benefiting from the impact of betting advertising on the value of TV contracts.

The new US sportsbooks don't follow the old Las Vegas model of simple point spread bets and a tolerance for large wagers. They are firmly in the "European soft bookmaker" space, acquiring customers via flashy bonuses and wall-to-wall advertising and imposing strict stake restrictions for winners.

Across Europe, policymakers are increasingly worried about this model, citing high levels of problem gambling. Momentum is building for reform and regulation of the sector. In contrast, the US has legalised with very few guardrails. As of now, America appears set to be a super-lucrative Wild West of the sports betting industry.

II. The Basics

This part of the book starts where I started: figuring out what betting odds mean and what we can learn from them.

Chapter 3 introduces betting odds and shows how the work of a 17th century mathematician, Jacob Bernoulli, helps us to think clearly about bets. Chapter 4 shows how economists' ideas about financial markets provide a useful way to think about betting odds. Chapter 5 explains a way to estimate the average profit bookmakers earn on bets and to translate odds into probabilities. Chapter 6 uses these ideas to show why accumulator bets typically generate big average losses.

CHAPTER 3

Odds and Win Rates

Let's start with the obvious: the odds and what they mean. We'll look at three different ways of quoting odds and how to use them to answer a key question: how often do you need to win to break even? Then we'll shift to something deeper – how a 17th-century mathematician, Jacob Bernoulli, would think about sports betting and how following his approach helps avoid many common mistakes.

What Are the Odds?

Around the world, bookmakers differ in the way they quote odds. Depending on where you are from, you might be used to one of these conventions but not the others. Here, I'll describe three kinds of odds and explain why this book sticks with just one of them.

Fractional Odds

If you live in the UK or Ireland, these are the odds you will be familiar with. At their simplest, they are easy to understand. 4/1 means that if you place a £1 bet and it wins, your profit will be £4. You will be paid back £5 by the bookmaker – your original £1 stake and the £4 profit.

That's easy enough but fractional odds come with conventions that can sometimes make things a bit trickier. The terminology isn't always as clear as "something-to-one." You rarely see odds quoted as 1/1 (bet £1 to win £1); instead, this is quoted as "Evens." If a bet is likely to win, you will see odds like 4/9 (bet £9 to potentially win £4) but in conversation people will say the odds are "9/4 on."

One thing we will be interested in is whether odds reflect the underlying probabilities that events will happen. The conventions around fractional odds restrict their accuracy in reflecting the underlying probabilities. British and Irish bookies tend to use only relatively small whole numbers in the fractions, so they quote odds that aren't quite right but are easy to read. Instead of quoting 287/100 (even if they think these are the right odds) bookies would probably go with 3/1 (equivalent to 300/100) or perhaps 11/4 (equivalent to 275/100).

These small differences between the odds a bookmaker might want to set versus what is "socially acceptable" in the land of fractional odds are a potential source of vulnerability for bookmakers. They can either lose business from odds that are priced a bit too low or lose money on odds that are a bit too generous. Even small mispricings can be picked off by well-informed bettors who spot value. For this reason, sharp bookmakers around the world do not use fractional odds. And neither will we.

Decimal Odds

Throughout this book, I will use decimal odds. These odds tell you, up to two decimal places, what your payout will be if you win after placing a bet of one unit. It's the amount of money you get back after winning, inclusive of your original one-unit bet. These are the odds quoted in most of the world, including mainland Europe, Australia, New Zealand and most of Asia.

It is easy to go from fractional odds to decimal odds. A 3/1 bet in fractional odds is decimal odds of 4. You just add one to include your original bet that you get back and express it in decimal numbers to two digits. These odds are not restricted to fractions involving low numbers, so if a bookmaker wants to raise the odds on this bet, they can set them to 4.01 despite 301/100 being socially unacceptable as fractional odds.

This way of quoting odds never caught on in the UK, perhaps because many British people view all things decimal as some kind of European plot. (In the UK, these are often called "European odds.") But in addition to being more useful for bookmakers, decimal odds have a big advantage for bettors. They immediately tell you what fraction of your bets you need to win to break even.

Suppose you place four £1 bets at decimal odds of 4, winning one and losing the other three. That means that in return for your £4 in bets, you got back £4. You broke even. The general principle is that if the odds are D, you need to win $1/D$ of the time to break even. These *breakeven win rates* are extremely helpful for understanding betting and this is one reason why we use decimal odds throughout this book.

Breakeven rates provide a simple way to think about why people place bets. If the breakeven rate on a bet is 25% and someone thinks the actual probability of the bet winning is greater than 25%, they might decide to take the bet because on average they would win money taking bets of this sort. Someone else could look at the same bet, figure the probability of winning is less than 25% and pass it up. Their disagreement about probabilities is central to betting markets.

American Odds

American odds, as the term suggests, are principally used in America and aren't going to be an exporting success. They work like this. If you are making a bet where your potential profit is larger than the amount you are staking, the odds are quoted with a plus sign. Odds of +150 mean a successful $100 bet will earn you a profit of $150.

Now, you might imagine that if a $100 bet wins you $80, that the odds would be +80. But you'd be wrong. If the potential profit from a bet returns less than the amount you've risked, American odds switch to a different convention. Instead of telling you how much your $100 bet wins, they tell you how much you need to bet to win $100. So, odds of -150 means you need to bet $150 to potentially win $100.

I have no idea why this system switches from "profit on $100" to "stake needed to win $100." But this system doesn't lend itself to clear thinking about breakeven win rates and assessing whether a bookmaker is offering good value. This perhaps explains much of the confused thinking that you see in online discussions of betting in the US.

From a practical perspective, my recommendation if you are confronted with American odds is to convert them to decimal before making any decisions.

Win Rates and Returns

If you make a series of £1 bets, then the average amount of money you will get back per bet placed – what we'll call the *average payout* – is the fraction of times the bets win (f) times the decimal odds (D). If this amount is £1.05, then you can think of your £1 bets as investments that made an average 5% *rate of return.*

There is a useful link between the average return on your bets, the fraction of times you win and breakeven rates. Your average payout on a £1 bet ($f \times D$) is the same thing as the fraction of times you win (f) divided by the breakeven rate ($1/D$). Calculate your win rate; divide it by the breakeven rate and this tells you your average payout and thus your rate of return.

Why is this a useful insight? Well, bettors often think about how they will do in terms of their percentage "edge". How much bigger is your winning percentage than the breakeven rate? But it's your average payout that determines how well you'll do. What matters isn't the difference between your winning rate and the breakeven rate but the *ratio* of your winning rate to the breakeven rate.

To give an example, suppose you repeatedly bet on draws at decimal odds of 5 and you win 22% of the time. The odds imply a breakeven rate of 20%, so you only have a two-percentage point edge. But this translates into an average payout of $f \times D = 0.22 \times 5 = 1.1$. You get a 10% rate of return because your winning rate is 10% bigger than your breakeven rate. With this strategy, you would lose 78% of the time but these would not be bad bets. At this rate of return, they'd all be bets worth making.

In contrast, consider the same 2% edge on a toss-up bet with decimal odds of 2. Those bets have a breakeven win rate of 50%. A 2-percentage-point edge would mean winning 52% of the time, which would translate into an average payout of 1.04 (52 divided by 50 is 1.04) and thus a smaller 4% rate of return.

Breakeven rates provide a way to summarise how you are doing with your bets. Whatever your reasons for betting, it's worth knowing how you're really doing. I recommend recording your bets – the odds you got and whether they won or lost. Group them by odds range to see how often they won. It's not much hassle: most bookmakers let you download your betting history straight into a spreadsheet. If your bets win more often than their average breakeven rate, then you may have a good strategy. If they win less, it's worth asking whether the fun is worth the cost.

Thinking Like Jacob Bernoulli

When you're betting on a football match, you might think about a hundred things: team form, tactics, pitch size, weather, injuries and so on. But once the match kicks off and your bet is placed, it's best to treat the outcome like the flip of a weighted coin.

That might feel like a simplification. But this mindset - treating the outcome of each match as a probabilistic event determined by random chance - is your best defence against some common fallacies that people fall into when betting. And it connects you to a tradition of mathematical thinking that dates back centuries.

Jacob Bernoulli was a Swiss mathematician and part of a prolific scientific family. Working in the late 1600s, he laid the foundations for modern probability theory. He introduced the idea of repeated, independent events with only two possible outcomes: success or failure. He imagined each success would happen with probability p and failure with probability $1-p$. However complex the forces leading to success or failure might be, these events were treated as though somebody decided their outcome by rolling a weighted dice. These events - now called *Bernoulli trials* - form the basis of many modern probability models.

Why does this matter for betting? Because once your bet is placed, the outcome is out of your control, and you should think of it as a Bernoulli trial. You win or you lose and there is a set probability for each outcome.

You lose your bet because a 94th-minute goal turns a home win into a draw? You didn't "almost win" and you weren't unlucky. You lost. Football matches are unpredictable, and one reason is the frequency of late goals - especially when the score is close. Teams that are behind often throw everyone forward, sometimes equalising, sometimes conceding another.

If you place enough bets, some will go into the 94th minute and win, which doesn't mean you're a genius. And some will go into the 94th minute and lose, which doesn't mean you've been unlucky. Thinking in terms of Bernoulli trials means you don't go into your next bet feeling that the near win means you're on the right track and the next one is likely to be a winner or that the gods have cursed you and you're doomed never to win.

The truth is that your bets are independent. The coin doesn't care whether you won or lost the last toss. Neither does the ball. If your bet has a 20% win probability, then that's the number - no matter how the last few bets went.

The Gambler's Fallacy and The Law of Large Numbers

One of the most persistent myths in betting is the belief that past results somehow influence future outcomes in situations that are actually independent from each other.

Suppose you're making a series of even-money bets that should win about half the time. You lose your first four bets. You reason that you're likely to win the next one because things must even themselves out. Nope. You're engaging in what is known as *the gambler's fallacy*.

The most famous example of the gambler's fallacy took place in 1913 at the Casino de Monte Carlo. A roulette wheel landed on black again and again - 26 times in a row. Convinced that red was "due," players piled on, doubling and redoubling their bets as the streak stretched out.

The odds of such a run were about 1 in 66 million: incredibly rare, but not impossible. To borrow Aristotle's phrase, "the improbable is probable." Randomness guarantees that somewhere, sometime, even the most unlikely sequences will happen. And when red finally appeared, it wasn't because it was due. It was just as likely as black on every single spin.

You might imagine that this kind of flawed thinking is rare. But the evidence suggests it is pretty common. For example, researchers have found that when lottery numbers come up, those numbers were less likely to be picked in the following weeks. Players reckon those numbers have "had their turn" and it's the other numbers that are probably going to come up next.[9]

People sometimes justify gambler's fallacy thinking via an appeal to some kind of "law of averages". They think: "I've lost four of these even-money bets – that must mean a win is coming soon, because the law of averages will kick in." A recent study of American online sports bettors found that about 15% of them agreed with the statement: "My chances of winning get better after I have lost."[10]

Well, there is no "law of averages" of this type. But there is a real mathematical law that explains how things even out over time. It is due to Jacob Bernoulli and is known as the *Law of Large Numbers*.

Bernoulli proved that in a long sequence of independent trials, the fraction of successes will converge toward the true probability as the number of trials increases. Things eventually "even out" over time but the trials are still independent: past losses don't foreshadow future wins.

This has crucial implications for gambling. You may believe your bets at decimal odds of 5 have a greater than 20% chance of winning and that, so far, you have been unlucky in only winning 19% of them. But as you place more bets and that average doesn't budge upwards, the Law of Large Numbers is telling you something vital. Your chance of winning isn't greater than 20%. It's almost certainly 19% and your strategy is a loser. You're not unlucky. Unfortunately, you're just wrong.

CHAPTER 4

Market Efficiency and Margins

There are many reasons why people bet but a key motivation is that they might win money. The bet is a financial investment. That doesn't mean it's a good investment, but the theory of financial markets provides a useful baseline for thinking about how betting markets work.

This chapter starts with the idea of financial market efficiency. We trace its journey from initial obscurity to the dominant framework for thinking about financial markets and then describe how the idea can be applied to betting. We also discuss bookmakers' profit margins and the crucial role they play in affecting your ability to win.

Financial Market Efficiency

The idea starts with a little-known French mathematician called Louis Bachelier. In 1900, Bachelier wrote a PhD thesis on the "theory of speculation." He argued that if there were predictable patterns so that the price of an asset was likely to go up tomorrow, speculators would pile in to buy it today, pushing the price up; similarly, if there was a predictable fall tomorrow, it would end up getting pulled forward to today.

The outcome of this logic was that prices for financial assets should follow a *random walk*, meaning changes in prices were unpredictable. Prices will still move, because new information arrives all the time, but the direction of each move is essentially unpredictable.

Bachelier's work was remarkable: his mathematics anticipated results that appeared five years later in a famous physics paper by Albert Einstein. But his examiners were not sure what to make of this work and his thesis received only an "honourable mention" rather than the top grade. For decades, his insight that competitive markets should produce price changes that look random was largely forgotten. Half a century later, it came to the attention of Paul Samuelson at MIT.

Samuelson, perhaps the greatest economist of the twentieth century, was the first American winner of the Nobel Prize in economics and wrote the best-selling and most influential textbook of his time. Samuelson had a special ability to use mathematics to clarify ideas rather than obscure them. In the 1960s, he took Bachelier's insights and provided a more general way to show that if market prices already reflect the available information, then price changes should indeed look random.

A younger economist from the University of Chicago, Eugene ("Gene") Fama, took this logic to the data. Using US stock-market prices, he documented how hard it was to find reliable, exploitable patterns in returns. From this work came the language of the "Efficient Markets Hypothesis": the idea that financial market prices reflect all useful information.

Fama and his co-authors tested this idea repeatedly. Were there simple trading strategies that beat the market? Did prices tend to drift up or down after good or bad news? In study after study, they found that such strategies either didn't work or offered gains too small to survive real-world costs like brokerage fees. Other work focused on "event studies": how quickly did prices respond to earnings announcements, dividend changes and other public news? The studies showed market responses were rapid, and it was difficult to impossible to make money trading on publicly available information. This evidence helped make the Efficient Market Hypothesis the dominant view in financial economics, and in 2013, Fama won the Nobel Prize in economics for this work.

Ironically, Fama shared his Nobel Prize with Yale's Robert Shiller, who made his name showing that financial markets could deviate dramatically from fundamentals. Where Fama emphasised how quickly prices of individual shares responded to new information, Shiller documented how prices for the market as a whole could drift away from rational values – creating bubbles and crashes. The "irrational exuberance" associated with the tech stock bubble and crash of the early 2000s is the classic example.

Fama dismissed talk of irrational bubbles, arguing these were just periods where people had more relaxed attitudes to risk. Fama and Shiller's debates are a classic case of two smart people looking at the same data and coming to very different conclusions – and if Nobel laureates can look at the same evidence and disagree, it's no surprise that bettors do too.

Efficiency in Betting Markets?

The Efficient Markets Hypothesis provides a benchmark for thinking about sports betting odds. Like financial markets, betting involves buyers and sellers, large financial stakes, and a constant flow of information. Team news, player injuries, weather, historical stats. If odds reflect all of that, they should give us a clean signal about the true probabilities of various outcomes.

But there's one big difference. Buying a share is an investment in a company. If the company makes profits, they will share them with you by paying you dividends; and if the company is successful, its share price will go up. You can always lose money by investing in shares, but the average return on these investments is positive. In contrast, in betting markets, bettors collectively lose because the bookmaker wins on average.

This means that, for most people, the financially efficient choice is not to bet. This immediately raises the question: why do so many people do it? We'll tackle this in Part III.

That bets lose on average has caused some to dismiss betting as a puzzle that can't be solved with the tools of economics. Still, economists Richard Thaler and William Ziemba decided betting markets were an interesting test case for assessing people's behaviour.

Thaler is not a believer in the efficient market hypothesis. He has devoted his career to showing that people were prone to predictable biases and that markets often reflected those mistakes. Unlike Fama, Thaler believed people's irrationality made it possible to make money from some market opportunities and built a successful investing career on that belief. He moved in the mid-1990s from Cornell to the University of Chicago – working in the same building as Fama – and won a Nobel Prize in 2017 for his work on behavioural economics.

Ziemba combined academic credentials with a fascination with horse racing. He was part academic, part high-stakes bettor and was a legend in gambling circles, having written a book under the name "Dr. Z" recommending a pari-mutuel racetrack betting system based on his own research.

In a 1988 paper, Thaler and Ziemba discussed the idea of betting market efficiency.[11] They defined *weak betting market efficiency* as holding when bets had negative expected profits. Finding sure-fire winners with positive expected profits is difficult enough for this idea to not be of much interest to us. Of more relevance is their idea of *strong betting market efficiency.* If a market satisfied this condition, it meant that all bets on the same event had the same *expected return.*

A word on terminology. By the *expected value* of something, I mean its long-run average. This is the average of the different possible outcomes weighted by their probabilities. For instance, if you roll a fair six-sided dice, the expected value is 3.5 – you'll never roll a 3.5, but that's the average across many rolls.

If you stake one unit at decimal odds D with a win probability p, then a fraction p of the time you will get a payout of D and the rest of the time your payout will be zero. Weighing up the two possible payouts by their probabilities, the expected value of your payout will be $p \times D$. I will call this the *expected payout rate.*

Of course, in reality you either get back nothing or D – you don't *expect* to get $p \times D$ as an outcome from any given bet. But the Law of Large Numbers implies that your average payout over many similar bets will converge to the expected payout. Your average return on this investment will converge to the expected return, which is $(p \times D) - 1$. This will be positive if $p \times D$ is above one and negative if it is below one. Online discussions often refer to bets with positive $(p \times D) - 1$ as being bets with "positive EV."

Strong betting market efficiency implies the expected return is the same on all bets on an event. The implications are stark. If this holds, then over time you'd end up with the same returns whether you backed the favourite, the longshot, or a mix of both. The odds already reflected all the available information. There is no edge to be gained in studying the form or building models - the market has already done the work.

This definition of strong betting market efficiency was a clever way of incorporating Fama's idea of prices reflecting all available information into a betting context. And it did so while side-stepping the thorny question of why anyone should ever bet in the first place.

Fair Odds and Bookmakers' Margins

Betting odds are innately linked with probabilities. Suppose a bet is offered at *fair odds* - meaning the expected payout on a £1 bet is precisely £1. In this case, the bookmakers, on average, take in as much money as they pay out, not taking a profit for themselves. You can immediately use the odds to calculate the probability that a bet will win. If the decimal odds are D, then the fair odds assumption of $p \times D = 1$ means the bet's chance of winning is $1/D$.

Alas, the world is not fair - neither in general, nor in the sense that bookmakers decline to take a profit - and this makes mapping odds into probabilities trickier. To figure out the link between odds and probabilities, we need to estimate how much profit the bookmaker is keeping.

A note on terminology. Gamblers use various terms to describe the profit earned by bookmakers. Americans often refer to it as "the hold" (the amount held back by the bookies), or "the juice" (who knows?), and most intriguingly, the "vigorish" - or just "vig" - a term that apparently came from Russian, passed through Yiddish, and ended up as underworld slang. But I will follow UK conventions and refer to the profit rate earned by the bookmaker as their *margin*.

Whatever term you use, the bookmaker's profit margin is often explained with examples like the following. Suppose Sinner plays Alcaraz in the Wimbledon final and bookmakers think it's a toss-up. The fair decimal odds would be $D = 2$, so you would get paid back £2 half the time on your £1 bets. But to make a profit, the bookmaker might instead offer $D = 1.9$ on each. Suppose they took in a £1 bet on Sinner and a £1 bet on Alcaraz. The bookie would take in £2 in bets and pay out £1.9 on whoever won, keeping the remaining 10p.

In this case, we can say the bookmaker earned a 5% profit margin on the £2 in bets taken. But sometimes, simplifying examples like this mislead more than they help. We don't see the volumes that bookmakers take on each side. What if they took in more money on Alcaraz and then he won? Bookmakers do not come out ahead on every event in the simple way this example suggests.

To calculate the bookmaker's margin, we need to make some assumptions. We show in the next chapter that strong market efficiency is precisely the assumption that allows us to calculate it.

What Margins Are

If bookmakers set odds of $1/p$, where p is their estimate of the probability the bet wins, they would be setting odds believing they are only going to break even on average.

Bookmakers do not set prices like this - they offer less generous odds so they can make a profit. And here is a really important point. Every odds quote you see from a bookmaker has been set as $(1-m)/p$ where m is a positive number between zero and one. The bookmaker believes the expected payout rate to bettors is

$$p \times D = p \times \frac{1-m}{p} = 1 - m$$

This means m represents the *expected profit margin* per unit staked for the bookmaker and the expected loss rate for the bettor.

Keep this equation in mind

$$D = \frac{1-m}{p}$$

Whenever you see odds, you're seeing the influence of both a probability estimate p and a built-in margin m. This simple formula turns many things in betting that look complicated into straightforward calculations, including bookmaker margins, parlays and the value of free bets.

This idea that odds are set with a specific margin built into each bet *in advance* of the event by the bookmaker is sometimes missed because margins are typically explained using examples like the one we just went through with Sinner and Alcaraz. In that case, whatever happened, the bookmakers came out *afterwards* with a 5% profit. But that's not how things work in the real world.

Instead, bookmakers set their margins knowing that if they are correct in their probability estimates, then over many bets, the Law of Large Numbers implies they will keep a fraction m of what is staked. So whatever the outcome ends up being, be sure that the bookmaker believed your bet had a specific probability p of winning and attached an intended profit margin of m to it. You might win this time, but the odds are set for them to win overall.

What Margins Mean for Winning

We have already introduced the breakeven win rate. If the odds are D, then you have to win a fraction $1/D$ of the time. With odds of $(1-m)/p$, you have to win at least p / $(1-m)$ of the time. For any given value of p (the bookmaker's estimated probability), higher margins m mean you need to win more often to break even.

Let's work through a concrete example. Suppose the bookmaker thinks the true win probability is $p = 0.60$. The fair odds would be 1.67 = 1/0.6 and you would need to win these bets 60% of the time to break even. But if the bookmaker incorporates a 5% profit margin (m = 0.05), then the odds are $(1-m)/p$ =0.95/0.60 = 1.58. At those odds, your breakeven win rate is 1/1.58 = 0.632. For these bets to be profitable on average, then their true probability of winning must be 3.2 percentage points higher than the bookmaker's assumption of 60%.

Now suppose the bookmaker sets a 10% profit margin. Then the odds are $(1-m)/p$ =0.90/0.60 = 1.5 and now your breakeven rate is 1/1.5 – you need to win two-thirds of the time to break even. The bookmaker's assumed probability needs to be nearly 7 percentage points too low.

The general rule is that if we convert the margin m to a percentage value, call it x% (so $m = 0.1$ means $x = 10$), then winning on average requires your bet's true probability of winning to be roughly x percent higher than the bookmaker had assumed. In other words, the margin sets a *hurdle* for your betting. The higher the margin, the more wrong the bookmaker must be for you to profit.

Bigger margins thus make it less likely that you can come out ahead on average. You might think you have better judgement than the bookmaker and can make profits with a 2% margin. But when the margin is 7%, what is the chance that your judgement that a bet is profitable is correct? The bookmakers are professionals at odds setting and you can only win over time on those bets if they are way off in their calculations.

This is why the starting point for winning is simple: Know what the historical margins are on your bet. Bookmakers don't publish their margins, but later chapters in this book will provide lots of information about how margins vary across different kinds of bets.

Who Really Pays the Margin?

Some online discussions of betting – especially American ones – say things like "the loser pays the margin." Is that right?

Consider the following scenario. Chad and Brad watch football games together and each put $11 on the table and whoever wins gets to keep all $22. Then one day, a new guy called Paddy shows up offering to act as a middleman.

Chad wins the bet. But instead of getting $22, this time he gets only $21 because Paddy is keeping the other $1 as his middleman fee. Paddy has taken Brad's $11, kept $1 of it and passed the rest over to Chad. In this sense, it seems like the loser "paid" the margin.

But then Chad says, "hey Brad, you didn't pay the margin, you just lost $11 like you always do when your pick doesn't win. How come I only get $10 profit for my win instead of $11? I'm pretty sure it's me who's paid this Paddy dude."

The point is that it's not useful to think of one side or the other as "paying the margin." Margins exist because, on average, payouts are smaller than the amounts staked. The larger the margin, the more the bookmaker is holding back on average – and the less you get when you win. Given that you will often lose your bets, making sure you get back as much as possible when you do win is crucial for breaking even or making a profit. And typically, that means seeking out the lowest possible margins. In the next chapter, we will show a method for calculating margins.

On Shopping Around

Knowing that bookmakers build in profit margins when they set their odds, an obvious piece of advice is to shop around for the best price. Clearly, if two bets are identical in every respect, the one with the higher odds is better.

But how much does this matter in practice? To answer this, I gathered data from The-Odds-API.com on quotes from UK bookmakers for every Premier League match from the 2022/23 season to the 2024/25 season – just over 53,000 individual price quotes from about 60 minutes before kick-off. On average, there are fifteen quoted prices per possible outcome, and they are tightly clustered. The typical dispersion across bookmakers is small: four-fifths of quotes sit within about 0.2 in decimal odds of the average. Bookmakers are largely pricing off the same view of the game, with roughly the same margin layered on top.

The larger gaps you sometimes see tend to come from a small number of outliers rather than widespread disagreement. There are some very good prices and some very bad ones, but not many. And the larger quote differences are heavily concentrated on longshots – I will explain later why even attractive-looking quotes on these bets may not be enough to win.

The benefits of shopping around are also more limited than the raw figures suggest. The "best odds" in a market are often promotional, limited in size, or available only briefly. They are not usually prices you can bet at repeatedly or at scale. Consistently turning up only when a bookmaker is offering the standout price also gets noticed, and you get limited or banned.

So yes, shopping around on your chosen bet is one of the fine margins you can use to improve your returns. But you can make bigger gains by only choosing bets that have lower margins across all the bookmakers or avoiding bookmakers altogether and using betting exchanges. More on this later.

CHAPTER 5

Calculating Margins and Probabilities

If you've ever stared at betting odds - twenty horses, three options on a football match, a list of candidates competing in an election - and wondered, "How big is the bookmaker's cut here?", I have something useful to show you. When betting markets are strongly efficient, you can recover the bookmaker's margin and their implied probabilities from nothing more than the posted odds.

How to Spot Margins

If bookmakers set fair odds, you could take the inverse of the decimal odds and calculate the bet's chances of winning. If $D = 5$, it would have a 20% probability of winning. But in reality, if you add up all those implied probabilities, they sum to more than one.

This is the tell-tale sign that the bookmaker has added a margin. That $D = 5$ bet really had less than a 20% chance of winning. This discrepancy - how far that sum exceeds one - is exactly what allows you to calculate the bookmaker's margin.

We will show precisely how to do the calculation. The method comes from my research with Tadgh Hegarty. Explaining it involves some equations, so I will go through it slowly, step by step. But if you just want the punchline - how to calculate the bookmaker's margin and their assumed probabilities – you can skip that bit and go straight to the "Overround" section. It's ok – there won't be a test.[12]

Margins in Efficient Betting Markets (Maths Alert!)

Suppose Chelsea are playing Arsenal in the FA Cup and you are betting on which team will go through to the next round (so there is no draw outcome). Strong betting market efficiency means the bookmaker sets the odds so expected payout rates on both bets are the same.

Assume the bookmaker's margin is m, so the expected payout rate is 1-m. Now let P_C be the bookmaker's estimate of the probability that Chelsea will go through. Strong market efficiency implies that they set the decimal odds on Chelsea (D_C) so that the expected payout rate on the bet is

$$P_C \times D_C = 1 - m$$

This means the bookmaker's estimate of Chelsea winning can be related to the odds and the margin as follows

$$P_C = \frac{1 - m}{D_C}$$

And the same applies to the probability of Arsenal winning

$$P_A = \frac{1 - m}{D_A}$$

Now, here is an important trick. The bookmaker's probabilities must sum up to one. This means

$$\frac{1 - m}{D_C} + \frac{1 - m}{D_A} = 1$$

And from that we can calculate the margin from the odds. Divide both sides by 1-m and you've got

$$\frac{1}{D_C} + \frac{1}{D_A} = \frac{1}{1 - m}$$

Flip both sides and we get

$$1 - m = \frac{1}{\frac{1}{D_C} + \frac{1}{D_A}}$$

which means the margin is

$$m = 1 - \frac{1}{\frac{1}{D_C} + \frac{1}{D_A}}$$

We've figured out what fraction of money gets paid back to punters and how much the bookmaker keeps. And we got it just from the odds and the assumption of strong betting market efficiency. We didn't have to make up a story about how much money came in on Chelsea compared to Arsenal.

The Overround

The equation we derived for the bookmaker's margin looks forbidding, but the calculation is not so hard once you take it step by step. The steps are

1. Convert the odds on each of the competitors to decimal odds.
2. For each of the odds, calculate 1 divided by the decimal odds
3. Sum up each of those fractions. That number is known as *the overround.*
4. Now divide 1 by that sum.

This will tell you what one minus the bookmaker's margin is, i.e. it tells you (1-m). If it's 0.95, then the bookmaker's margin is 0.05, i.e. 5%.

A quick concrete example. A standard American point spread bet offers both sides at -110, which is decimal odds of 1.909. The overround, calculated as the sum of the inverse of the decimal odds is 1/1.909 + 1/1.909 = 1.0476. Calculating 1/1.0476 we get 0.9545, so the margin is m = 0.0455. In other words, on average, the bookies keep 4.55% of the money placed with them.

This example has just two possible outcomes, but the method generalises to events that have any number of competitors. If there are 10 horses, you just sum up the inverses of the 10 decimal odds.

Calculating overrounds and converting them to margins might seem tricky at first but experienced punters across the world do these calculations every day. Once you've figured out an overround a few times, you get used to it. Justin Wolfers - a quick-witted Australian economist and TV regular - once worked as a teenage runner for Sydney bookmakers. Speaking to a journalist years later, he recalled: *"There was a time when I could walk past the bookie's board and tell you the bookie's winning percentage."*[13]

In other words, he was calculating the overround in his head. You don't need Justin's gift for mental arithmetic to figure out the overround - a spreadsheet will do just fine. You can access a free spreadsheet that will do these calculations on my website at www.karlwhelan.com/sports-betting/margin-calculator.

When you start working out overrounds and realise some bookmakers or certain events have higher ones than others, then give them a skip if you care about the bottom line.

A health warning on using overrounds instead of following all four steps above. Many bettors assume an overround of 1.0x means the bookmaker keeps x% of the money. That's usually close but not quite right. The bettor's average payout is one divided by the overround (the last step above). For small margins, this error isn't too big. For example, if the overround is 1.02, then the true average payout for bettors is 0.9804, not 0.98, so the typical calculation is essentially correct.

However, if the overround is 1.1, then the implied average payout for bettors is 0.909, not 0.9. In this case, the margin implied by the overround is closer to 9% than 10%. Close enough for back-of-the-envelope maths - but it's worth knowing the difference.

The Margin Calculation as a Reality Check

So, you've got an estimate of the profit margin the bookmaker is keeping on average. What do you do with that information? You run the calculations above and find out the implied margin is 7% and you still think you're on to a winner?

Well, you might want to be honest with yourself about what kind of edge you have. If the bookmaker has built in a 7% margin on your bet, then it having a positive expected return means they must be 7% too low in their estimated probability that it will win. How probable is it that you have this kind of edge?

A profile of Gadoon Kyrollos, the legendary American professional gambler known in betting circles as Spanky, reported that at his peak he earned between a 1% and 2% profit margin on average across his bets.[14] Using the typical US market margin of 4.5%, then his edge on judging probabilities was about 6%, in the sense that the outcomes he was betting on were about 6% more likely to happen than bookmakers had assumed.

So that's world class betting skill, backed up by a staff collecting data and running models, all of which he had to pay for. Are you sure you have more of an edge on this bet than Spanky in his prime? Of course, it may be that the margin on your chosen bet is lower than the overround implies. But, as you will see soon, there is also a decent chance that it is higher.

Application: Should You Take the Boosted Odds?

Here is a useful application that comes from calculating margins. Sometimes bookmakers offer you boosts on the usual odds. These might be offered to everyone or perhaps just to a selected group of customers. Boosted odds are clearly better than the regular odds but that doesn't mean they are worth taking. Knowing the margin on the original bet will tell you whether the boosted odds have a positive expected profit.

The first thing to do to figure this out is to convert the regular and boosted quotes into decimal odds and calculate the percentage increase implied by the boost. So D is the original offer and $b \times D$ is the boosted offer, where b represents the scale of the boost. Assuming the original odds satisfy strong betting market efficiency, the expected payout rate on your boosted bet is

$$b \times p \times D = b \times p \times \frac{1-m}{p} = b\,(1-m)$$

This will be greater than one as long as

$$b > \frac{1}{1 - m}$$

So, if betting markets are strongly efficient, you can check whether your boosted odds have a positive expected profit as follows

1. Convert the original odds to decimal odds.
2. Calculate the margin m from the original unboosted odds.
3. Figure out the boost factor, b, as the ratio of the boosted decimal odds to the original decimal odds.
4. Calculate whether b is greater than 1 / (1-m). If it is, then the boosted bet has positive expected profit.

To give an example, suppose you get offered a 10% boost and you figure out that the original odds implied a margin of 10%. Plugging m = 0.10 into our formula shows you needed the boost to be 11.1% for it to have a positive expected profit. So you should turn down the boost offer.

Note something interesting: the percentage boost in decimal odds has to be greater than the bookmaker's profit margin for your bet to have a positive expected return. This gap isn't too big when margins are low but explodes for bets with big margins. For example, suppose a bet has a one-third profit margin for the bookmaker (m = 1/3). Then you need a 50% boost just to break even on average. You're only getting two-thirds of your money back; you need an extra one-third to break even, so the odds need to be 50% better. More on this kind of thing later.

In practice, many boosts are smaller than needed to offset the margin, so the bets still have negative expected profit. And when large boosts are offered, they tend to be associated with markets that have big margins. Of course, if you only take boosted bets when they have positive expected profit, your days of receiving odds boosts offers are unlikely to last long.

Calculating Probabilities

The assumption of strong betting market efficiency allows us to see the bookmaker's margin. It also means we can see what they had assumed about probabilities. Remember that strong market efficiency implies the bookmaker believed the probability of Chelsea going through was

$$P_C = \frac{1-m}{D_C}$$

We see the odds, D_C and now we know what $1\text{-}m$ is, so we can directly calculate the probabilities used by the bookmaker.

For example, suppose the bookmaker's odds on Chelsea winning are 2. Without any margin, that suggests a 50% chance of winning. But if we know the margin is 10%, then that means the bookmaker thinks the probability of the home team winning is 0.9 / 2 = 0.45, so Chelsea have a 45% chance of winning, quite a bit less than 50%.

This might be your first time seeing this way to calculate probabilities - working out the bookmaker's margin and then combining that with the odds. But I suspect some of you have seen this kind of calculation before, just approaching it from a different angle.

We just showed above that the average payout was

$$1-m = \frac{1}{\frac{1}{D_C}+\frac{1}{D_A}}$$

Plug this into the first equation above in this section for P_C and we get

$$P_C = \frac{\frac{1}{D_C}}{\frac{1}{D_C}+\frac{1}{D_A}}$$

This calculation is known as a *normalised probability*. You first divide one by the decimal odds to get an initial "raw" estimate of the probability. Since these raw estimates typically sum to more than one, you then "normalise" them by dividing each by the total sum. By construction, your new normalised probabilities reflect the information in the odds, but they also sum to one.

To give an example, suppose a bookmaker offers decimal odds of 1.36 on Arsenal to go through and 3.17 on Chelsea. The "un-normalised" estimated probabilities are 1/1.36 = 0.737 and 1/3.17 =

0.316. Add those up and you get 1.053. You then get normalised probabilities by dividing 0.737 and 0.316 by 1.053 to get 0.7 for Arsenal and 0.3 for Chelsea.

Many regular bettors are able to do rough calculations of normalised probabilities in their heads. They don't think of it as an application of strong betting market efficiency, just a convenient way to use the information in the odds. They figure that in an ideal world with no bookmaker's margin, they could calculate the probabilities as $1/D$, but they know we don't live in that ideal world, so you have to adjust this first set of estimates to make them sum to one, as probabilities must.

What we've shown here, however, is that normalised probabilities are not just a convenient way to approximate the bookmaker's probabilities. If the betting market is strongly efficient, *normalised probabilities are the bookmaker's assumed probabilities.* By the way, the free spreadsheet that is on my website at www.karlwhelan.com/sports-betting/margin-calculator that calculates margins also reports normalised probabilities.

An Example and a Warning: EPL v Horse Racing

Calculating the profit margin implied by strong market efficiency allows you to figure out quickly that some kinds of bets offer considerably worse value than others.

For example, compare betting on the English Premier League to British horse racing. For the Premier League, I collected data on results and average betting odds from www.football-data.co.uk, an incredible resource run by Joseph Buchdahl, an expert on gambling and author of some excellent books on the topic. I calculated average bookmaker margins implied by overrounds for 7,600 matches over the period 2005-2025.

For horse racing, I used a dataset from Kaggle, a site where data scientists share data and code. Made available by the mysterious Nikolay Kashavkin, who did not respond when I sent him some questions via Kaggle, it contains odds for over 400,000 horse races around the world. I've checked many of the races against the Racing Post's database and the key data are all correct, with the occasional error for supplementary details like the dates of the races. I calculated the average margins for about 260,000 British races from 1990 to 2020.

The results show the average margin implied by the odds for bets on the Premier League was 5.3% while the average for racing was 20.7%. This is a huge difference – your money is likely to disappear four times faster betting on horses than on football.

These datasets also record the outcomes of the events, so one calculation we can do is the average loss you would have recorded from placing a £1 bet on all of the different possible outcomes. Think of this as what your average loss rate would have been if you had picked your bets at random. For football, this average loss rate would have been 7.3%. For horse racing, it would have been 27.8%. The overround-based margin was correct in telling you which sport was the superior one to bet on, but it was too low in predicting average losses across all bets.

This isn't a statistical accident. The sample sizes are huge: if the estimated margins were correct, you would not have errors this large. The problem is that the overround only lets you measure the bookmaker's margin correctly *if the betting market is strongly efficient*. And the bad news is ... betting markets generally are not strongly efficient. For some bets, the overround calculation of the bookmaker's margin will be too low and for others it will be too high. But, as we will see later, for a randomly picked bet, it will be too low.

Similarly, because they depend on the accuracy of the estimate of the bookmaker's margin, normalised probabilities don't tell you the probabilities the bookmaker had in mind when setting the odds.

So, overrounds and normalised probabilities are useful tools. In particular, comparing overrounds across bookmakers and events can help you see which are offering good or bad value. But these calculations don't let you look at odds and read off the bookmaker's p and m. To get a better idea of these, you need to dig a bit deeper. We will return to these issues in Part 4.

CHAPTER 6

The Grim Arithmetic of Accumulators

This chapter shows how bookmakers' margins affect average returns on one of the most popular products in the industry: Accumulators. They may be fun, but here we show how expensive that fun is.

How Accumulators Work

Accumulators (Accas, known as parlays in the US) work as follows. You back outcomes for a set of matches at a specified set of odds and if your first bet wins, your return rolls on to your second pick and if that wins your money is placed on the third pick and so on. You only get money back if all your picks win. This is pretty unlikely to happen but the payout if you do win is substantial.

Accas are hugely popular with bettors. But first let's discuss why they are so popular with bookmakers. The first hint is the advertising spending - as the guy in All the President's Men said, if you want to understand something, you need to follow the money. Accas are widely advertised and that costs money, so you can be pretty sure that this extra cost is covered by bookmakers earning higher profit rates on these bets.

Here's why they do. Suppose you place a series of bets where you have a 50% chance of winning (W) or losing (L).

Let's work out what the different possible outcomes will be through the first four legs.

After one leg, these 2 outcomes are equally likely:
W, L

After two legs, these 4 outcomes are equally likely:
WW, WL, LW, LL

After three legs, these 8 outcomes are equally likely:
WWW, WWL, WLW, WLL, LWW, LWL, LLW, LLL

After four legs, these 16 outcomes are equally likely:

WWWW,	WWWL,	WWLW,	WWLL,
LWWW,	LWWL,	LWLW,	LWLL,
WLWW,	WLWL,	WLLW,	WLLL,
LLWW,	LLWL,	LLLW,	LLLL

After each leg, only one of the possible outcomes sees you winning all the bets. Your chance of winning the first bet is one-half. Your chance of winning the first two bets is one-quarter. Your chance of winning the first three bets is one-eighth. Your chance of winning the first four bets is one-sixteenth. The pattern is clear – when the probability of winning each bet is 1/2, your chance of winning all of N different bets is 1/2 to the power of N. As you can see, this quickly becomes a very small number.

There is nothing special here about the probability being one-half. If you have N bets each with a probability p of winning, then your chance of winning all N of them is p^N. More generally, if you place N different bets with probabilities $p_1, p_2, \ldots., p_N$, then your probability of winning all of the bets is found by multiplying all the probabilities together. With all the probabilities being less than one, the chance of winning all the bets gets really small really quickly.

Of course, most Acca bettors know they are very unlikely to win. But when they do, they win big, so perhaps this makes up for it? Well, let's calculate how much you would win if you placed N different bets at decimal odds of D.

You place a one-unit bet and win the first leg. Your payout would be D but you have picked an accumulator so that money is placed on the second leg. If that wins, your original one-unit bet has turned into D^2 to be placed on the next leg. If you win all N legs, your payout is D^N. This could be a big number, so you get an exciting win.

For example, suppose you pick a series of 50/50 bets that the bookmaker has priced with a margin of 5%, so the decimal odds are 1.9. Winning a six-leg accumulator will turn your one unit bet into $1.9^6 = 47$. £6 placed on this accumulator instead of spread across six separate bets gives you a profit of £276 while winning the six separate bets would have won you only £5.40. Surely if you've got six bets that you are confident in, you should go with the accumulator?

Well, unless they really are sure-fire bets - and they probably aren't - you're much better off placing those six bets separately than combining them in an accumulator.

The $p \times D = 1 - m$ framework helps to explain why. If the bets have a probability p of winning, then you have a probability p^N of getting a payout of D^N and a probability $1 - p^N$ of getting nothing. This means your expected payout rate is $p^N \times D^N$ which is simply $(p \times D)^N$. And $p \times D$ is less than one because the bookmaker has incorporated a margin: it equals $(1-m)$, meaning your expected return on your N-leg Acca is $(1-m)^N$.

This shows how you are compounding the bookmaker's margin into bigger losses. As you add more legs to your Acca, its expected payout rate equals higher and higher powers of a number less than one. This falls in value quicker than you might think. That £6 six-leg Acca has an expected payout of £4.40 which is about 20% worse than the expected payout of £5.70 from placing six separate £1 bets.

Boosts and Insurance

This explains why plain vanilla Accas are bad, but bookmakers tend to offer more attractive versions than simply combining the individual bets at their separate odds. For example, many bookmakers offer odds "boosts" if you place an accumulator, with bigger boosts the more legs you add. This sounds great - the prospect of a big win and you're getting boosted odds. The table below shows an example of Bet365's "Acca boost" percentages. They go from a modest 2.5% boost on two legs to a massive 55% boost if you take fifteen legs.

Bet365's Accumulator Boost Percentages (as of October 2025)

Number of Legs	*Percentage Boost*
2	2.5%
3	5%
4	7.5%
5	10%
6	12.5%
7	15%
8	20%
9	25%
10	30%
11	35%
12	40%
13	45%
14	50%
15	55%

Less popular these days but still available are "insurance" offers – you get your money back if you win all but one leg of the Acca. These are usually only offered if you have picked at least five legs.

The second column of the table below shows how expected payout rates for a standard accumulator change as the number of legs increases if all bets pay out 1.9 with a probability of 0.5. The third column shows expected payout rates if you get Bet365's odds boost. The fourth column shows expected payout rates if you get Acca insurance.

The precise numbers for the pure Acca depend only on the expected payout rate of each leg (in this case 0.95). The others depend a bit on the mix of probability and odds but the overall pattern is the same for any realistic set of odds, probabilities and margins. In other words, the exact numbers will vary slightly depending on which specific bets you choose, but the fundamental pattern shown here always holds.

The bottom line is that expected payout rates on Accas drop disastrously as you add more legs. Despite the modest 5% margin on each leg, you are losing 23% on average playing a five-leg Acca and 40% when you go up to ten legs.

Boosts like those offered by Bet365 slow the decline in expected payout rates as you take on more legs, but they don't reverse it. Popular Acca lengths like four to six legs still offer bookmakers profit margins of 13% to 17%, about three times the usual profit margin on bets. So even with the boosts, these are great products for bookies.

Acca insurance is better than the boost for five or six legs but then becomes pretty useless afterwards. With four to six legs being the most popular length for Accas, bookmakers may have moved away from these because they were slightly more expensive than boosts. And for longer-legged Accas, punters may have largely figured out getting back your original stake from the insurance isn't something that is going to happen very often – unlike the boosts, this insurance does little to reduce the disastrous plummet in expected payout rates as the number of legs gets big.

These calculations show that despite their superficial appeal, Accas offer terrible returns and most bettors will lose a lot more money playing them instead of placing money separately on matches. This is why bookmakers are so enthusiastic about them and place them front and centre of their advertising campaigns.

Expected payout rates on accumulators from a £1 bet with each leg having decimal odds of 1.9 and a 50% probability of winning

Number of Legs	*Acca*	*Acca with Boost*	*Acca with Insurance*
2	0.903	0.919	
3	0.857	0.894	
4	0.815	0.871	
5	0.774	0.848	0.930
6	0.735	0.825	0.829
7	0.698	0.802	0.753
8	0.663	0.795	0.695
9	0.630	0.787	0.648
10	0.599	0.778	0.609
11	0.569	0.768	0.574
12	0.540	0.756	0.543
13	0.513	0.744	0.515
14	0.488	0.731	0.489
15	0.463	0.695	0.464

Near Wins

The arithmetic is simple enough and grim. But people often still feel like they have a better chance of winning than they do. One reason for this is Acca bettors sometimes experience "near wins" which convince them they might win next time.

But frequent near wins on modest-sized Accas are a feature. Look at the equally likely outcomes above after four legs of an Acca where each leg has a 50% chance of winning. Four of the sixteen possible outcomes showed all but one leg winning but only one out of sixteen won every leg.

This generalises to adding more legs. You place a five-leg Acca and all of them win apart from one. So close, right? But that situation will happen five times more often than winning all five legs, so maybe not so close. As you add more legs, being one leg short becomes increasingly more likely relative to winning them all.

Higher Margin or Higher Volumes?

American betting industry experts Ed Miller and Matthew Davidow's books, *The Logic of Sports Betting* and *Interception*, are excellent reads, full of insight on how the betting industry works. But I think regular bettors need to be wary of some of their advice.

Accas are an example. Miller and Davidow believe these bets get a bad rap. They say the view of them as bets with high margins is incorrect; instead, they argue you should view Accas as having *higher volume*. Consider an example of a five-leg Acca with each leg at decimal odds of $D = 3$. Suppose these bets have a 30% chance of winning so $p = 0.3$. The expected payout rate on each of the individual bets is $p \times D = 0.3 \times 3 = 0.9$. Individually, the bets have a 10% profit margin for the bookmaker. And our calculations show that the expected payout rate for the Acca is $(p \times D)^5 = 0.59$, so on average Acca bettors will lose 41% of their money.

Miller and Davidow say you should think about this differently: you are placing an initial £1 bet, then you have a 30% chance of placing a £3 bet on the second leg, a 9% chance of placing a £9 bet on the third leg, and so on. The expected volume of money placed in the five-leg example is

$$1 + (0.3 \times 3) + (0.3^2 \times 9) + (0.3^3 \times 27) + (0.3^4 \times 81) = 4.1$$

And on this £4.1 in "expected volume" you expect to lose 41p. That's 10%, just like the regular bets. Looked at this way, maybe the bookie isn't taking a huge profit on your accumulator, they're just applying the same margin to a higher volume.

For regular bettors, this debate – do Accas have higher margins or higher volumes? – is largely semantics, a bit like the "who pays the margin, the winner or the loser?" discussion from earlier.

Of course, the higher volume point is technically correct. But the bets have a house edge. If you do win, the bookmaker wants you to place your winnings back with them. By getting you to keep rolling over your money, it becomes more probable that the house wins and you lose. Inducing you to bet more is precisely how they make more profits on Accas.

So, if you want to think of your £10 Acca as "effectively" a £41 bet with a 10% margin, go ahead if that makes you feel better. But the reality of your account statement is that you are handing over £10 and on average only getting £5.90 back.

Hiding Among the Suckers?

Miller and Davidow have other reasons to praise Accas. As industry professionals, they believe it is possible to systematically find bets that are winners on average. In other words, bets with $p \times D > 1$. If you can find many such bets, then the multiplicative maths above tell a different story. Your expected payout rate on an N-leg Acca of $(p \times D)^N$ now increases with the number of legs.

Miller and Davidow also suggest other advantages to placing Accas with soft bookmakers who like to restrict or ban successful bettors. You might want to place £300 on a bet and find that soft bookmakers won't take a bet of that size from you. But you can place it as the last bet in a five-leg accumulator with only £10 initially placed down - because if the first four legs win, you'll have £300 down on the final leg. Plus, Miller and Davidow point out that the industry views people who place Accas as "suckers", so placing some of these bets helps profile you as unlikely to be a sharp bettor, thus perhaps postponing the day you get shown the door.

In reality, this kind of advice has limited practical value. There is an old story about economists and their reliance on unrealistic assumptions to arrive at their conclusions. Two economists are washed up on a desert island with bare trees and a bunch of tins of soup that floated over from the ship. "What shall we do?" says the first economist. "Let's assume a tin opener" says the other.

Assuming you have a steady supply of bets with $p \times D > 1$ is a classic assume-a-tin-opener approach. If you can consistently pick bets with $p \times D > 1$, whether you should place them on Accas is a second-order issue to the important things you have to consider, like which kind of superyacht you're going to buy with your winnings.

The recommendations about beating the soft bookmakers don't make much sense either. In practice, if you win even a small number of accumulators, you are probably going to get limited or banned. And, in any case, what is a genius like you doing hiding among the suckers betting on Accas with Paddy Power? If you think the odds offered by Paddy satisfy $p \times D > 1$, then you'd be even better off taking the superior odds offered by Pinnacle or available on Betfair Exchange. And they won't throw you out for winning.

There is some interesting economics on what to do if you have an edge but the answer is not to bet on Accas. We'll return to this later.

III. Beliefs and Betting

We have discussed how to use the odds to estimate probabilities and profit margins. But how exactly do odds get set? To answer that, we need a working model of how bettors behave.

This part of the book focuses on how beliefs drive betting decisions. We assume people take bets when they think the bet has a positive expected profit. This is contrasted with how economists have usually thought about decisions to gamble. We provide worked examples of how people will bet when quoted specific odds and show how this approach solves an old puzzle that economists struggled with for 80 years – why pari-mutuel betting odds are biased.

CHAPTER 7

Beliefs, Risk and a Rule for Betting

Bookmakers set odds expecting to make a profit on average, and they do. But they're not infallible. Their probability estimates can be wrong, and that possibility is the basic motivation for betting: on average bookies get it right, but maybe they've got *this* one wrong.

Over the next few chapters, I'm going to use a simple rule of thumb to describe when people decide to place bets.

People place a bet when they believe its expected profit is positive.

In the terms we have been using, we assume that if someone believes their bet has a probability p of winning, they will accept a bet with decimal odds of D provided $p \times D > 1$.

Before applying this idea, here we discuss some other factors that may influence the decision to bet, such as attitudes to risk and the enjoyment of betting as an activity. I will contrast this simple rule with how economists have thought about how people take risky decisions and about gambling decisions in particular.

What About Risk?

One thing missing from our simple rule is what economists call *risk aversion*. We are assuming people place bets based on their expected profit. But taking these bets creates uncertainty. And there is lots of evidence to show that people usually don't want to introduce more uncertainty into their lives.

Economists explain risk aversion using an idea called *diminishing marginal utility*. The insight goes back to Daniel Bernoulli, Jacob Bernoulli's nephew, writing in 1738. He was considering the famous St. Petersburg puzzle in which you win one ducat if you tossed heads once, two ducats if you tossed it twice in a row, four ducats if you tossed it three times in a row and so on. The expected payoff from playing the game is infinite but not many people seemed willing to pay much to play it.

Daniel figured out it was because they didn't place much additional weight on the huge but unlikely possible riches the game offered. As you get a bit richer, it makes you happier, but each extra bit of wealth adds a little bit less happiness than the last one. Going from £10,000 to £20,000 in wealth feels more significant than going from £100,000 to £110,000. Diminishing marginal utility makes people turn down gambles with equal chances of winning or losing the same amount – the extra happiness (or utility as economists call it) they would get from winning is smaller than the reduction in happiness they would get from losing.

Bernoulli also described how risk aversion generalises beyond 50/50 gambles. He argued that people take decisions based on maximising their *expected utility*: weighing up the utility from each of the options by their likelihood.

Risk-averse people will turn down a bet with decimal odds of $D = 10$ and a probability of $p = 0.1$ of winning. The bet has $p \times D = 1$ so it is fair, but the drop in utility from losing is more than nine times the gain in utility from winning. This means 90% of the potential loss in utility outweighs 10% of the potential gain, so the better option from an expected utility viewpoint is to not take the bet.

Applications of risk aversion aren't limited to coin-tossing games or bets on sport. It explains a wide range of human behaviours. Risk aversion explains why people buy insurance – even though the insurer expects to profit. Many people would rather pay a modest, guaranteed cost than face a small chance of a big loss. It explains why employees prefer a stable salary over bonuses; why many of us shy away from entrepreneurship, even when the average payoff is high. Across the economy, risk carries a price – and people need compensation to bear it.

You can particularly see risk aversion in financial markets. The key model of financial markets used today stems from Nobel Prize winner Harry Markowitz's work in the 1950s. He started from the simple assumption that risk-averse people liked higher average returns on assets but disliked higher *variance*, a statistical measure of how widely returns fluctuate around their average.[15] His work laid the foundation for the kind of diversified investment funds - which reduce variance without giving up returns - that are so popular today.

Given all this evidence that most people are risk averse, the most common explanation among economists for why people gamble has been that gamblers must have different preferences to everyone else. They must have *increasing marginal utility* as wealth gets higher. This means they actively enjoy taking risks, including even taking some gambles with a negative expected value. What else could explain why someone would bet on sports with bookmakers, when these bets clearly lose on average?

I won't list the cast of highly eminent economists that have put forward this theory over the years, but I think it's wrong, both in theory and in practice.

Small Stakes

Survey evidence published by the UK Gambling Commission shows that one in ten adults had placed a bet on sports over the previous four weeks. What is the chance that one in ten people have a strange enthusiasm for taking risks purely for their own sake?

Of course, some bettors fall into the abyss of gambling addiction but most people who bet are perfectly normal. They routinely make decisions that reflect risk aversion. They buy insurance products. They choose their investments carefully. They avoid unnecessary risks in their everyday life.

And the idea that sports bettors have increasing marginal utility in wealth doesn't match their everyday behaviour. Someone with increasing marginal utility in wealth would simply enjoy adding risk to their life. Sure, they'd like betting on sports. But if they truly loved risk for its own sake, they wouldn't need a bookmaker. You'd expect to see them flipping coins with their risk-loving friends at coffee breaks, just for fun.

As Richard Thaler and William Ziemba noted in their classic 1988 paper *"groups of friends that attend the track together rarely bet among themselves, although they could thereby guarantee a zero sum game for the group and increase variance as much as they wanted."* There have to be some other explanations for why they bet on sports, beyond the idea that they just enjoy taking risks.

And there is nothing in economic theory that says risk-averse people won't ever take a risk. Many people are risk averse but still make risky investments in shares because they believe they have a high expected return. Indeed, there is a simple result from economic theory, due to Nobel Prize winner Ken Arrow, which states that a risk-averse person will always accept a positive-expected-value gamble once the stakes are small enough relative to their wealth.[16] Small stakes allow rational, risk-averse people to take gambles they think are likely to be profitable without risking financial distress.

The evidence confirms that most bettors risk very modest stakes. A team of Harvard psychologists found the average bet size with *bwin*, a European bookmaker, was €18.[17] This average, however, was heavily influenced by a small number of gamblers who placed large bets. The median bet size was €6, meaning half of the bets placed were bigger than €6 and half were less. A recent survey of American online sports bettors reported the median amount staked was $10.[18] Reports from Betfair, the betting exchange, show the average bet size is about £13. So, across different countries and different platforms, there is a clear pattern that most bets placed are relatively small.

Why does someone choose to bet £5 rather than £10 when the bigger bet would potentially offer more profit? The most reasonable answer is that they didn't want to risk the larger amount. The very fact that people tend to bet small amounts points to risk aversion as playing a key role in their decision making.

Beliefs and Rationality

Our decision rule - take the bet if you think it offers a positive expected profit - is consistent with the idea of rational behaviour. It assumes people take what they think is the best decision. But there is one natural objection.

On average, sports bettors lose and bookmakers win. Otherwise, bookmakers wouldn't be in business. Given this, you might think a common line of reasoning would be: "If bookmakers offer odds of D, the chance of success must be less than $1/D$ so this bet must be a loser." This, in all likelihood, is exactly how most people reason. Betting on sports is popular. 10% of UK adults do it regularly. But that means 90% don't. The most likely reason is they think they will lose money.

Does that mean people who bet are acting irrationally? Not necessarily. The question of how publicly available prices should influence your beliefs goes back to the classic work of Sanford "Sandy" Grossman. Awarded his PhD from Chicago in 1975 at age 22, his research posed a simple question: if prices already reflect all available information, as Gene Fama argued, why does anyone trade? If a share is priced at £10, people should just look at it and say "yep, that's the right price." Nobody should want to sell it to make a better investment or buy it because they think it's superior to other investments.

Grossman showed, however, that even when everyone sees the same market price and understands that it communicates information, people with different pre-existing beliefs will still end up with different assessments after seeing the price - and so they keep trading. The price doesn't erase their initial differences in opinion - it might update them, but they still disagree about whether the asset is over or underpriced.

Sports betting works the same way. Bettors know that bookmakers earn profits. But they also know that this is a profit earned across all the bets, not this specific bet that they are about to make. They may have carefully selected the 49ers to beat the Bears as the one bet today where they think the bookmakers have got their probabilities wrong.

There is some recent evidence that sports bettors do indeed think like this. A remarkable study by three Stanford economics PhD students — Matthew Brown, Nick Grasley, and Mariana Guido — surveyed American online sports bettors who agreed to share their account data in return for some financial incentives.[19] The bettors had, on average, lost 7.5 cents per dollar staked. But when asked how they expected to do in the future, their average prediction was a small profit. Remarkably, even when explicitly shown their past losses and asked to revise their forecasts, the respondents held onto their beliefs that they would come out ahead.

We are clearly reaching the limits of normal ideas of rationality here. Acknowledging that you didn't win in the past while expecting to win in the future probably reflects a behavioural bias. And that's ok. We are not going to assume that bettors are hyper-rational. But the idea that people take the actions they think are best given their beliefs explains much of what we see in betting markets.

Betting for Enjoyment

There is, of course, another simple explanation for why people bet on sports: They enjoy it. I don't mean they enjoy it for its own sake in the sense of "they have increasing marginal utility of wealth." I mean they are normal risk-averse people who also get a buzz from placing bets on sports.

Survey evidence makes clear that this is one of the factors motivating the decision to bet. A UK Gambling Commission survey found that 72% of regular bettors listed "Because it's fun" as one of their reasons for betting. 35% answered that they bet "Because it's something I do with my family and friends."[20] The Stanford study also asked this question, and the most popular answer - given by 80% of respondents - was "It makes watching sports more fun."

Is this the real explanation then? People don't bet to make money; they do it because it's fun? Well, like the cute kid in the meme says, "Why not both?" And that's exactly what the survey responses show. 63% of bettors in the UK Gambling Commission's survey listed "To make money" as one of their motivations for betting. In the Stanford study, 40% agreed that "To win money on average" was one of their motivations. Another American survey showed 71% of sports bettors cited "winning money" as a major reason for betting, a higher number than the 61% agreeing that doing it "for the thrill" was one of the reasons.[21]

As we'll discuss more in the next chapter, there is nothing incompatible about someone betting for enjoyment while also picking the bet they think will win money. If Arsenal are playing Chelsea, I might enjoy betting on either team. But what makes me pick Arsenal, you pick Chelsea, and someone else decide not to place a bet? Our differing beliefs.

Loss Aversion

Bernoulli's idea of diminishing marginal utility explains why you would turn down fair bets: the expected reduction in utility from losing is greater than the expected extra utility from winning. But in the 1970s, psychologists Daniel Kahneman and Amos Tversky argued that this didn't go far enough. In their view, many people don't just dislike losses — they hate them.

Kahneman and Tversky weren't economists, but their research had a profound influence on economics. They uncovered systematic patterns in how people make choices under uncertainty that couldn't be explained by traditional models. Kahneman was awarded the Nobel Prize for economics in 2002 for this work.[22]

Perhaps their most influential idea, known as *loss aversion*, suggests that losses carry extra psychological weight. Losing £10 doesn't just feel worse than gaining £10 - it feels *much* worse.

Loss aversion goes beyond standard risk aversion. Risk aversion is about how people value levels of wealth - each additional pound means less to someone who is already wealthy. Bernoulli's theory of diminishing marginal utility implies that as your wealth declines, losses become increasingly painful. Losing £100 when you're poor matters more than when you are wealthy because each dollar matters more when you have less.

But loss aversion is subtly different. It's not the level of wealth that matters most — it's the fact of the loss. Gains are valued in line with

Daniel Bernoulli's predictions, but losses trigger a different kind of response. Beyond the loss of utility from being poorer, the very fact that you have lost money feels bad. Kahneman and Tversky proposed something quite different to diminishing marginal utility. They suggested that the pain of losing the first £10 is greater than the extra pain of losing £10 more on top of already losing £100.

Part of the reason losses from gambles or investments sting so much may be that they don't just feel like bad outcomes – they feel like mistakes. People often experience regret or even guilt if they make choices that cause them to lose money. We will see later that loss aversion probably influences the decisions people take on some bets.

On Lotteries

Lotteries are by far the world's most common type of gambling. A UK Gambling Commission survey showed that 36% of people in Britain reported buying lottery tickets over the previous four weeks, almost four times as many as bet on sports.

What explains this popularity? It could be that people really think lottery tickets are good investments. One of the many important contributions of Kahneman and Tversky was demonstrating that many of us are poor at judging small probabilities. When you ask people how likely it is that events like earthquakes or tornadoes will happen where they live, they substantially overestimate the probabilities. People have little feel for just how rare these events are, beyond a vague sense of "not too often."

In the same way, it could be that people's subjective estimates of the probability p of winning a lottery could be high enough that they believe $p \times D > 1$.

After all, the D for a lottery win is huge. There is also evidence that lotteries with higher expected payout rates (for example, when rollovers increased the prize pool) generate greater demand for tickets, suggesting lottery players are capable of making rough calculations about expected returns.[23] So it could be that our framework also explains why people buy lottery tickets.

Except it doesn't. Average payouts on lotteries are terrible. Typically, only about half the amount collected in ticket sales is paid out in prizes. And the evidence suggests people know that lotteries are a bad investment. Indeed, survey evidence points to lottery players being even more pessimistic than is warranted. One survey of American lottery ticket buyers showed 70% thought the average payout was less than one quarter of the cost of the ticket and only 8% thought it was three-quarters or more.[24]

So, if people know lottery tickets are bad investments, why do they still buy them? The best explanation is that, for a small price, they get to spend some time imagining how life might change - paying off debts, buying a house, quitting their job. To use the phrase coined by economists David Forrest, Robert Simmons and Neil Chesters, lottery players are "buying a dream" not making an investment.[25] And to the extent that loss aversion shapes gambling decisions, it doesn't apply here: nobody dwells on the regret of losing money on a £2 ticket.

Even the evidence that lottery demand is sensitive to their expected payout rates points towards the dream-buying explanation. Demand seems to respond to the size of the jackpot (the bigger the jackpot, the bigger the dream) and not to other improvements in expected payouts, such as more generous secondary prizes.[26]

Lotteries are a fascinating subject. But I don't think the dream-buying explanation sheds much light on how odds are set on most sports bets.

CHAPTER 8

Betting and the Wisdom of Crowds

This chapter explores the implications of differences in beliefs for betting. We do this by providing worked-out examples of how people will bet on the available options given the odds.

Two Simplifying Assumptions

In showing the implications of our framework for betting, we are going to make two simplifying assumptions that make it easier to go from the framework to concrete predictions.

The first is that we assume a *uniform distribution* of beliefs about probabilities. This means there are equal numbers of people with each of the possible beliefs in between the highest and lowest values. To give a quick example, suppose people's beliefs about a probability range from 0.4 to 0.6. Then a uniform distribution implies three-quarters of people have beliefs above 0.45 because the space between 0.45 and 0.6 is three-quarters of the space between 0.4 and 0.6.

The second assumption is that each bettor places the same size bet. This means we can go straight from the number of bettors to the total volumes placed on each outcome. We will come back later to the question of how much people should bet based on their beliefs near the end of the book.

The Wisdom of Crowds

Figuring out probabilities is hard and most people are probably wrong in their estimates. But something strange and encouraging happens when you combine all those individual guesses: on average, the crowd tends to get things right.

A well-known example involves Francis Galton, a brilliant scientist, but also a leading promoter of eugenics. At a country fair in 1906, Galton came across a contest in which you could win an ox if you made the best guess of its weight. He collected the tickets, with around 800 guesses. Holding a dim view of most humans, he expected the average to be way off. It was 1,197 pounds. The true weight was 1,198.

Today, we see the same phenomenon in many real-world betting markets, where the collective judgement of thousands of bettors often does a remarkable job of matching the true probabilities - so much so that bookmakers regularly rely on this wisdom of crowds when setting their odds. Given this, our baseline assumption will be that the public's average belief about a probability is correct. I'll be clear when this matters for conclusions and when it doesn't.

Would You Bet on Arsenal or Chelsea?

Let's return to the Arsenal v Chelsea FA Cup example and assume that Arsenal have a 70% chance of winning. Let p represent people's subjective beliefs about the probability that Arsenal will win. In line with the wisdom of crowds idea, let's assume the average value of p is 0.7 and that beliefs range from a low of $p = 0.64$ to a high of $p = 0.76$. This means the person who is most optimistic about Arsenal is off by the same amount as the person who is most optimistic about Chelsea.

Assume also that people's subjective probability assessments are always two-digit decimal numbers (like 0.64, 0.65, 0.66 ...) This means there are 13 possible beliefs going from 0.64 up to 0.76 and the uniform distribution assumption means each of those possible beliefs is held by 1/13 of the potential bettors.

Assume also that the bookmaker knows the probability of success of each bet and, for now, that there is zero margin. This means they set fair decimal odds of

- Arsenal: 1 / 0.70 = 1.43 = D_A
- Chelsea: 1 / 0.30 = 3.33 = D_C

Given odds of D_A, only those who have $p > 1/D_A$ will bet on Arsenal. By the same logic, only those with $1-p > 1 / D_C$ will bet on Chelsea. For the edge case of $p \times D = 1$, we assume people don't bother betting since they don't expect to earn a profit.

Let's see what this implies. The table below shows what happens as we vary the bettor's belief about Arsenal's chances, from 64% to 76%. For each belief, we compute the expected payout rate from betting on Arsenal at odds of 1.43 and from betting on Chelsea at odds of 3.33.

The table shows that those who believe Arsenal's chances of winning are greater than 70% bet on Arsenal to win and those who believe Arsenal's chances of winning are less than 70% bet on Chelsea. The small number of people who believe the probability is precisely 70% don't bother betting. I've put this line in bold to highlight those who don't bet.

So almost everyone places a bet: only those who believe $p = 0.70$ don't bet. Because we've assumed that beliefs are uniformly spread from 0.64 to 0.76, it follows that the same number of people bet on Arsenal as on Chelsea. Note that each person here is being rational given their own beliefs; this *rational disagreement* is what drives betting markets.

Betting decisions by belief: fair odds (no margin)

Belief about probability Arsenal win	*p × 1.43 for Arsenal*	*(1-p) × 3.33 for Chelsea*
0.64	0.91 (Don't bet)	1.20 (Take bet)
0.65	0.93 (Don't bet)	1.17 (Take bet)
0.66	0.94 (Don't bet)	1.13 (Take bet)
0.67	0.96 (Don't bet)	1.10 (Take bet)
0.68	0.97 (Don't bet)	1.07 (Take bet)
0.69	0.99 (Don't bet)	1.03 (Take bet)
0.70	**1.00 (Don't bet)**	**1.00 (Don't bet)**
0.71	1.01 (Take bet)	0.97 (Don't bet)
0.72	1.03 (Take bet)	0.93 (Don't bet)
0.73	1.04 (Take bet)	0.90 (Don't bet)
0.74	1.06 (Take bet)	0.87 (Don't bet)
0.75	1.07 (Take bet)	0.83 (Don't bet)
0.76	1.09 (Take bet)	0.80 (Don't bet)

Adding a Bookmaker's Margin

Time to get more realistic. Bookmakers set odds that are less generous than fair odds so that they will, on average, make a profit. Let's assume this is a strongly efficient market with a 5% profit margin.

Since the true probability of an Arsenal win is 0.70, the odds for Arsenal are now

$$D_A = 0.95 / 0.70 = 1.36$$

And for Chelsea, whose true win probability is 0.30, the odds are

$$D_C = 0.95 / 0.30 = 3.17$$

What does the introduction of the margin do to betting behaviour? The table below shows how people bet when offered these less generous odds. The break-even condition for betting on Arsenal is no longer $p > 0.70$. Instead, you need a higher belief to justify the bet. We can work out what this higher belief is as follows

$$p \times 1.36 > 1 \text{ which means } p > 1 / 1.36 = 0.735$$

Similarly, for Chelsea, the break-even condition becomes

$$(1-p) \times 3.17 > 1 \text{ which means } p < 1 - 1/3.17 = 0.685.$$

This means people place a bet if their belief about p is one of the following

- Above 0.735, in which case they bet on Arsenal
- Below 0.685, in which case they bet on Chelsea.

Those with beliefs from 0.685 to 0.735 don't place bets. Again, we have highlighted those who don't bet in bold.

Now, let's count how many people fall into each group.

- Chelsea bettors: beliefs from 0.64 to 0.68 → 5 people
- Non-bettors: beliefs from 0.69 to 0.73 → 5 people
- Arsenal bettors: beliefs from 0.74 to 0.76 → 3 people

Notice that the margin doesn't just reduce the number of people who bet (from 12 in the fair-odds case to 8 now). It also shifts the balance of bets toward the underdog. Even though the bookmaker's edge is the same for both teams, and beliefs are spread evenly, more people end up betting on Chelsea than on Arsenal.

This asymmetry, arising naturally from how margins interact with beliefs, is key to understanding bookmaker pricing. We will come back to it when we explore how they set odds, and why bets on favourites give better returns than bets on longshots.

Betting decisions by belief: adding a 5% margin

Belief about probability Arsenal win	$p \times 1.36$ *for Arsenal*	$(1\text{-}p) \times 3.17$ *for Chelsea*
0.64	0.87 (Don't bet)	1.14 (Take bet)
0.65	0.88 (Don't bet)	1.11 (Take bet)
0.66	0.90 (Don't bet)	1.08 (Take bet)
0.67	0.91 (Don't bet)	1.05 (Take bet)
0.68	0.92 (Don't bet)	1.01 (Take bet)
0.69	**0.94 (Don't bet)**	**0.98 (Don't bet)**
0.70	**0.95 (Don't bet)**	**0.95 (Don't bet)**
0.71	**0.96 (Don't bet)**	**0.92 (Don't bet)**
0.72	**0.98 (Don't bet)**	**0.89 (Don't bet)**
0.73	**0.99 (Don't bet)**	**0.86 (Don't bet)**
0.74	1.01 (Take bet)	0.82 (Don't bet)
0.75	1.02 (Take bet)	0.79 (Don't bet)
0.76	1.03 (Take bet)	0.76 (Don't bet)

Factoring in Excitement

One motivation we discussed earlier is that people enjoy the excitement that comes with betting. We can factor this into how betting decisions are taken by focusing not just on the expected payout rate $p \times D$ but also adding an "excitement element" e, so people will take a bet whenever $(p \times D) + e > 1$. There is likely to be a limit on how much people are willing to lose just for the thrill, so we model this in the next table with the relatively small value of $e = 0.02$. This means, for example, that someone who believes that $p \times D = 0.99$ will now take the bet, because adding the excitement element brings the combined total over one.

Adding $e = 0.02$ excitement from betting

Belief about probability Arsenal win	*p × 1.36 + 0.02 for Arsenal*	*(1-p) × 3.17 + 0.02 for Chelsea*
0.64	0.89 (Don't bet)	1.16 (Take bet)
0.65	0.90 (Don't bet)	1.13 (Take bet)
0.66	0.92 (Don't bet)	1.10 (Take bet)
0.67	0.93 (Don't bet)	1.07 (Take bet)
0.68	0.94 (Don't bet)	1.03 (Take bet)
0.69	0.96 (Don't bet)	1.00 (Take bet)
0.70	**0.97 (Don't bet)**	**0.97 (Don't bet)**
0.71	**0.99 (Don't bet)**	**0.94 (Don't bet)**
0.72	**1.00 (Don't bet)**	**0.91 (Don't bet)**
0.73	1.01 (Take bet)	0.88 (Don't bet)
0.74	1.02 (Take bet)	0.86 (Don't bet)
0.75	1.04 (Take bet)	0.81 (Don't bet)
0.76	1.05 (Take bet)	0.78 (Don't bet)

The table shows that adding some excitement doesn't change much. Two people change their decision - both had previously not backed either team but one now bets on Chelsea, one on Arsenal. Everyone else takes the same decision as before and the balance of bets is similar.[27] Crucially for our later discussions of bookmakers' pricing strategies, you can also work out that the pattern of demand for bets as the odds change is essentially the same.

This shows "people bet for the excitement" is not a full explanation of betting behaviour. Yes, they do. But that doesn't explain *which* bets they choose to take, or the crucial role played by the odds in that decision. And there is no contradiction between "enjoying betting" and "expecting to win", something we saw in the survey evidence. In this example, of the ten possible beliefs consistent with placing bets, only two of them were from people who thought the bet had a negative expected profit.

None of the messages that follow in the rest of the book would be changed by continuing to add in an excitement element to the decision-making process, but it would make the calculations messier. So, while getting enjoyment from betting is clearly part of the reason people do it, in the rest of the book we'll focus largely on people betting because they expect to win on average. Models in economics are most useful when they explain things in the simplest possible way that still works. Excitement about placing bets is real but we won't use it in the models.

And the payoff comes immediately. In the next chapter, we'll see how our rational disagreement framework - combining the $p \times D > 1$ rule, disagreement in beliefs and the wisdom of crowds - explains a well-known puzzle about parimutuel betting.

CHAPTER 9

Solving an Old Puzzle: Bias in Pari-Mutuel Odds

Joseph Oller's invention of the pari-mutuel system in 1867 quickly spread around the world, becoming the dominant way to bet on horse races. In many countries, it was the only legal way to place a wager. As a result, when social scientists began studying sports betting in the 20th century, their attention naturally focused on pari-mutuel racetrack betting.

One pattern kept showing up, no matter the track, the year, or the type of race: longshot bets lost more money on average than bets on favourites. This persistent result became an enduring anomaly in economics, defying satisfactory explanation from the economic theory of rational behaviour for over half a century. For us, this is where the framework we've built – differences in beliefs, $p \times D > 1$ and the wisdom of crowds – starts to pay off. It can explain this famous result without assuming any strange or irrational behaviour on the part of bettors.

The Favourite-Longshot Bias

In 1949, psychologist Richard Griffith produced a paper based on odds and results from 1,386 races at three American tracks.[28] Overall, he concluded that the odds were pretty good indicators of the likelihood that a horse would win. Grouping together horses with similar odds, he found that the longer the odds, the less likely the horses were to win. However, the odds were not perfect indicators of the true probabilities. Backing out the implied probabilities using the normalisation method described earlier, he found that horses with decimal odds below 6 won more often than the implied probabilities, while those with odds above 6 won less often.

Both economics and psychology have had problems over the years with replicability. Empirical studies appear to show something interesting but then other studies looking at different times and places don't produce the same results. But Griffith's finding - what is known now as *the favourite-longshot bias* - proved to be incredibly robust. The largest-scale study came in 2010, when Erik Snowberg and Justin Wolfers examined odds on over 5.6 million American horses from 1992 to 2001 and found the same favourite-longshot bias in pari-mutuel odds, consistent across tracks and time.

The evidence also showed that loss rates rose sharply as the odds lengthened. Snowberg and Wolfers reported that across all bets, the average loss per dollar staked was 26% - a reflection of the extremely high "takeout" rates of that era, when limited legal betting options allowed tracks to set steep margins. Bets on favourites lost only 5% on average. But once the odds climbed above 10, losses accelerated quickly, and wagers on horses priced over 100 lost more than 61% on average.

What drove this remarkable pattern?

Thaler's Anomalies

During the 1970s and 1980s, Richard Thaler worked with the psychologists Daniel Kahneman and Amos Tversky to build a systematic case for behavioural economics.[29] They argued that deviations from the *homo economicus* model of rational maximisers were not just small random errors that could be ignored but were important to understanding key aspects of the economy.

In 1987, the American Economic Association set up a new journal, the *Journal of Economic Perspectives,* with the aim of communicating important research to economists and non-economists in a less technical form than found in other journals. The editor, Joe Stiglitz, was not a "markets always work" economist and he hired Thaler to write a regular feature called *Anomalies*, to highlight the evidence that people did not always follow the textbook economics model.

One of Thaler's first *Anomalies* columns was the 1988 paper co-authored with Ziemba, which defined strong betting market efficiency. Thaler focused on betting markets because they helped to rebut a common criticism of his ideas from critics like Gene Fama. Sceptics would read studies based on small-stakes laboratory experiments – the staple of Kahneman and Tversky's work – and dismiss them as not going to apply once people were playing for "real" money.

Well, betting markets featured lots of real money but still generated a result that didn't seem consistent with Fama's ideas. Thaler and Ziemba defined strong market efficiency so that they could immediately point to the favourite-longshot bias in pari-mutuel markets as a case where it didn't hold. Quite clearly, the expected return on all bets was not the same.

Thaler and Ziemba then discussed the potential explanations for the favourite-longshot bias. Leading economists like Richard Quandt had argued that the bias existed because gamblers had increasing marginal utility in wealth – in other words, they just loved risk.[30]

Quandt's argument was as follows. Longshot bets involve far more uncertainty than bets on favourites. Two bets can have the same average payout but very different levels of variance: a series like 0, 2, 0, 2, 0, 2, 2, 0, 0, 2 has an average of 1 and modest ups and downs, whereas 0, 0, 0, 0, 0, 10, 0, 0, 0, 0 also has an average of 1 but bigger variation. Risk-averse people dislike high variance. But risk-loving bettors have the opposite taste, so they actively seek it. All else equal, they would prefer the longer-odds bet that wins big a small fraction of the time.

Quandt reasoned that you couldn't have everyone in a pari-mutuel market all picking the same bet. The only way for the market to be in "equilibrium" was for longshots to offer a lower average return, so they would no longer be more attractive than other bets. In short, if gamblers actively chase long odds bets as their preference, then the market will make the payoff on those bets worse, so the thrill comes at a cost. The lower average return will offset the higher variance.

Thaler and Ziemba did not buy this argument. They observed that the small average size of bets and the absence of random coin tossing games amongst racetrack bettors both pointed against bettors having increasing marginal utility of wealth.

But Thaler and Ziemba's own arguments for the bias were not much more convincing. They pointed to people perhaps having difficulty judging small probabilities, an idea that Kahneman and Tversky had promoted. But the evidence shows favourite-longshot bias applying to bets whose chances of winning are not that low. Empirical studies showed win rates were too low for bets with decimal odds as small as 6. A one-in-six chance is not exactly hard to grasp; most people can figure out how likely you are to roll a 3 on a dice. It's unlikely that the psychology research on struggles to put correct numbers on low-probability events applies to this case.

Thaler and Ziemba's other argument was that perhaps it was fun to bet on longshots so you could brag to your friends when it came in. Well, ok, maybe. But I don't think many people are placing bets thinking *"I will lose 50% of my money on average but man think of the bragging when I win."*

Ironically, an explanation for the favourite-longshot bias in pari-mutuel betting that would have satisfied both Thaler's belief that markets often deliver the wrong outcome and Fama's conviction that people act rationally, had already been published in a leading journal but it was almost entirely ignored.

Mukhtar Ali: A Missed Insight

In 1977, economist Mukhtar Ali published a paper in the *Journal of Political Economy* that contained an idea that, had it been properly understood, might have reshaped how economists thought about betting markets.[31] The paper was read by some, but the insight was mostly missed.

As with our framework, Ali assumed rational bettors would only take bets they believed had a positive expected profit. He showed that even if bettors satisfy the wisdom of crowds, so they are on average correct in their beliefs, pari-mutuel markets would still produce biased odds. The classic favourite-longshot bias could arise not because people are irrational, or biased in their average beliefs, or risk-loving or want to brag about winning a big bet. It arose simply because people differed in their beliefs.

Unfortunately, Ali didn't explain his idea well and the second half of his paper wandered into a standard treatment of gamblers as risk lovers. So, his insight never caught on. Let me try to explain it here more clearly.

How Differences in Beliefs Lead to Biased Odds

Before explaining Ali's argument, a quick technicality. When you place a pari-mutuel bet, you don't know the odds you will get if your horse wins. That's only settled after everyone has placed their bets. The operator displays the odds you would get based on the volume placed so far but you could imagine you're getting a good price and then a flurry of last-minute bets on your horse might mean the odds are not so great after all.

Ali assumed that people know the pari-mutuel odds when they place their bets. This was a reasonable simplification. Big last-minute moves in pari-mutuel odds can happen but they are unusual, and most people have a very good idea of the odds they will be getting when they place their bets.

His argument about favourite-longshot bias went like this. Consider a race with two horses where the favourite has probability q of winning. Let's stop for a second. Why q? Haven't we been using p for the probability? Nope. We have been using p as people's *subjective* assessments of probabilities. In contrast, q is the *actual* probability that the favourite wins - the true underlying number that people are trying to estimate.

Ali assumed the pool of potential bettors disagree about how strong the favourite is. They each have their own subjective value of p, which is their estimate of what q is. But, on average, they satisfy the wisdom of crowds, so their median belief about the favourite's probability of winning is also q. This means half the bettors have values of p greater than or equal to q and half of them have values less than or equal to q.

Assume the track take is zero so, on average, every £1 bet placed will return £1 and let D_F be the decimal odds on the favourite and D_L be the decimal odds on the longshot. This market will be strongly efficient if $q \times D_F = 1$ for the favourite and $(1-q) \times D_L = 1$ for the longshot. This would imply fair odds of $D_F = 1/q$ for the favourite and $D_L = 1 / (1-q)$ for the longshot.

At those odds, half of those who bet - those with a subjective belief p that is greater than q - will want to take the bet on the favourite because they believe $p \times D_F > 1$ so the expected return on the favourite is positive. By the same argument, the same number of bettors - those with a subjective belief p that is less than q - will take the bet on the longshot, believing it to have a positive expected return.

But wait a minute. This can't be the outcome. Pari-mutuel odds depend on the volume of bets placed and if the two horses each have the same number of backers the odds for both will be the same. Without a track take, odds will be $D = 2$ for both. And since the public on average correctly assesses that the favourite is more likely to win, then at these odds more people will want to back the favourite which stops the odds being $D = 2$. So, equal volumes can't be the outcome.

These contradictions show pari-mutuel betting markets will not be strongly efficient when bettors disagree. The efficient odds produce betting volumes that are not consistent with those odds. Ali recognised that pari-mutuel betting featured more people backing the favourite than the longshot. This meant the odds for the favourite had to be a bit higher than $1/q$ and the odds for the longshot had to be a bit lower than $1 / (1-q)$. This in turn implied that bets on favourites had to do better on average than bets on longshots.

Without assuming the betting public loved risk, or systematically misunderstood small probabilities or loved bragging about unlikely wins, Ali had explained why pari-mutuel markets had a favourite-longshot bias. All you needed to assume was that people had differing beliefs.

Consistent Pari-Mutuel Odds and Volumes

Ali showed that differences in beliefs implied pari-mutuel betting markets would not be strongly efficient and their odds could not be simply mapped into true probabilities. But he did not provide concrete examples showing exactly what the odds would be and how badly longshot bets would perform. Let's show how it works.

Fair odds can't be the outcome of pari-mutuel betting markets because they imply an inconsistency: The betting volumes generated by fair odds were not consistent with the pari-mutuel odds implied by those volumes. The outcome of the market needed to be a set of volumes and odds that were compatible with each other.

Figuring out this kind of thing is a standard problem in economics. Consider the most famous economics model of them all: supply and demand. Higher prices discourage people from buying: This implies a *negative* relationship between the quantity of a good purchased and its price. But higher prices attract more firms to supply the good: This implies a *positive* relationship between the quantity purchased and its price. Generations of economics students are familiar with the graph showing a downward-sloping demand curve and an upward-sloping supply curve. The *equilibrium* is at the intersection of the two curves: The prices and quantities that are consistent with the behaviour of both consumers and firms.

In the same way, we have a positive relationship between pari-mutuel odds and volumes stemming from how people decide to bet, since the higher the odds, the more willing people are to back the horse. And we have a negative relationship from the pricing formula: pari-mutuel pricing means a higher volume of bets implies lower odds. You can use the same methods that solve the supply and demand model to figure out the pari-mutuel odds and volumes that are consistent with each other within the rational disagreement framework.[32]

Let's provide a concrete example by going back to our two-horse race. Assume the track take is 10%, the true probability of the favourite winning is $q = 0.55$ and the public's beliefs about this probability range from 0.45 to 0.65. Using algebra to work out the odds and volumes that are consistent with each other, the market produces odds for the favourite of D_F = 1.66 and odds for the longshot of D_L = 1.96. From these odds, we can figure out the average payout on a £1 bet on the favourite as

$$q \times D_F = 0.55 \times 1.66 = 0.913$$

meaning bets on the favourite lose 8.7% on average (because 0.913 - 1 = - 0.087). This is less than the track take percentage.

In contrast, the average payout on a £1 bet on the longshot will be

$$(1\text{-}q)\ D_L = 0.45 \times 1.96 = 0.882$$

meaning an average loss rate on these bets of 11.8% (because 0.882 - 1 = - 0.118).

But how do we know these are the right odds? Let's do a quick check to see they are correct.

First, how many people bet on the favourite? You will take this bet if your judgement is that $p \times D_F > 1$, which here means $p > 1 / 1.66 = 0.602$. The upper limit on beliefs is 0.65, so those with beliefs between 0.602 and 0.65 will back the favourite. That's 24.1% of the full "space of beliefs" between 0.45 and 0.65, so 24.1% of the potential bettors will back the favourite.

A similar calculation for the longshot shows that only those with $p < 0.491$ would take that bet. With beliefs going down to 0.45, you can work out that 20.4% of potential bettors will back the longshot.

The pari-mutuel system means the ratio of the odds on the favourite to the odds on the longshot D_F / D_L should equal the ratio of total bets on the longshot to total bets on the favourite. Let's check this out. First, the ratio of the odds

$$D_F / D_L = 1.66 / 1.96 = 0.846$$

Now let's check the ratio of the volumes, using the percentages of people that choose each bet

$$20.4 / 24.1 = 0.846$$

So it all hangs together. The odds and the betting volumes are consistent.

Disagreement and the Longshot Loss Curve

What if the favourite's probability of winning was higher? The table below shows the model's predicted loss rates for both bets for different values of the favourite's probability of winning (q). We assume again that beliefs are at most 0.1 away from the true value.

The striking pattern is that as the longshot's chances of winning fall, loss rates from betting on it rise at an accelerating pace. The 11.8% loss rate when the longshot has a 45% chance of winning moves up to 19% when they have a 30% chance of winning and to a 46% loss rate when they have only a 10% chance of winning. The model reproduces the evidence of sharply increasing losses for longshot bets as they become less likely to win.

What drives this pattern? In pari-mutuel markets, high odds signal that very few people are willing to back the horse. And the fewer people betting on it, the more extreme those bettors' beliefs must be. Those who take the bet are the small minority whose beliefs were far enough from reality that they are willing to take what are objectively very bad odds.

Odds and loss rates for different values of the favourite's probability of winning (q) with uniform beliefs on [q-0.1, q+0.1] and a 10% track take

Favourite's probability (q)	*Favourite Odds*	*Longshot Odds*	*Favourite Loss Rate*	*Longshot Loss Rate*
0.55	1.66	1.96	8.7%	11.8%
0.60	1.54	2.16	7.4%	13.6%
0.65	1.44	2.40	6.4%	16.0%
0.70	1.35	2.70	5.5%	19.0%
0.75	1.27	3.09	4.7%	22.8%
0.80	1.20	3.60	4.0%	28.0%
0.85	1.14	4.32	3.4%	35.2%
0.90	1.08	5.40	2.8%	46.0%

IV. How Bookmakers Set Odds

We've worked out a framework for why people bet and used it to explain how pari-mutuel betting markets work. Now we use it to figure out the economics of how bookmakers set odds. When dealing with customers who behave like those we have described, what should their strategy be?

My approach is to assume that bookmakers are just like any other business, seeking to maximise profits. So, I start this part of the book by addressing the popular idea that bookmakers instead focus on "balancing the books" and show why this is misleading. I then explain the economic forces that have produced a two-tier system for the global sports betting industry, a competitive one serving sharp bettors and another less competitive one serving retail punters. We conclude with how bookmakers use the differences in beliefs across customers to set odds that maximise profits.

CHAPTER 10

The Balanced Book Myth

I have described how bookmakers set odds as

$$D = \frac{1 - m}{p}$$

They estimate the probability that the bet will win and then add a margin. But there is a commonly discussed alternative idea about how odds are set that you can see all over the internet – that odds are set to "balance the books" so whoever wins, the bookmaker earns the same profit. This chapter addresses this idea and explains why it does not describe how bookmakers set odds.

What the Internet Says About Bookmakers

If you ask the internet how bookmakers set odds, you get a consistent answer. When I asked Google "how do bookmakers set odds?" its AI summary told me about bookmakers "*tweaking the lines ... to balance their books and ensure profit regardless of the result. They aim to create a "fair book" where they take in balanced money on all sides, making money from the commission, not just picking winners.*"

The top answer to this question on Reddit also affirms "*They don't care about the outcome. Their goal is to find odds that result in an equal amount of money being bet on both sides. They tweak the payouts so that no matter the outcome, one side is paid out less than the other side bet leaving them a profit.*"

And Wikipedia, on its "Mathematics of bookmaking" page asserts that "*A bookmaker strives to accept bets on the outcome of an event in the right proportions in order to make a profit regardless of which outcome prevails.*" This idea has also appeared in many papers that academics have written about bookmakers.

The book balancing idea implies bookmakers set odds very differently from how I have described them so far. I have said they start with an estimate of the probability that a bet will win. But if bookmakers adjust their odds so they have an equal exposure whichever team wins, then they don't even factor probabilities into their pricing. They take a lot of money on Brentford to win at odds of $D = 3$, which they think is consistent with a healthy profit margin for them? The book balancing idea implies their judgement about the profitability of these bets doesn't matter. They just reduce the odds to get the exposure on Brentford down and less money starts flowing in on Brentford.

Google, Reddit, Wikipedia, decades of academics. They can't all be wrong, can they? Well, it turns out they can.

Bookmakers Tell Us They Don't Balance Books

I think most people who claim bookmakers focus on balancing books have never spoken to one about this. I have. When I started asking Tadgh how the betting world worked, one of my first questions was "do bookmakers adjust odds down when volumes go up so they have balanced books?"

He could not have been clearer: *Hell no, that is not what we do.* Taking risk on individual events is just part of being a bookmaker. He told me the goal was to make as much profit as possible averaged over all the bets, not to minimise the risk for each event.

I began reading more about the subject. I read an interview with Jay Kornegay, longtime head of the Westgate Superbook and perhaps the most famous Las Vegas bookmaker, about how he set odds.[33]

When asked about balancing books, Jay said "*I think there's a little urban legend that's out there, that we just want to balance every game ... In a perfect world, yeah. But ... it just doesn't happen. You go through every single game today and probably none of them ... are balanced on both sides. That scenario right there, it just doesn't happen. I don't want to sound corny but it is somewhat of an art form. You're dissecting the money, you're dissecting the market, you're dissecting the betting patterns that we're seeing between the sharps and the general public. What we're trying to do is put ourselves in the best possible position to win, not necessarily balancing both sides."*

Between Tadgh's explanations and Kornegay's discussion of his strategy, I realised my earlier line of questioning didn't really make sense.

I am an economist. We teach our students that businesses seek to maximise profits. Bookmakers are businesses. Why would they operate in a way that focuses on minimising risk? Why would they not seek to maximise profits? I suspect the reason people focus on the book balancing idea is because it is easy to understand. And there was no established research out there on how a bookmaker that wanted to maximise profits might go about doing it. That's something we will come back to soon.

Brooklyn Gangsters

As I kept digging, I found two papers from people I remembered as fellow students at graduate school at MIT, each questioning the "bookmaker as risk-avoiding book balancer" story. Both were smart and interesting guys who went on to academic careers devoted to researching unconventional topics.

Steve Levitt had published a paper in 2004 using evidence from a quasi-legal online "betting competition" that used Vegas odds. He showed that most people were betting on favourites, so bookmakers were definitely taking on risk on each game.[34] Steve suggested bookmakers were probably setting odds to maximise profits, since they did not seem to be minimising risk. Soon after, he wrote a book called *Freakonomics* that you might have heard of.

Koleman Strumpf's research relied on a remarkable dataset.[35] From 1995 to 2000, the Brooklyn District Attorney's office prosecuted a series of illegal bookmakers and made their records available after the cases had been resolved. That the illegal bookmakers kept such detailed records raises the question associated with Stringer Bell from

The Wire: "Is you takin' notes on a criminal f---in' conspiracy? What the f-- - is you thinking, man?" But thankfully for us they did, and Koleman found a treasure trove of data showing how actual real-world bookmakers ran their businesses.

Strumpf's evidence showed the conventional wisdom among economists about bookmakers was completely wrong. He wrote *"Bookmakers are thought to be perfectly diversified and to profit only from commissions. This would require implausibly risk averse preferences and is inconsistent with actual practices. I find that bookmakers gamble and take positions on games. The resulting variation in net revenues is substantial, with one large bookmaker often winning or losing one hundred thousand dollars per day on a daily bet volume of a half million dollars."*

Koleman found that bookmakers made high profit rates. But he also showed that the week-to-week variance in the profits and losses of the bookmakers was large enough that investors with typical preferences – the kind modelled years previously by Harry Markowitz – would require high returns for taking this level of risk. Harry's mean-variance theory worked well even for mobsters.

The Total Goals Scored Market

If you're not convinced by Brooklyn bookies from three decades ago, here is a more recent example.

One of the most popular football bets is the total goals scored market. You bet on whether the total goals scored in the game will be above or below a certain figure. The average number of goals scored in a football match is 2.5, so above or below 2.5 goals is by far the most popular total goals market. Economists Raphael Flepp, Stephan Nüesch and Egon Franck used data from Tipico, a German bookmaker, to study bets on the 2.5 goals market.[36]

If you think about it, backing goals not being scored isn't much fun. You're watching the game cheering the time wasting at throw-ins and celebrating missed shots. And you don't know you've won for sure until the end of the game, so you're hanging on in added time when it's 1-1 hoping that literally nothing happens. In contrast, backing the over means you cheer when goals go in and celebrate your win when that third goal hits the back of the net. This seems more like the experience that most bettors enjoy.

Well, sure enough, Flepp, Nüesch and Franck found that over 80% of all betting volume in the 2.5 goals market was on the over. This meant that bookmakers were exposed to risk on every match. When over won, the bookies lost money. When under won, the bookies made a profit. This is a high-volume market where the bookmakers are making no attempt to cover themselves on the risk inherent for them in every game.

Looking at the odds on the two types of bets and the outcomes of the games, the economists found the average return on both over and under bets was about the same, with both being negative because of the bookmaker's margin. So the bookie lost sometimes and won sometimes but on average they came out ahead.

You might be surprised that the returns to the two types of bets are equal. Couldn't bookmakers make a bit more money by setting worse odds on the over and punters would still take them because it's more fun? I think this example shows the limits of fun as a motivation for betting. The fun element influenced *which* bet they take, but betting based on the expected return dictated the overall market price.

Evidence from Betfair Volumes

Unless you are like the economists we just discussed and get a special deal to access a bookmaker's data on a specific market, it is impossible to know the volumes that bookies take on specific bets. Later, however, we will discuss betting exchanges where, instead of betting with a bookmaker, two people agree to take the opposite sides of a bet. And the leading betting exchange, Betfair, provides full information on the volumes on all the events on its platform.

Typically, the odds offered on the Betfair Exchange are better than you can get with a bookmaker, but the overall pattern for the odds is similar. If we find that 60% of bets on Betfair are on the home team, then bookmakers who are quoting the same relative odds on a match will probably also have a similar pattern of unbalanced betting.

Using a large dataset from Betfair on football matches from 2022 to 2024 and matching it with the average odds from the data from www.football-data.co.uk, I was able to construct a dataset for about 32,000 matches, from 27 countries around the world, that had both the average odds from bookmakers and volumes from Betfair Exchange.

I found that 59% of the volume of bets backing outcomes on Betfair Exchange was placed on the favoured team to win the game; 21% was on the underdog to win the game and 20% was on the draw. Using average bookmakers' odds and knowing the outcomes of the game, assuming these same betting volume patterns applied to bookmakers would imply that bookies lost an average of 14% of the total amount placed with them when favourites won but they won 20% when the underdog won and won 25% when the match ended in a draw. It turns out that draws are the bookmaker's friend!

Weighing up the different outcomes, the bookmakers made an average return of 4.2% on bets taken on the matches in this sample, a bit lower than the average margin of 5.9% implied by the overrounds.

This evidence also suggests that bookmakers' profits are incredibly volatile across matches. And this volatility doesn't disappear when profits are aggregated up to a weekly basis. Aggregating across each of the weeks in our dataset of 32,000 matches (an average of 205 matches per week), the results show the standard deviation of the weekly profit rate was 7.4%. Losses over a whole week on these games were common: about one-third of weekly outcomes showed a loss for bookmakers.

Evidence from New York

Some other useful data that has become available in recent years comes from the US. Bookmakers like to be pretty secretive about the profits they make. You can tell from the financial statements in their annual reports that they are usually pretty profitable, but you don't get much detail.

However, some US states, one of them New York, require bookmakers to provide them with weekly data on their total volume of bets taken (which they call "wagering handle") and their gross pre-tax profits (which they call "gross gambling revenue").

For an example of what these data look like, consider the three biggest bookmakers in New York: FanDuel, DraftKings and BetMGM. The table below shows their weekly profit margins for the first twelve weeks of 2026 – the ratio of gross gambling revenue to wagering handle, expressed as a percentage. If these are "book-balancing" firms taking very little risk, then we would expect to see fairly steady profit margins. But that is not what we see. Instead, the weekly margins bounce around substantially. Some weeks the profit margins are well above 10%; other weeks they are far lower. In the week ending February 8, which included the Super Bowl, BetMGM even lost money on its New York sports betting operations.

These profit margins are also clearly correlated with each other. The sportsbooks all post similar odds, and their customers tend to bet on many of the same events. This means some weeks work out better for the sportsbooks than others. Depending on the differences in their odds, promotions and customer betting patterns, individual operators can occasionally have a particularly bad week. But over the course of a year, all three are consistently highly profitable businesses.

Weekly profit margins in 2026 in New York state (%)

Week	*FanDuel*	*DraftKings*	*BetMGM*
Jan 4	17.1%	11.2%	4.5%
Jan 11	10.2%	5.0%	0.9%
Jan 18	21.7%	17.7%	10.9%
Jan 25	5.6%	4.5%	3.7%
Feb 1	12.1%	10.3%	7.1%
Feb 8	11.2%	9.2%	-3.2%
Feb 15	10.3%	8.5%	7.5%
Feb 22	11.0%	9.2%	2.6%
Mar 1	11.4%	8.8%	4.2%
Mar 8	10.5%	10.7%	3.6%
Mar 15	8.7%	10.5%	11.5%
Mar 22	12.6%	10.5%	7.4%

Don't Upset the Customer

A last point on this topic. A soft bookmaker's main asset is its customer base. They spend heavily to acquire customers with free bets and odds boosts, and once they're in the door the bookmakers want them to keep coming back, steadily losing money.

Now imagine Ladbrokes has more volume on Liverpool than they are comfortable with. For book-balancing purposes, they start offering terrible odds on Liverpool so no one else will take that bet with them. A loyal customer logs on, sees those odds on Liverpool, checks another bookmaker, and finds a much better price. Sayonara Ladbrokes – nobody likes to be ripped off.

This is a critical part of customer retention strategy: bookmakers have to post odds that are at least some way reasonable, even on exposed positions, because aggressively balancing the book would damage the long-term value of their customer base.

Beyond Book Balancing

Like many people, my initial guess as to how bookmakers operated was that they tried to balance their books. But I hope that the stories and evidence here will convince you that this idea, while superficially attractive, is actually a myth. In reality, bookmakers set odds using their estimate of the probability that the bet will win, p, and a profit margin, m. This raises some key questions – how do bookmakers estimate p and how exactly do they set their margins? This is where we go next.

CHAPTER 11

How Information Shapes the Global Betting Market

We have seen that odds are not just mechanically determined by betting volumes. Bookmakers set them based on their estimated probabilities p and a specified profit margin m. Here, we discuss how those probability estimates are formed and how the process by which information is gathered to do this task has produced the two-tiered (sharp versus soft) global bookmaker market that we see today.

Hayek: Markets and Information

After the Second World War, there were intense debates about whether capitalist or communist models of the economy worked best. Perhaps the single most influential argument among economists in favour of capitalism came from Friedrich Hayek (1899-1992). Hayek argued that capitalism allowed prices to reflect information about products in ways that centrally planned economies could not.

His argument went like this. Consider what happens when floods strike potato fields in Ireland. Farmers see their crops waterlogged. The wholesale price of potatoes begins to rise, and by the time Walkers place their next big order, they find prices have gone up. They raise the price of a bag of crisps.

Most people, of course, will never learn the details of what happened. Yet within weeks, the effects are felt in supermarkets across Britain and Ireland. Checking the shelf, some customers decide to switch to peanuts.

The waterlogged fields set in motion a chain of transactions with each step involving people acting on their limited slice of knowledge. None of them had the full story, but the price system stitched the fragments together. There are fewer potatoes available, so people need to consume fewer potato-based products.

For Hayek, this was the decisive edge for capitalism. Prices were not just numbers; they were messages. Without a decentralised system in which people react to information by setting their own prices at each stage of the production process, a central planner was not going to do a good job of matching supply with demand.

Competition Makes Betting Odds Reflect Information

Betting markets provide a clear illustration of Hayek's ideas. Just as no one person knows everything about potato harvests, the costs of shipping bags of crisps and the operational costs facing supermarkets, nobody knows the true probability that a team will win.

Information is scattered. Some people hear a rumour about a striker's injury. Others collect lots of data on recent performances. A few watch training footage released by the teams, looking for signs someone looks sharp or off it. Most of us know far less. And the odds offered by bookmakers - who are smart but not geniuses - adjust to absorb all this information in ways that make it very difficult to ever beat them.

How can these odds be so good if nobody, including the bookmaker, has the whole picture? The answer is partly competition among bookmakers and partly the wisdom of crowds.

Economists use the term *perfect competition* to describe a market with two key features. First, firms are price takers: they can't set whatever price they like because customers will walk away if a better deal is available elsewhere. Second, there is free entry and exit. When profits are unusually high, new firms are attracted in, increasing supply and pushing prices and profits down. When losses mount, firms exit, reducing supply and allowing prices and profits to recover. This keeps profit rates from ever getting too high or low.

Imagine a bookmaker posting odds that undervalue a team's true chances of winning. Punters rush to place bets at these generous terms. The bookmaker has seen this scenario before and remembers they typically lost money on these bets. They quickly adjust the odds downward. They are already operating on a tight margin and can't afford to be vulnerable to poorly set odds. Conversely, if odds are too low relative to competitors, nobody wants to back the team at poor odds. Without any demand, the bookmaker has to lengthen the odds to attract bets.

The effect is that even though no individual bookmaker or bettor knows the exact winning probability, the odds in a competitive market converge toward it. "Wrong" odds act like a magnet for smart bettors who step in and exploit the discrepancies when odds are too high and shun odds that are too low. Their actions pull the odds back into line with the underlying reality.

This is Hayek's argument brought to life, operating in real-time on betting odds screens all around the world. Scattered pieces of knowledge, none decisive on their own, come together through the competitive push and pull of the market. Odds, like potato prices, become signals that summarise information.

How Sharp Bookmakers Set Odds

The world's sharpest bookmakers operate from offshore tax havens, serving a clientele of professional gamblers and syndicates rather than weekend punters. Their strategy is to take huge volumes of wagers from a customer base they know to be highly informed and extremely price sensitive. With operational costs that are low relative to volumes, and customers who will shun bad prices, sharp bookmakers come close to the textbook model of perfect competition.

The huge sums placed with these bookmakers provide an opportunity for them to earn big profits. But their informed customer base means there are also clear vulnerabilities. If odds are posted that understate a team's true chances, syndicates will pounce immediately, placing heavy bets until the odds move. A small mistake can quickly become expensive.

To manage this risk, sharp bookmakers rely on a combination of internal modelling and careful monitoring of the behaviour of their customers. After the book on an event has been opened, when uncertainty is highest, they limit stake sizes to reduce exposure. Then they watch closely. They know which of their customers have good records and which don't. When smart money flows heavily in one direction, they treat that as an information signal, adjust their models, and move the odds. Later, as they become more confident in their estimated probabilities, they raise the limits. High-stakes bets from sharp customers are not just tolerated but actively valued because they help to sharpen the bookmaker's own prices.

Pinnacle, the best-known of the sharp operators, is famous for this strategy. When betting lines open on a Champions League match – perhaps three days before kick-off – customers may only be able to wager a few hundred dollars. As the odds settle and information accumulates, the limits are raised again and again. By the day of the match, Pinnacle is often willing to take six-figure bets from professionals. It even advertises its "winners welcome" policy, a stance that would be unthinkable for a retail bookmaker. The reason is simple: winners bring information and information improves prices. A bettor who consistently finds weak prices is effectively pointing out the bookmaker's errors.

The result is that, as the match approaches, sharp bookmakers' odds reflect not only their own statistical models but also the dispersed knowledge of bettors. By the time play begins, the odds stand as clear signals of the way markets aggregate dispersed knowledge – exactly the kind of information machine Hayek described.

Costly Information and the Grossman-Stiglitz Paradox

In most of the examples used to illustrate Hayek's ideas, the information is revealed to people free of cost. You can read online about the flooded potato fields in the newspaper. But not all information is freely available. If you are trying to work out whether a company is worth investing in, it requires effort – collecting and analysing information – and this costs time and money.

Sports betting is the same. Sure, when Everton play Burnley, anyone can freely access the information that Everton are mid-table and are probably a better team than bottom-of-the-league Burnley. But that's hardly the kind of granular information that will give anyone an edge. Those guys watching practice footage? That takes time and time is money. The nerds that build statistical models to figure out if the odds are right? That eats up even more time and is even more money.

Why do people expend this time and effort and what are the implications of costly information for market prices? The answer can be found in a famous 1980 paper called *On the Impossibility of Informationally Efficient Markets*, written by Joe Stiglitz with Sandy Grossman, who we saw back in Chapter 7 explaining how people disagree about the right prices for financial assets.[37] Their paper set out what became known as the *Grossman–Stiglitz paradox*.

The paper's starting point was simple: If prices fully reflect all available information, then there is no reason for anyone to spend time or money gathering information. The price already transmits it.

But if nobody gathers information, then prices can't reflect it. For costly information to be collected at all, it must be profitable to do so. Prices need to be just imperfect enough that informed traders can earn a return by exploiting small discrepancies that others miss. And the cost matters. When information is cheap, more people collect it and prices move closer to efficiency; when it's expensive, fewer do, and prices are less accurate.

This paradox – we rely on financial market prices to reflect information but if they did it perfectly nobody would collect the information – left a lasting mark on how economists thought about the efficiency of financial prices. It showed that "fully efficient" markets, in the sense imagined by Fama, could not exist in the real world. Instead, markets must always leave some room for mistakes – for informed traders to profit – otherwise the whole system breaks down.

Grossman-Stiglitz and the Two-Tier Betting Market

The global betting market provides proof that the Grossman–Stiglitz paradox is not just an ivory-tower curiosity but a description of how actual markets work.

Sharp bookmakers operate on razor-thin margins. If prices really were perfectly efficient, there'd be no point in paying for models, data feeds, or teams of analysts to closely analyse the performance of their customers and the flow of money on an event. Yet they do it anyway. Why? Because the information they collect pays twice.

First, it pays in the core business of taking bets. Sharps use their own models to set opening prices, but then they carefully watch how their most informed customers react. This is another example of where the pure "volumes move odds" story is wrong. What matters isn't total volume - it's *who* is betting. If sharp money flows one direction, odds move. If casual punters pile onto a team at odds where the bookmaker is confident of profit, those odds stay the same even if the volume is lopsided.

Second, it pays again when sharps sell that information. Once they have adjusted odds on a team, you'll often quickly see the same adjustment on a dozen soft bookmakers' apps. Those firms aren't necessarily reacting to demand from their own customers.

Indeed, some don't employ teams of quants to crunch the numbers themselves. It's sometimes cheaper and easier to buy information that others have already figured out. Real-time feeds of sharp prices have become a business in their own right, with sharps supplying the information and softs packaging it into the products most bettors see. For example, Pinnacle sells a "Pinnacle Solutions" product to other bookmakers around the world that provides them with odds and handles the technical side of things, which allows the bookmakers to focus on the retail side of the business.

Other firms like Genius and Kambi also sell these products. They use modelling but also incorporate information on betting patterns from their bookmaker clients giving them access to huge amounts of data. For example, Kambi have openly stated they categorise some bettors as "*players that are proven to damage margin*" and that "*To ignore their business would be costly ... we alter probabilities on the back of action from highly informed bettors, whose stakes are carefully managed.*"[38]

The result is a two-tier system. At the top are the sharps, the information creators who invest heavily in models, data and monitoring the behaviour of the savviest bettors to generate the most accurate prices. Below them sit the softs, the information distributors. Their business is packaging betting in a way that appeals to customers, while relying on the sharps to do the hard work of pricing.

From the outside, betting markets look like dozens of independent firms all setting their own prices. In reality, it's this hierarchy that makes them work. Odds end up being pretty accurate but only because sharp bookmakers or other firms that focus on gathering information are compensated, directly through betting volume and indirectly through selling their odds, for the costly work of producing information. That's Grossman–Stiglitz brought to life: markets can't always be perfectly efficient, because somebody has to be paid to gather the information that keeps them running.

Remember that odds are set as

$$D = \frac{1 - m}{p}$$

We have seen how bookmakers arrive at their estimates of p via a global system of processing information. What about m?

Well, this is another way in which the two tiers of bookmaking markets differ. I have emphasised here how the sharp bookmakers operate off thin margins in a hugely competitive environment. But the second tier – retail bookmakers – operate in a very different market structure, far removed from the ideal of perfect competition, and this allows them to have higher margins and also to vary them more across bets. We will look at the factors shaping retail betting markets in the next chapter.

CHAPTER 12

Barriers, Frictions and Competition in Betting Markets

We have described how an ideal competitive betting market would work, with cut-throat competition cutting margins down to the bone. But the retail markets where most people bet fall well short of this competitive ideal. Here, we describe the factors that make retail bookmaking throughout the world an imperfectly competitive market. In the next chapter, we will describe the consequences of this for how odds are set.

Legal and Regulatory Hurdles

In theory, any of us could be a bookmaker. You put up a website, write some code to copy Ladbrokes' odds, and start taking bets. In practice, you'd be shut down within hours and potentially face criminal charges. Bookmaking is one of the most tightly regulated industries in the world, and the barriers to entry begin long before you ever take your first wager.

The first hurdle is compliance. Regulators expect operators to monitor every transaction, flag suspicious activity, and keep detailed records for inspection. That requires compliance officers, reporting systems, and a willingness to submit to regular audits. None of this comes cheap.

Perhaps the most visible element is the Know Your Customer rules. Before you can place a bet, you are asked to upload documents to prove your identity and address. From the bookmaker's side, this is the front line of regulation, designed to prevent underage gambling and fraud. Behind the scenes, anti-money-laundering requirements demand constant monitoring of deposits and withdrawals and reports of any unusual patterns.

The penalties for getting this wrong are severe. In 2023, Entain – the parent company of Ladbrokes, Coral, BetMGM and other major brands – paid a record £585 million in penalties for failures in anti-money laundering systems. On top of that come responsible-gambling obligations. Operators must provide deposit limits, cooling-off periods, and self-exclusion tools. They are expected to train staff to recognise signs of problem gambling and intervene when customers show signs of distress. These rules are well-intentioned, but they add another layer of infrastructure that every entrant must build before they can sign up a single customer.

The United States provides the clearest demonstration of how regulation shapes competition. Since the repeal of PASPA in 2018, legal sports betting has spread through a state-by-state process, with each jurisdiction setting its own licensing rules and fees. Entry into new states is often costly: license fees can run into the millions (New York charges $25m per operator) and application processes require extensive lobbying resources and legal expertise. These fixed costs tilted the playing field towards well-capitalised firms, discouraging marginal entrants and leaving the sector dominated by a small set of national operators.

Two companies, FanDuel and DraftKings, leveraged a head start from their existing daily fantasy sports operations (very much a grey area under pre-PASPA-repeal law) to dominate early. With existing customer databases and brand recognition, they converted fantasy players into sportsbook customers when legalisation arrived. Both then deepened their positions through major capital injections and acquisitions of expertise.

FanDuel is part of Flutter, a global betting conglomerate best known for their Paddy Power brand. DraftKings raised substantial outside capital and acquired a leading betting-technology provider, enabling a product suite and in-house pricing capability comparable to the major European bookmakers. The result has been that FanDuel and DraftKings take about two-thirds of legal betting volumes with the remainder split among BetMGM, Caesars, and a long tail of small brands.

Complexity

Once you clear the regulatory hurdles, running a bookmaking business is enormously complex. Modern sports betting isn't run out of a back room with a few actuarial types setting odds. It is, at its core, a technology business. You need a reliable website and a phone app that can take thousands of bets every second without crashing. Those bets must be quoted at up-to-the-second odds, which are either pulled from external feeds or generated by in-house models. Beyond the challenge of finding customers, lots of work goes into making sure the system stays fast, safe and able to handle huge volumes without breaking down.

It is also a retail business. Bookmakers track their customers closely, offering free bets or enhanced odds to some, restricting others, and investing heavily in advertising and brand recognition. Like any retailer, they segment and manage their customer base - but here the product involves risk, and mistakes can be costly.

And it is a financial business. Bookmakers process huge volumes of payments in and out every day. They must reconcile accounts, manage flows across different currencies and payment systems, and ensure that money is always where it needs to be. In many ways, the back office looks more like a mid-sized bank than a leisure company.

The sheer difficulty of integrating all these functions is well described by Ed Miller and Matthew Davidow in their book *Interception*, a study of modern US sportsbooks. They note that, for anyone but the largest operators, "*running a modern sportsbook is largely an exercise in piecing together a Frankenstein of technology components and then praying the monster comes to life.*" Only a small number of global brands can afford the luxury of their own in-house technical infrastructure. As they put it, "*this technical flexibility tends to entrench their already enriched advantages over the rest of the pack.*"

That last point matters for competition. Complexity isn't just a barrier to entry; it also acts to preserve a structure in which a small number of firms play a dominant role. The result is a market where a few big names dominate, not because they offer better odds, but because they have mastered the machinery of the business.

Complexity, then, doesn't just make entry difficult. It ensures that a small group of large operators enjoy structural advantages that smaller rivals can rarely overcome.

Customer Frictions

Even when multiple retail bookmakers operate in the same market, competition is far from perfect because customers are rarely willing to spend time and effort seeking out the best odds. Know Your Customer rules mean opening a new account involves sending in documents, waiting for approval, and setting up payment methods - often taking several days. That process is not something most people want to repeat again and again.

On top of the paperwork comes the mental cost. Serious bettors may juggle ten or more accounts, each with its own password, two-factor authentication system, and quirks about deposits and withdrawals. Keeping track of it all is exhausting and often the payoff is meagre: a slightly better price here or there, rarely enough to justify the hassle.

Two different studies based on bank transaction data reported that the typical UK gambler has accounts with two gambling operators, including online casinos.[39] This puts a hard limit on how much odds-shopping is going on. And surveys from the US also report the typical sports bettor as having two accounts, often the big two of FanDuel and DraftKings. Only 31% of US bettors say they shop for the best odds.[40]

Bookmakers know this and design their strategies around it. Promotions, free bets, and loyalty schemes are designed to keep customers from straying. Once you are locked into one or two accounts, inertia does the rest. The result is a market where customers don't shop around as much as the textbook perfect competitive model assumes, and where firms can hold margins above competitive levels without losing their business. These frictions don't just make life inconvenient for bettors; they are another force sustaining imperfect competition in retail betting markets.

Brand Advertising

With customers reluctant to switch and odds that differ only marginally across firms, the most visible competition among bookmakers is their brand advertising strategies.

For smaller firms, the advertising strategy serves a simple purpose: to let potential customers know they exist. In a market where the products are essentially identical, name recognition is the first hurdle. Hence, the explosion in shirt sponsorships and advertising on pitch-side boards all screaming "We exist."

For larger firms, the advertising strategy takes on a different logic. They are not competing on price but on personality. Economists studying oligopolies have long noted that when firms sell near-identical products, competition shifts away from price toward persuasion – think Coca-Cola vs Pepsi, or Nike vs Adidas. Advertising doesn't inform customers about concrete things like prices; it reassures and entertains. Bookmakers follow this pattern exactly.

Paddy Power is the clearest example. Its campaigns are intentionally cheeky and provocative, projecting an irreverent personality that invites some customers and repels others. The point is not to promise better prices but to create a sense of belonging and humour that keeps customers loyal.

Ladbrokes generally emphasises the "lads enjoying betting together" aspect, presumably inspired by the first three letters of their name. Other firms stress reliability and safety or lean on celebrity endorsements or big-event sponsorships. What they share is an emphasis on identity rather than value. Despite an appearance of competition, retail bookmaking's intense advertising is proof that it is far removed from the textbook ideal of perfect competition.

Exceptions

US President Harry Truman famously asked for a one-handed economist so he couldn't be told "on the other hand." Here's my "on the other hand" for retail bookmaking.

Even in an imperfectly competitive market, bookmakers sometimes price particular events very aggressively. For some types of bets, being seen to have "the best odds" can be worth more as marketing than the extra profit from a fatter margin. In those cases, the bookmaker is happy to give up some edge because the bet is really doing double duty as an advert. We will see later that some sports get priced more competitively than others.

Taken together, the factors discussed in this chapter explain why retail sports betting markets fall well short of the perfectly competitive ideal. Regulation, operational complexity and customer frictions all hold back the forces that would otherwise force price competition and push margins down. Brand advertising keeps the big incumbents ahead and makes it difficult for new firms to succeed. The next question is what this means for how odds are set.

CHAPTER 13

How Far Will You Stretch? Bookmakers and Elasticity

We have a model for how bettors take decisions and we have described the market structure for retail bookmakers. The next step is to show what this means for how these bookmakers set odds. We know odds depend on both the estimated probability that a bet wins p and the built-in profit margin m. We've discussed where p comes from; now let's look at how m gets set. We start here with three long-dead thinkers whose ideas explain how firms in "imperfectly competitive" markets set prices. We then apply these ideas to explain how bookmakers set odds to maximise profits.

Cournot, Marshall and Lerner

As odds flash on betting screens around the world, few punters or bookmakers realise that the logic behind pricing rests on ideas developed long ago by three economists who never placed a bet in their lives.

The first was Antoine Augustin Cournot, a French mathematician and civil servant. Cournot spent most of his life in provincial academic posts and bureaucratic appointments. Yet in 1838, he published *Recherches sur les principes mathématiques de la théorie des richesses* – a book that laid the foundations for the modern economics of firms and markets.

In the idealized world of perfect competition, the price is set by the market and firms either sell at that price or don't produce. But, in the real world, most firms have some control over the price they sell. A higher price might see you lose some of your customers, but not all of them.

Cournot figured out a key condition for how a firm could set its price to maximise profits. As you sell more units, you usually have to cut the price to attract additional customers, so the extra revenue from each sale - the marginal revenue - falls as output rises. And producing those extra units adds cost. At what point have you produced enough? Well, if your goal is to maximise profits, you don't want the marginal revenue of the next unit you sell to be below its marginal cost. If producing one more widget costs you £5 but only brings in £4, you shouldn't make it. The optimal point is where that last unit just breaks even: marginal revenue equals marginal cost. Today, $MR = MC$ is the most famous rule in microeconomics.

Cournot used calculus to formalise this reasoning. It was a breakthrough, but one that few appreciated. Cournot's contemporaries were not ready for mathematics in economics. His book made little impact and went out of print. Late in life, he sadly admitted that his ideas had left no mark on economic thinking.

The second ingredient came from Alfred Marshall, whose *Principles of Economics* (1890) was the first globally read economics textbook. Marshall invented the idea of *elasticity of demand.* This measures how sensitive buyers are to price — the percentage fall in sales when the price rises by one percent. This concept became a central part of every economist's toolkit.

But it was a third economist, Abba Lerner, who put these pieces together into a clean and insightful rule. Lerner was born in 1903 in Bessarabia, in what is now Moldova, and grew up in a poor Jewish immigrant family in London's East End. His path into economics was anything but conventional. He worked in manual jobs, including as a machinist, and was largely self-taught in mathematics before eventually studying at the London School of Economics at the age of 26.

In 1934, Lerner showed how Cournot's condition, combined with Marshall's idea of elasticity, implied a powerful result: a profit-maximising firm sets price as a markup over marginal cost, and the size of that markup depends on its elasticity of demand.

If a firm is faced with highly price-sensitive customers, then even if it was a monopolist, the lack of competition it faced would not help it charge high prices. But the firm with customers whose demand is not that sensitive to price can set a high markup and make big profits.

Today, this formula is taught in economics degrees and MBA classes around the world. And whether they know it or not, when firms tweak their prices, they are implementing a formula established by a former East End machinist.

Applying Lerner's Rule to Bookmakers

Cournot's ideas can be applied directly to thinking about a bookmaker setting odds. If they set higher odds, then they will attract more bets. That's marginal revenue. But if those bets win, they have to pay out more. That's marginal cost. The profit-maximising odds will balance those elements.

That describes a condition for odds to maximise profits, but it is Lerner's formula that says precisely what those odds should be. A 2021 paper by a young economist, Maurizio Montone showed that a bookmaker's profits were maximised by setting odds as a fraction of the odds that would imply zero profits.[41] And this fraction depended on the elasticity of demand for bets relative to odds.

Proving this requires using calculus but the result is completely intuitive. A bookmaker that faces very price-sensitive customers can't set poor odds because their customers will desert them. But if they are setting odds on a bet where the customers are not so price-sensitive, they can afford to set low odds and make large profits.

Montone's paper proved this as a general result without specifying what determines the elasticity of demand for bets. But the true power of the result comes from specifying the demand for bets. Our rational disagreement model does this.

How Far Will Bettors Stretch?

Let's recap two results we've already seen. In Chapter 8, when we introduced a bookmaker's margin into the Arsenal-Chelsea example, remember how more people dropped out who had backed Arsenal (the favourite) than had backed Chelsea, leaving the book unbalanced? And remember how, in Chapter 9, the pari-mutuel system also left longshot enthusiasts accepting worse odds than people who backed the favourites? These hinted at something important: **demand for longshot bets is less elastic than demand for bets on favorites**.

We can explain this again using our example where Arsenal had a 70% chance of going through in their FA Cup tie against Chelsea. Suppose beliefs about Arsenal's probability of going through ranged from 0.6 to 0.8.

Consider first the bet on Arsenal. The fair odds that would see this bet break even on average are $D_A = 1/0.7 = 1.43$. But, in our example, the most optimistic person thinks they have an 80% chance of winning. They think they have a profitable bet at odds all the way down to $D_A = 1 / 0.80 = 1.25$. If they took a bet at those odds, their average payout would be $0.7 \times 1.25 = 0.875$. Getting only 0.875 back for every unit you stake means an average loss rate of 12.5%.

But now consider the other side of the bet, the person who is most enthusiastic about Chelsea. They have a 30% chance of winning, so their fair odds are $D_C = 1/0.3 = 3.33$. But the biggest Chelsea optimist believes they have a 40% chance of winning so they will accept bets at odds all the way down to $1/0.4 = 2.5$. Such a bet would give an average payout of $0.3 \times 2.5 = 0.75$. They will lose an average of 25% on their bets, twice as bad as the worst-case scenario for even the biggest Arsenal optimists.

This gap between potential loss rates for the two types of optimists widens as the favorite becomes more likely to win. Suppose Arsenal have an 80% chance of going through and the spread in beliefs goes from 70% to 90%. Their most optimistic believer (who thinks they are 90% likely to win) now thinks they are worth backing at $D_A = 1/0.9 = 1.11$. They would get an average payout of $0.8 \times 1.11 = 0.89$ if they accepted that bet, losing an average of 11%, a bit less than when Arsenal are 70% likely to win.

In contrast, the most optimistic believer in Chelsea, who thinks they are 30% likely to win, believes they are worth backing at $D_C = 1/0.3 = 3.33$. They would get an average payoff on that bet of 0.2×3.33

= 0.66, losing an average of 34%. That's three times as bad as even the worst case for the extreme Arsenal optimists.

These calculations illustrate the elasticity of demand for bets and how bookmakers can use it. People who are enthusiastic about longshots are willing to continue placing their bets even as the odds objectively become very bad, while those who are enthusiastic about favourites are far less willing to accept bets with objectively bad terms. This difference in elasticity – highly elastic demand for favourites and low-elasticity demand for longshots – explains why the profit-maximising strategy for bookmakers is to set odds with a favourite–longshot bias.

Note the prediction does not rest on assuming people love taking riskier bets. It also does not rely on assuming people are systematically bad at judging small probabilities. We just needed to assume that people differ in their beliefs about the likelihood of outcomes, which after all, is the essence of why betting markets exist.

Something more subtle is at work in relation to small probabilities. We assume that people are correct on average in their beliefs but essentially everyone is incorrect in their own specific belief. In some cases, this is harmless. Those with beliefs close enough to the truth can scan the odds and, with the bookie's margin factored in, figure out correctly that they won't make money. But inaccurate beliefs do not all have equal consequences. Being overly optimistic about bets with a low probability of winning is more harmful to your finances than excessive optimism about bets that are likely to win.

Profit-Maximising Odds for Bookmakers

We've reached the point where it helps to express the ideas just explained as an equation. Don't worry, there are almost no equations in the book after this and more importantly, you don't need to master these formulas to understand what follows. But they give us a concrete way to tie together everything we've said about bookmaker pricing and differences in beliefs, and they will be useful for the applications in the chapters that follow.

Let's assume that an event has a probability p of happening and there is a single monopoly bookmaker who knows this value. With only one bookmaker, the market demand for bets we have been describing is also the firm's demand for bets.

Let's also assume the public's beliefs about this probability are spread evenly between two points, with the higher point being $p{+}w$. I use w here because it represents the *width* of the gap between the most optimistic belief and the truth.

Under this assumption, and allowing for a per-bet operational cost of c (to cover staff costs, technology, advertising etc.), the profit-maximising decimal odds a monopoly bookmaker will offer on this bet are[42]

$$D = \sqrt{\frac{1-c}{p} \times \frac{1}{p+w}}$$

This looks a bit intimidating and almost physics-like! But we will apply this formula repeatedly in the next section of the book, so it is worth explaining carefully what it means.

The formula says the profit-maximising odds equal the *geometric average* of two benchmarks. The first is $(1-c)/p$, the odds that generate zero expected profit. The second is $1/(p+w)$, the odds that the most optimistic bettor would be willing to accept. The geometric average of two numbers comes from multiplying them together and then taking the square root. In some cases, this can differ noticeably from the more familiar arithmetic average (adding two numbers and dividing by two), but for realistic values for betting markets, the difference is very small.

This means the monopoly bookmaker sets odds that are essentially the average of the zero-profit odds and the odds that the most optimistic bettor would accept. We can see now that our earlier examples showing what the most optimistic bettors would accept were not just indicative stories. With evenly spread beliefs, they are *exactly* what determines the bookmaker's odds. The more optimistic the bettors, the further the bookmaker can push odds down.

A story that helps explain this formula comes from a podcast series on sports betting in the US from Michael Lewis, author of *The Big Short.* Lewis interviewed Rufus Peabody, perhaps the famous modern

American gambler, who told a story about when he went to work as a college intern for the firm that set odds for Vegas casinos. Rufus asked them why they always set the odds based only on the probability that a bet would win. He told them his theory that "if they know the public is biased, they can make more money setting the price between the true price and the price the public thinks." The story goes that a veteran oddsmaker told Rufus where he could stick his theory.

Rufus was definitely onto something, but our formula shows the logic behind true profit-maximising odds relies on something more subtle. Even if the public is on average correct, you don't have to set odds based purely on the true probability. Instead, you maximise profits by setting odds between the breakeven odds and the odds that the most optimistic people would take. And we will see that modern bookmakers follow precisely this logic.

What Determines Profit Margins?

The bottom line for both bookmakers and bettors, of course, is the bookmaker's margin - the fraction of each pound staked that disappears, on average, into the bookmaker's profits. This is simply $m = 1-(p \times D)$, which, from our formula above, works out to

$$m = 1 - (p \times D) = 1 - \sqrt{\frac{(1-c) \times p}{p + w}}$$

This tells us that the bookmaker's margin depends on three things – the true probability of the bet winning (p), the gap between the most optimistic person's beliefs and the true probability (w) and the bookmaker's per-bet operating cost (c).

To see how this works, suppose the upper bound of beliefs has $w = 0.05$ and there are no operating costs ($c = 0$). If the true chance of winning is only 10% ($p = 0.1$), then the margin is

$$m = 1 - \sqrt{\frac{0.1}{0.1 + 0.05}} = 1 - \sqrt{\frac{0.1}{0.15}} \approx 0.18$$

meaning bettors will on average lose 18% of their money taking this bet. Now take the case where the true chance of winning is 90% (p = 0.9), again with w = 0.05 and c = 0. This implies a margin of

$$m = 1 - \sqrt{\frac{0.9}{0.9 + 0.05}} = 1 - \sqrt{\frac{0.9}{0.95}} \approx 0.026$$

so the average bettor loses only about 3% of their stake.

An important thing to emphasise here is that while we have called the pattern of longer-odds bets losing more the "favourite-longshot bias", it is not whether a bet is on a favourite or not that matters. All that matters for this comparison is the probability that a bet will win. If that probability is relatively high, this reduces losses and if it is low, this increases losses.

We can also use the formula to illustrate how the extent of over-optimism affects average loss rates. To give an example, suppose the true probability of winning is 40% with no operating costs (c = 0). If w = 0.05, the margin is

$$m = 1 - \sqrt{\frac{0.4}{0.4 + 0.05}} = 1 - \sqrt{\frac{0.4}{0.45}} \approx 0.057$$

so the average bettor loses only about 6% of their stake. But if over-optimism is greater, say w = 0.10, then the formula gives

$$m = 1 - \sqrt{\frac{0.4}{0.4 + 0.1}} = 1 - \sqrt{\frac{0.4}{0.5}} \approx 0.106$$

which means the average loss jumps to about 11%. The greater the optimism, the heavier the losses for bettors as a group.

We've perhaps reached (or gone beyond) your tolerance for equations, so we won't work through multiple cases for the operational cost parameter. But the economics is simple: the bigger the expected costs for bookmakers, the lower odds must be to cover these costs.

To go beyond plugging in a few numbers, the table below shows the average loss rates predicted by the model for c = 0.03, for different probabilities of winning and three different values of w. I picked this value for c based on information in public financial reports from bookmakers about their basic operational costs due to staff, IT and data acquisition. Another justification for a 3% cost figure is that you can see margins as low as this among sharp bookmakers and they presumably can still make a profit with this pricing. This suggests an upper bound of 3% on basic operational costs, at least for high-profile large-volume sporting events.

The table illustrates the model's core prediction: expected loss rates rise sharply as the probability of winning declines, and this effect intensifies when bettors are more optimistic. Bets with a 10% chance of winning loses more money than bets with a 30% chance and the gap widens as the biggest optimists become more confident. And like the pari-mutuel markets we examined earlier, losses accelerate as your chance of winning falls.[43]

Average loss rates on bets predicted by the monopoly bookmaker model with $c = 0.03$

Probability of Winning	$w = 0.03$	$w = 0.06$	$w = 0.12$
10%	13.6%	22.1%	33.6%
20%	8.2%	13.6%	22.1%
30%	6.1%	10.1%	16.8%
40%	5.0%	8.1%	13.6%
50%	4.3%	6.9%	11.6%
60%	3.9%	6.0%	10.1%
70%	3.6%	5.5%	9.0%
80%	3.3%	5.0%	8.2%
90%	3.1%	4.6%	7.5%

When the Crowd Is Not So Wise

When figuring out what caused bias in pari-mutuel markets, we relied on the wisdom of crowds assumption that, on average, the public are correct. But the predictions of our monopoly model don't rely on this assumption. They can be applied just as easily to situations where the crowd are wrong on average.

The results just presented did not rely on specifying the lower bound of probability beliefs. All we needed was that the most optimistic bettor thinks they have a probability of $p+w$ of winning. I didn't say exactly how pessimistic the person with the most negative assessment was. And that's because it doesn't matter to the bookmaker. Someone who thinks the bet has a smaller chance than p of winning won't place the bet even at fair odds, so they certainly won't take the odds chosen by a profit-maximising bookmaker.

This means our formula applies whether the public is wise – in the sense of being on average correct – but it also applies in other cases. The square root formula would be the same if the public's beliefs were biased.

This matters because it's not hard to find examples where many bettors are systematically over-optimistic about certain teams. Despite the historic evidence that England never win major football tournaments, sixty years of hurt and all that, they will start the next tournament at impressively short odds because there are enough believers. And the English are not alone in allowing nationalism to affect their betting. A study of bets on Euro 2008 qualifiers found that bettors tend to get worse odds on their own country's football team.[44]

This was precisely the intuition the young Rufus Peabody had when talking to the Vegas odds setters. If the public is biased, bookmakers should lean into that bias and set worse odds for a public that is overly optimistic about a particular outcome.

The opposite applies, of course, when the public are overly pessimistic about a competitor. In that case, the bookmaker will make lower profits. For example, studies have shown that you will lose a little less betting on horse racing if you back female jockeys.[45] Another study showed that bets on NBA teams with more white players tend to out-perform.[46] These findings are unlikely to reflect bias by bookmakers, who will set whatever price maximises profits. Instead, they stem from biases in the population that unfairly under-rates female jockeys and perhaps thinks "White Men Can't Jump" somehow applies to NBA players.

More generally, the model suggests you should be wary of betting on events that draw in a lot of poorly informed members of the general public. The Grand National, for example, attracts the most betting of any horse race in the UK but it is also the worst to bet on, with the highest overround. The occasional dabblers placing a recreational bet know little about the horses so the bookmakers set terrible odds knowing that enough overly optimistic punters will accept them.

Why Bookmakers Don't Want Zero Risk

In Chapter 10, we saw that the popular image of bookmakers "balancing the books" isn't how they really operate. In principle, they could behave like pari-mutuel operators and set odds so that, whatever the outcome, the house collects the same percentage of the money placed. That would mean zero risk. But the odds that achieve this are not the profit-maximising odds, so zero risk would mean smaller profits.

This is because a pari-mutuel operator has only one knob to turn: the overall "take percentage" deducted from the pool. A bookmaker, by contrast, has as many knobs to turn as there are potential outcomes of the event. By adjusting all these odds, the bookmaker can do far more than skim a uniform margin: they can exploit the shape of demand that comes from bettors disagreeing about the chances of different outcomes.

How much smaller would zero-risk profits be? To get an answer from the model, we will go back to our previous assumption of an even spread of beliefs from $p-w$ to $p+w$.

First, we need to think about which zero-risk odds a monopolist would set. Profits depend on the "take percentage." As this rises, profits increase at first, but eventually a higher take drives away so many customers that profits stop rising. I worked out what the profit-maximising take percentage would be in our rational disagreement framework, so we can compare this to the case where odds are set separately on each option to maximise profits.[47]

Consider a simple two-competitor case with operational costs set at $c = 0.03$. The table below shows the best zero-risk expected profits as a percentage of the maximised expected profits implied by the square root formula. With the optimism parameter set at $w = 0.06$, the maximum possible profits are more than double the best zero-risk case when the event is a 50/50 toss-up, and over eight times higher when the favourite is 90% likely to win. With a higher optimism parameter ($w = 0.12$), the advantage is smaller. With lots of misinformed punters, even pari-mutuel systems generate big returns from setting high take rates. But the risk-free profits are still typically well below the profit-maximising level.

The message is clear: Risk-taking is profitable for bookmakers. They make far more money by exploiting the varying demand elasticities across different bets (turning multiple odds "knobs") than by sticking to the single, uniform margin of a pari-mutuel system. This profit advantage is the rational explanation for why bookmakers embrace risk instead of eliminating it.

Zero-risk expected profits as a percentage of maximum profits

Probability of Favourite Winning	$w = 0.06$	$w = 0.12$
50%	37%	86%
60%	35%	82%
70%	29%	72%
80%	20%	55%
90%	11%	34%

Point Spreads Versus Moneylines

Another useful application of our model comes from the widespread legalisation of sports betting in the US after 2018.

Traditionally, the most popular type of bet in the US was the point spread. This means you bet on the margin of victory, not which team wins. If the Lakers are getting 10 points versus the Celtics, then your bet on the Celtics requires them to win by more than 10 points and your bet on the Lakers requires them to do better than losing by 10 points. Typically, each team is equally likely to win these bets, so the odds offered on the teams are the same. This kind of betting dominated the offerings of traditional Las Vegas bookmakers.

However, point spreads are not the preferred product for the new

US sportsbooks. Their advertising and promotional strategies are focused more on encouraging bets on teams to win, which they call "moneyline" bets. There are two reasons for this, one explained by our model and one not.

The one not explained by our model is that Vegas point spreads were typically priced at -110, equivalent to decimal odds of 1.91. Richard Thaler has long documented that ideas about fairness can have a big influence on firms' pricing strategies. For example, in surveys he carried out with Daniel Kahneman and Jack Knetsch, people judged it "unfair" for a hardware store to raise the price of snow shovels after a blizzard, even though supply and demand would justify a higher price.[48] Customers have a reference point for what feels like a normal price and resent deviations from it, even when the economics are perfectly rational.

In US betting, odds of about -110 on each side of a two-way market act as a psychological anchor. Bettors have come to see -110/-110 as the "fair" going rate for a bet, so bookmakers are cautious about straying too far from that anchor.

But while the 4.5% margin implied by these odds might have been fine for Vegas bookmakers – operating as a small part of a wider casino business – it is less attractive for the new sportsbooks who often have higher tax rates on profits, and substantially higher marketing and promotional costs compared with casinos who had the tourists already in the building and ready to gamble.

The second reason is explained by our model. When we look across the different levels of competitive imbalance in an event, 50/50 bets like point spreads have the lowest profit margin. The rising profit as contests become more uneven is a nonlinear effect. Relative to a 50-50 bet, a 60%-40% probability split earns more profit on the 40% bet and less profit on the 60% but the extra profits on the longshot outweigh the lower profits on the favourite. And the more uneven the event, the higher the bookmaker's profits will be. Hence, the move to push customers away from point spreads to betting on who will win.

From Monopoly to Multiple Bookmakers

So far, we've looked at two extremes. At one end is the textbook case of perfect competition, where many firms compete profits away until only operating costs are covered. At the other is a single monopoly bookmaker. Real betting markets fall in between. A small number of firms dominate. Economists have a name for this: *oligopoly*.

One possibility in an oligopoly is that firms compete intensely on prices, forcing profits down to the minimum level that allows them to survive. But the evidence clearly suggests this is not how bookmakers behave. Their financial statements report substantial profits. To understand why, it helps to get Cournot back on stage.

In a remarkable chapter in *Recherches*, Cournot worked out a model of non-price competition among a small number of firms. He assumed that each firm chooses the quantity it will supply, taking the other firms' choices as given. This work was even more ahead of its time than his famous $MR = MC$ rule. The idea of each firm doing their best, taking the other firm's strategy as given, anticipated modern game theory and the model was not commonplace in textbook economics until at least the 1970s.

Our rational disagreement model can be solved under Cournot's oligopoly structure. In this setup, each bookmaker sets the same odds and decides how many bets to take, taking the other bookmakers' actions as given but also accounting for how its own decision influences the overall market odds. The outcome is that odds and loss rates are in between the monopoly case and the perfectly competitive case, depending on how many competitors there are. With not many firms, there is a strong favourite-longshot bias. As the number of firms increases, the bias narrows but does not disappear.[49]

What determines the level of competition in a betting market? The number of firms in the market depends on the factors we have already discussed, such as regulatory requirements. But remember also that the number of firms isn't necessarily a useful indicator of the level of competition if most customers only use one or two apps to check odds. The result is prices that are a lot closer to monopoly than perfect competition.

This gives us a framework for thinking about the strategies adopted by real-world bookmakers. The precise numerical predictions of the monopoly model might not hold in the real world but the mechanisms driving pricing - cost, differing beliefs, the favourite-longshot bias - will still drive pricing in an oligopoly betting market. Next, we assess how well our framework does in explaining the odds.

V. Evidence on Bets with Bookmakers

We have built a framework to understand how bookmakers set odds. Here, we put that framework to work. No new theory, just practical questions. What is the evidence on returns to betting on favourites and longshots? When is backing the draw the best option? What are Asian handicap bets on football and how are they priced? What do insiders and corruption do to betting odds and should you be concerned about it? How do bookmakers' profit margins differ across markets?

You will see that our model's predictions generally do a good job of explaining the world of betting, with the odd curiosity that doesn't fit with the rational disagreement approach we have developed.

CHAPTER 14

Evidence on Odds and Information

It's Friday evening in late August 2025. Chelsea are playing West Ham. The television cameras catch Chelsea's star attacking midfielder Cole "Cold" Palmer limping off during the warm-up. The probability of Chelsea winning just fell. Within seconds, Chelsea's odds have lengthened and West Ham's have shortened. That instant adjustment is a classic example of the kind of market efficiency that Gene Fama often documented for the stock market.

In this chapter, we will see that odds are efficient in the weak sense described by Thaler and Ziemba. Simple strategies don't beat bookmakers. And the odds react quickly to new information and get more accurate as game time approaches.

Beating the Bookmakers?

Fama's research showed there was no simple system for "beating the market" by picking shares that had particular features unless you were willing to take on extra risk. And research also showed that the market generally priced risks fairly. There was no free lunch in picking riskier stocks.

Similarly, the first studies of betting market efficiency examined whether you could systematically make money betting with bookmakers. The first rigorous research appears to have been a 1968 paper by Lyn Pankoff, a junior professor at Washington University in St. Louis who had just graduated from the University of Chicago with a

PhD in Economics.[50] He had been influenced by Gene Fama's ideas about market efficiency and his paper applied these ideas to betting on NFL games with bookmakers.

While operating as a bookmaker was illegal, it wasn't against the law for the sports pages to publish the terms offered on bets. Pankoff collected this data and, in line with Fama's ideas, found that "*systematic market error patterns are not large enough to be profitable to bettors.*" Later studies backed this up across a range of sports and samples. A well-known 1989 article on English football odds by economists Peter Pope and David Peel reported that the market "*appears to meet the arguably most important criterion for market efficiency, namely the absence of a trading rule that generates abnormal profits.*"[51]

You get the idea. It's hard to just rock up, do some quick sums and beat the bookmakers. You'd probably already figured that out. Otherwise, there wouldn't be any bookies in business.

At the same time, that hasn't stopped some academics publishing papers claiming to have systems that beat the bookmakers. Some of these studies show that if you had picked certain kinds of bets at the best available odds, then you would have systematically made profits.

But as we discussed earlier, you'd generally find those extra-generous odds were promotions with very limited stake sizes. And if you kept showing up only when bookies were offering the most generous odds, you'd pretty quickly find yourself limited to tiny bets or banned. To my knowledge, the academics who published these papers never quit their ivory tower jobs to go full time into high-rolling professional gambling.

Elo v Bookmakers

The studies just described tested relatively simple strategies for trying to win by betting with bookmakers. When I first became interested in sports betting in 2022, I decided to use my statistical skills to see if I could build a model to provide forecasts that could match those implied by the sportsbooks' odds.

Armed with data from hundreds of thousands of football matches taken from www.football-data.co.uk, I built what is known as an Elo model to predict the outcomes of football games. It is named after Arpad Elo, a physics professor and chess master who devised it in the 1960s to rank chess players. After each match, player scores are updated based on the "surprise" element of the result. If a very strong player beats a very weak player, there is little surprise and almost no updating of scores. But if a weak player beats a strong player, they get a big boost in their score and the stronger player's score declines. Elo scores are used widely now to rate teams.

I designed my Elo model so that the updating element - how much the change in score responded to the surprise - was calibrated to produce the best possible forecasting performance with the historical data. Just a few days of work, but I was proud of this thing I'd built.

The result? My Elo model's forecasts failed to predict match outcomes better than bookmakers' odds. In fact, they added no useful forecasting value at all once you knew the odds.

Perhaps soccer's low-scoring nature makes it a particularly difficult sport to forecast using data. So I turned to modelling NBA games. Re-built my fancy Elo model and compared it with historical Vegas moneyline odds. The results were even worse for the Elo system.

I may have imagined myself as a clever quant, but the truth is that sportsbooks have quants too, with more sophisticated models than Elo's system. And they can make ad hoc adjustments based on injuries, the weather, and things like weird tactical matchups where some strong teams really hate playing specific teams they should beat (e.g. why do Spurs always do well against Manchester City?) They can also see where the weight of money is going, which provides its own signals. All this means beating bookmakers needs a lot more than a huge dataset and a fancy scoring system.

Event Studies and Covid Ghost Games

Event studies were another style of work that was popular in efficient market research. Researchers would check whether the market response to things like earnings announcements, or news like the approval of new drugs, were quick and efficient or whether you could make money systematically trading after these announcements. The typical finding was the markets reacted to news about companies very quickly, leaving little room for investors to profit after announcements had been made.

Similar findings exist for odds set by bookmakers. For example, a 2022 study of how bookmakers reacted to the announcement of injuries to star Aussie Rules players showed that the odds moved by just the right amount warranted by the impact of these players being missing.[52] Another study using real-time in-play information has shown that bookmakers adjust odds appropriately when goals are scored in football. There is no money to be made from believing the bookmakers have missed the "momentum" swing or some other failure to interpret the implications of goals.[53]

But my favourite event study of bookmakers is the one that started my research on sports betting. The idea that Tadgh and I joined together to work on in 2022 was inspired by the games played behind closed doors during the Covid lockdown.

Everyone knows there is a home advantage in team sports but there are so many different possible factors, it is hard to know which are the most important. Home teams don't have to travel as far and in sports like football or baseball where the size and shape of playing surfaces varies, getting to play in the stadium that you know well can be an advantage.

But another obvious factor is the presence of home fans. Players may be lifted by being cheered and perhaps put off by being jeered when they are playing away from home. The referees are also more willing to give decisions to the home team to avoid the crowd getting on their backs.

The lockdown situation thus provided a perfect "natural experiment" to figure out how much of the home advantage factor was due to the presence of fans. In addition to answering that question, our paper examined how well bookmakers did at figuring out the size of this effect when pricing the home advantage.

Using a large sample of pre-Covid football games, we found that the usual home advantage effect was worth an average of about an extra 0.3 goals to the home team. Our results showed that this reduced to about 0.15 goals in the absence of fans.[54] So the presence of supporters accounts for about half of the home advantage effect.

What about bookmakers? My original thought would be that bookmakers probably had no idea what the impact would be. An early study released in May 2020 (before lockdown games had begun) that looked at a small sample of previous games played behind closed doors, generally as a punishment for the home team for bad behaviour by their fans, had found no clear statistical effect on match outcomes.[55]

I expected to find that bookmakers had adjusted their odds to favour home teams a bit less but that this adjustment would change over time as they got more evidence about the impact of fans being absent. What actually happened was the adjustment applied by bookmakers from day one of the lockdown games was about 0.15 goals. It took our statistical methods hundreds of games to provide reliable evidence for this to be the best estimate but somehow, the bookmakers had figured this out from the start.

Odds Get More Accurate Over Time

A useful illustration of how bookmakers are always incorporating information into their odds comes from looking at their predictive properties as you get closer to the beginning of an event.

To illustrate this, I gathered a dataset on real-time odds from different bookmakers from The-Odds-API.com. This dataset includes quotes from different UK-based bookmakers on 1,120 English Premier League games and from US-licensed bookmakers on 3,669 NBA games. For both sports, we have quotes on all games from the 2022/23 seasons to the 2024/25 seasons. The quotes go from 48 hours before the match for the EPL and 24 hours beforehand for NBA, right up to 10 minutes before the games start.[56] On average, we have quotes for about 15 different bookmakers for each game.

To get a sense of how good the quotes are as predictions for the outcomes, we calculate normalised probabilities for each quote and then check the probabilities against actual outcomes, calling the outcome 1 if it happened and zero otherwise. We then calculate the *correlation coefficient* between normalised probabilities and the outcomes. The closer this correlation is to one, the better the forecast from the odds. If it's zero, then the odds were no use at all in forecasting the outcomes.

The table below shows the correlations between the normalised probabilities and outcomes. They show the predictive power of forecasts getting gradually better as we get closer to the game. The gains are not huge - most of the useful information is available by a day or two before a game starts - but it shows that new information is absorbed and the "wisdom of crowds" effect of aggregating information from the public is still at work even in the final hour before a game starts.

Correlations between normalised probabilities and outcomes for 1,120 English Premier League matches and 3,669 NBA games sorted by time prior to the start of games

	EPL	*NBA*
48 hours before	0.3951	
24 hours before	0.3959	0.3905
18 hours before	0.3974	0.3927
12 hours before	0.3986	0.3987
6 hours before	0.3992	0.4012
1 hour before	0.4021	0.4058
10 minutes before	0.4024	0.4073

Our model of profit-maximising pricing by bookmakers points to their assessment of the bet's probability of winning as a key determinant of the odds. Taken together, the evidence here builds a strong case that bookmakers' odds do a good job of communicating information about who is likely to win an event.

But the model did not predict that betting markets were strongly efficient. It predicted several ways in which margins would vary across different types of bets. Most importantly, it predicted average loss rates would be higher on longshot bets than on favourites. Let's look at the evidence on this.

CHAPTER 15

The Favourite-Longshot Bias and Its Implications

We have seen that closing odds do a good job of reflecting the information about sporting contests. Indeed, in the new US sports betting market, the "closing line" has gained an almost mythical status as the final diviner of all knowable truth. But typically, it isn't.

Despite the incredible efficiency with which bookmakers accumulate information when pricing odds, the strategy they use to maximise profits means their odds are not perfect guides to the probability that a bet will win. If betting markets are strongly efficient, the ratio of the odds tells you the ratio of probabilities of winning. But our model predicts that this doesn't hold with odds from bookmakers. Differences in odds don't just reflect differing estimates of probabilities. They also reflect variations in margins.

In this chapter, we will confirm the bias in bookmakers' odds with data. The favourite-longshot bias in pari-mutuel horse-racing odds is well known. There is a smaller literature documenting the same finding for odds quoted by bookmakers, but the evidence is a bit patchier and many of the studies are old.

To provide evidence that is both comprehensive and up to date, I compiled two types of datasets. First, I gathered historical datasets going back decades with odds on football, tennis, horse racing and golf. Second, I collected odds from licensed US sportsbooks from 2022 to 2025 for six different professional and amateur American sports. In each case, we can combine the odds with the actual outcomes to show the average performance of bets sorted by their odds.

Long Historical Data: Football, Tennis, Golf and Racing

We start with four datasets with odds on major international sports, each of which give us a long history of betting quotes. These odds largely come from "soft" retail bookmakers and the patterns documented here reflect the strategies of those firms.

The first is Joe Buchdahl's www.football-data.co.uk, which we have used a few times already. It contains quoted average odds and outcomes on bets on home, away and draw outcomes, what bookies call 1X2 bets. The dataset includes 211,840 matches from 38 football leagues throughout the world across 27 countries, starting with the 2005/06 season and ending with the 2024/25 season. That is 635,520 different quotes on possible bets that could have been placed.

The second, from Buchdahl's www.tennis-data.co.uk contains similar information for 130,245 tennis matches on the men's and women's professional tours. This provides another 260,490 quotes.

The third is the Kaggle data set with odds and results from 400,000 horse races around the world from 1990 to 2000. This has odds quotes and finishes for over 4 million different horses.

The final dataset comes from www.covers.com/sportsoddshistory. It records quoted odds and winners for 31,921 bets on individual golfers in major golf tournaments since 2007. The odds largely come from leading Vegas bookmakers, particularly the Westgate Superbook.

In each case, because we know both the odds and the outcomes of the events, we can figure out the average loss rates for different groups of bets.

I organised each of the datasets into five groups, sorted by odds, and calculated the average percentage loss on all bets in that odds range. The top rows show the average loss rates for those bets whose odds were in the lower fifth of the sample (the biggest favourites). The rows below show average losses for bets with odds in the second lowest fifth and so on, with the bottom row showing average losses when odds are in the top fifth (the biggest underdogs).

For each sport, the evidence is clear: as odds lengthen, average loss rates rise. The same principle holds across sports too. Bets offered at, say, decimal odds of 10 show similar average losses whether they're on horse racing favourites or football underdogs. This is consistent with our model's predictions. What matters for pricing is the probability of the bet winning, not whether it is labelled as a favourite or a longshot.

Another pattern to note is that the worsening loss rate as odds rise is not a steady trend. Loss rates get worse at an accelerating rate as odds get higher. This is precisely what our model of profit-maximising bookmaker pricing predicts. In fact, you generally only need small values of *w* to match this accelerating loss trend very well. In other words, the model's predictions are consistent with the evidence even if the most optimistic bettors are only modestly biased in their beliefs. For football for example, a value of $w = 0.06$ explains the data very well.

Average loss rates on football and tennis bets

Football (635,520 quotes)		*Tennis (260,490 quotes)*	
Odds Range	*Loss Rate*	*Odds Range*	*Loss Rate*
1.01 to 2.13	3.9%	1.01 to 1.35	3.2%
2.14 to 2.89	6.7%	1.36 to 1.66	5.0%
2.90 to 3.31	6.8%	1.67 to 2.19	5.3%
3.32 to 3.89	9.8%	2.20 to 3.13	6.4%
Over 3.89	15.3%	Over 3.13	17.6%

Average loss rates on horse racing and golf bets

Horse Racing (4,107,315 quotes)		*Golf Majors (31,921 quotes)*	
Odds Range	*Loss Rate*	*Odds Range*	*Loss Rate*
1.01 to 5.5	10.8%	1.1 to 41	33%
5.55 to 9.5	17.3%	43 to 101	69%
9.6 to 15.0	27.3%	102 to 201	66%
15.1 to 26.0	39.7%	202 to 501	93%
Over 26	59.2%	Over 501	100%

Evidence from American Bookmakers

The legalisation of sports betting in the US has provided a great opportunity to see how modern bookmakers set prices across lots of different markets. To check whether they also price with a favourite-longshot bias, I combined "moneyline" odds quotes for major American sports with data on results. The odds quotes are for licensed US sportsbooks and are taken from The-Odds-API.com

The key idea is the same as above: take a large sample of quoted odds and realised outcomes, sort bets by how long the odds are, and compute the average loss rate in each odds band. One difference here, however, is that instead of one set of "typical" odds for each match, we have multiple quotes from about 30 minutes before the matches start, each from separate US bookmakers.

The results below show college basketball, college football, the NHL and the NFL with the familiar pattern: as the moneyline odds get longer, the average loss rate gets worse. In particular, those bets with the highest odds suffer by far the largest loss rates. Worth noting is that the overround-implied margins on these bets don't vary across these different odds groupings. The bad pricing is well hidden.

The NBA and MLB look different. There is no evidence of a systematic worsening of returns as odds lengthen. In fact, there is some sign that longshot bets in the NBA do better than favourites.

Why might those two sports be the exceptions? I suspect it relates to the extent of competition among US sportsbooks for bettors in these markets. Favourite-Longshot bias can only prevail when markets are not highly competitive. But there is a good reason for the new US sportsbooks to price NBA and MLB bets competitively.

NBA and baseball seasons generate a relentless flow of games. For many customers they are the sports that keep the app open night after night. That makes them unusually valuable to American bookmakers. These companies are still in an aggressive expansion mode and attracting NBA and MLB bettors is a key marketing goal. When a product is that central to customer attraction and retention, it becomes a natural candidate for more competitive pricing: give up some margin in order to attract and retain high-volume bettors.

Average loss rates on NCAA college sports moneyline bets with US-licensed bookmakers, 2020/21 to 2024/25 seasons

Basketball (502,254 quotes)		*Football (54,850 quotes)*	
Odds Range	*Loss Rate*	*Odds Range*	*Loss Rate*
1.00 to 1.30	1.5%	1.00 to 1.24	3.4%
1.31 to 1.67	3.2%	1.25 to 1.62	5.5%
1.68 to 2.25	5.0%	1.63 to 2.35	3.6%
2.26 to 3.55	8.1%	2.36 to 4.18	2.2%
Over 3.55	24.5%	Over 4.18	15.0%

Average loss rates on NHL and NFL moneyline bets with US-licensed bookmakers, 2020/21 to 2024/25 seasons

NHL (121,518 quotes)		*NFL (28,236 quotes)*	
Odds Range	*Loss Rate*	*Odds Range*	*Loss Rate*
1.00 to 1.57	0.8%	1 to 1.41	3.5%
1.58 to 1.80	0.8%	1.42 to 1.69	4.2%
1.81 to 2.08	6.0%	1.7 to 2.22	4.8%
2.09 to 2.48	6.4%	2.23 to 3	2.7%
Over 2.48	10.1%	Over 3	11.0%

Average loss rates on NBA and MLB moneyline bets with US-licensed bookmakers, 2020/21 to 2024/25 seasons

Basketball (205,238 quotes)		*Baseball (219,290 quotes)*	
Odds Range	*Loss Rate*	*Odds Range*	*Loss Rate*
1.00 to 1.38	5.1%	1.00 to 1.62	4.6%
1.39 to 1.70	2.7%	1.63 to 1.81	3.0%
1.71 to 2.20	4.3%	1.82 to 2.05	4.2%
2.21 to 3.15	5.2%	2.06 to 2.36	3.7%
Over 3.15	0.9%	Over 2.36	3.4%

Back to Shopping Around

Earlier, I described how Premier League bookmaker quotes from one hour before kick-off were generally clustered quite tightly together. But that average hid an important pattern. Once we split the quotes by the level of the odds, the dispersion looks very different.

For short-priced outcomes, with average odds below 1.75, the central 80 percent of bookmaker quotes ranged only about 0.06 decimal-odds points from top to bottom, almost nothing. But for outcomes with odds above 4.0, the same central range spanned about 0.94 points. So shopping around matters far more once you move into longer-priced bets.

But we can now also see why that still doesn't help you much. Favourite-longshot bias means bookmakers build larger profit margins into longshot bets than into favourites.

It's not that getting better quotes on longshots doesn't help. In the Premier League data, bettors taking random bookmaker quotes on longshots with odds above 4 in that 2022/23 to 2024/25 dataset lost about 13 percent on average. Those who got quotes in the top 10 percent of available prices lost closer to 10 percent. Shopping around reduced their losses, but it didn't overcome the large margins built into these bets. For the bets where the apparent benefit of shopping around is the biggest, it still isn't nearly enough to allow you to make money.

Spreads versus Moneylines

Our model predicted that bookmakers should profit more on uneven moneyline bets than on evenly matched point spread bets. The US data provide a great test of this prediction because for each of the moneyline bets in the calculations above, The-Odds-API also provide odds and lines for point spreads. We know the scores for each of these games, so we can calculate how you would have done backing the same teams via point spread bets relative to how you would have done with moneyline bets.

The data bear out the model's prediction. Bookmakers make money from point spread bets, but they make more on moneylines because of large margins on longshots.

For example, consider again the 406,242 quoted bets on NCAA basketball from the table above. These bets had a significant favourite-longshot bias with loss rates going from 1.5% for the bottom fifth of odds to 24% for the top fifth of odds. The average loss rate across all these bets was 8.3%. For each group, the average loss rate from taking the corresponding point spread bet was about 4.5%, right in line with the margin implied by the overround. No wonder the US sportsbooks want their customers to take moneylines rather than spreads.

Implications for Margins Calculated from Odds

In Chapter 5, we showed that if betting markets were strongly efficient, we could use the odds to calculate the bookmaker's margin. But we have seen now that odds set by bookmakers do not satisfy strong efficiency, so the standard calculation, based on inverting the overround, does not measure a unique bookmaker's margin.

So what does it measure? Figuring this out involves some maths – skip down to the bit that says "In plain English" if it's not to your taste!

Let's go back to our Arsenal v Chelsea FA Cup tie example. We calculated the bookmaker's margin on this game from

$$1 - m = \frac{1}{\frac{1}{D_C} + \frac{1}{D_A}}$$

In other words, we computed the overround – the sum of the inverses of the odds – and then took the inverse of that to get the expected payout rate on bets.

Now, let's assume the bookie has set the odds to feature a lower margin on Arsenal because they are favourites. They set odds on Arsenal of

$$D_A = \frac{1 - m_A}{P_A}$$

and odds on Chelsea of

$$D_C = \frac{1 - m_C}{P_C}$$

where $m_A < m_C$ (a lower profit margin on Arsenal than Chelsea).

When the odds are set in this way, the standard calculation of the overround computes as

$$1 - m = \frac{1}{\frac{P_C}{1 - m_C} + \frac{P_A}{1 - m_A}}$$

That looks pretty awful. But when I stared at it long and hard, I thought – this is the inverse of a weighted set of inverses with the weights being the probabilities the bets win; maybe the two inverses cancel out and this is basically the same as just weighting the margins by the probabilities?

If that reads like a load of technical econ prof mumbo-jumbo, don't worry. The point is just that the margin you get from the usual calculation turns out to be almost exactly the same as calculating

$$m = P_A m_A + P_C m_C$$

In plain English, the standard overround calculation gives you a weighted average of the bookmaker's profit margins across all possible outcomes, with *the weights being the bookmaker's perceived probabilities* of each outcome.[57]

The first interesting implication of this is that you can have bets with huge profit rates for the bookmaker hiding behind perfectly reasonable overrounds. If the bookmaker thinks the bet has only a 10% chance of winning, then they can set a big margin on it and it still won't have much impact on the margin implied by the overround.

More generally, the margin implied by the overround will, in one simple sense, be too low on average. This is because it doesn't represent what you'll actually face on a randomly chosen bet.

To see this, suppose the bookmaker thinks Arsenal have a 75% chance of going through and sets their odds with a 4% profit margin in mind ($m_A = 0.04$) while Chelsea have a 25% chance of going through and their odds have a 10% profit margin ($m_C = 0.1$). When you calculate the bookmaker's margin in the usual way, starting with inverting the bookmakers odds, you will get a margin of 5.57%. Note how this is almost the same as you get from the approximation just mentioned where you'd add 75% of Arsenal's margin and 25% of Chelsea's

$$m = (0.75 \times 0.04) + (0.25 \times 0.10) = 0.055$$

The sense in which this is too low is as follows. If I randomly picked my bet on this game, flipping a coin and picking Arsenal if it comes up heads and Chelsea if it comes up tails, then the average bookmaker's margin on the bets I would pick is 7%. That's what you get from an equal weighting of the margins on each bet. But the overround-based calculation doesn't produce an equal weighting. It weights the margins by each bet's probability of success, so in this case it puts more weight on the lower margin on Arsenal than it does on the higher margin on Chelsea.

You can see how average losses across all bets are bigger than implied margins in the US sport tables above. For all the sports, the average implied margin was about 4.5%. For those sports with no favourite-longshot bias (NBA, MLB) that was also the average loss rate. For the others, the average loss rates across all bets were higher.

In another sense, the standard margin calculation might not be so wrong. The data from Betfair that we discussed in Chapter 10 showed more people bet on favourites than on longshots. If the fraction of people betting on Arsenal in this game is higher than 75%, then the average profit margin the bookmaker is earning across all bets placed will be lower than 5.5%.

Ultimately, you don't care about average margins across bets. You care about what the profit margin is on *your* bet. If you've picked a bet that has a relatively high chance of winning, the margin on it is probably lower than the overround implies. If you've picked a longshot, then it probably has a higher margin, potentially much higher.

Overround-based margins are useful as a yardstick for how competitive a bookmaker's pricing is. If one bookmaker's overrounds are consistently higher than others, you can be confident that they offer poor odds. But these calculations don't tell you the true margin on your bet.

Implications for Normalised Probabilities and Boosts

We showed in Chapter 5 how you could calculate the probabilities assumed by the bookmaker when the market was strongly efficient. This relied on using the overround to figure out the bookmaker's margin. And since we now know that estimate of the margin isn't correct, that means the normalised probabilities are also off the mark.

We showed before that once you have calculated the margin m, then the probabilities used by the bookmaker can be found as

$$P = \frac{1 - m}{D}$$

and that strong market efficiency means this calculation is the same as figuring out normalised probabilities.

But favourite-longshot bias means the m used when calculating normalised probabilities is not correct. As a result, normalised probabilities are lower than the probability estimates used by bookmakers for favourites, with the opposite applying for longshots.

If we go back to the datasets above and organise the bets by their normalised probabilities and then calculate how often they win, you see longshot bets win less often than the normalised probabilities predict and favourite bets win more often. This means normalised probabilities are useful as a back-of-the-envelope calculation, but they can't be trusted as true reflections of a bet's actual likelihood of winning.

Similarly, Chapter 5 also showed how to evaluate whether a bet with boosted odds had a positive expected profit when betting markets were efficient. The method involved checking whether the multiplicative boost factor was greater than 1 / (1-m). But favourite-longshot bias means there is no single value of m for all bets in the event, so you need to approximate the right value for your bet based on evidence on the separate margins bookmakers earn across different bets. You can use the tables here for rough estimates of the likely margin on bets at different odds across a range of sports.

CHAPTER 16

Backing the Draw?

When people consider betting on a football match, they usually focus on backing one of the teams to win. But what about the draw? How do you judge whether the odds on a draw are good or bad? Here we describe how to work out whether a draw is more or less likely and use the framework we have developed to show why sometimes betting on a draw is a reasonable bet and why other times it's a very bad one.

How Likely Is a Draw?

To work through what determines the likelihood of a draw, consider a hypothetical example. Suppose Arsenal are top of the table and they are playing bottom-of-the-table Sunderland at home.

Arsenal are clearly more likely to win. Everyone can agree on that. But what is the next most probable result? Well, Sunderland fans would happily admit before the game that they'd "bite your hand off" for a draw. Sunderland winning seems like the least likely outcome, so their hopes are focused on the possibility of a draw. We would expect these games to mainly end up with the favourite winning, for the underdog to get the odd draw, with upset wins being very rare.

In contrast, some matches are genuine toss-ups where each team's chance of winning is about equal. In those games, a draw is more likely than in uneven matchups, precisely because the teams are closely matched.

The table below splits our www.football-data.co.uk dataset of 211,840 football matches into five groups sorted by the normalised probability of the favourite winning.[58] It confirms the intuition just described. For matches where there is only a very weak favourite, draws and wins by underdogs (not really longshots in this case) happen about as often as wins for the favourite. Once one side becomes the clear favourite, draws happen less often, but what really collapses in these mismatches is the chance of an upset. The result is that the ratio of draws to longshot wins rises steadily as the favourite strengthens. By the time the favourite has a two in three chance of winning, a draw is about 60% more likely than an upset win.

How draws and longshot wins vary by average favourite strength

Favourite win probability	*Draw rate*	*Longshot win rate*	*Draw rate ÷ Longshot rate*
37%	30%	33%	0.91
41%	29%	29%	1.00
46%	28%	25%	1.12
53%	26%	20%	1.30
66%	19%	12%	1.58

Differing Beliefs About Draws

How do we fit this evidence about draws into the framework we've been using — bettors who disagree about probabilities and bookmakers who exploit that disagreement? Let's assume that both bettors and bookmakers know that the likelihood of a draw follows the pattern just described and bookmakers base their pricing strategy on this knowledge.

Think first about a well-balanced football match in which all three outcomes have about a one-third chance. Spurs are playing Aston Villa. One bettor thinks Villa's chance of winning is 43%, another thinks it is 23%. They disagree about which side will win, but they both put the probability of a draw at roughly the same level - just under a third. In matches like this, there is very little disagreement about the likelihood of draws. Bookmakers can't set a big margin on bets where everyone more or less agrees on their probabilities of success, so our framework predicts that draw odds in balanced games should be relatively good.

Now consider a mismatch, going back to our Arsenal vs Sunderland example. Here, the principal focus of disagreement is not about which team is more likely to win - everyone knows Arsenal are far stronger than Sunderland - but about the chance that Sunderland can snatch an unlikely draw. Since that's where the disagreement lies, bookmakers have significant scope to set higher margins on draw bets.

Up to now, we've stressed that the worst losses occur when betting on the least likely outcomes. But our framework predicts the extent of disagreement also matters. In this case, incorporating realistic beliefs about the likelihood of draws into our model produced a prediction: Outcomes from betting on draws could vary widely from generating small losses to much bigger losses even with very little variation in the bets' chances of success.[59] When favourites are very likely to win, draws should have a high loss rate and when the game is relatively evenly matched, draws should have a low loss rate.

This was a very specific prediction. I always worry when models generate very specific predictions.

Evidence on Returns to Betting on Draws

In this case, the evidence strongly confirmed the prediction. Again, we group the 211,840 matches into five categories, this time sorting them by the normalised probability of the favourite winning.

The table below shows that, in balanced contests, where the favourite has a limited edge, average losses from backing the draw are relatively small, only 5%. This makes backing the draw better than betting on the home or away teams in these matches, which have average loss rates of 8%.

By contrast, in games where there are strongly fancied favourites, losses from betting on draws average 15%, three times worse than when there are only weak favourites.

Even though the likelihood of draws doesn't vary much across these different groups of bets – the average share of draws ranges only from 19% to 30% – the loss rates vary widely. That is exactly what our model predicts: what matters is not only the probability of a draw, but the extent of disagreement about that probability.

Average loss rates on draw bets and the fraction of draws as the average normalised probability of a favourite win changes

Probability of favourite winning	*Fraction of draws*	*Loss rate on draw bets*
0.37	30%	5.3%
0.41	29%	6.5%
0.46	28%	6.2%
0.53	26%	9.2%
0.66	19%	15.1%

Risk-Loving Preferences Don't Explain This

One reason Tadgh and I felt these results were useful was they provide some decisive evidence for our rational disagreement approach. Our approach could explain the favourite-longshot bias, both in pari-mutuel markets and in bookmaker odds, including its distinctive shape: average losses on longshots increasing faster as the probability of winning falls. These puzzles are "the holy grail" of the economics of sports betting so we were pleased our approach explained them without assuming bettors are irrational or have strange preferences.

Still, when presenting our work, we found some economists preferred the theory that bettors just like taking risks. Risk-loving preferences can in principle explain why longshots do badly as well as the shape of the bias: as a bet's probability of winning falls, the variance its payoff accelerates, so people who like risk may be willing to accept steadily worse average returns to make these riskier bets.

The evidence on draws shows, however, that our framework explains an important pricing pattern that can't be attributed to variations in the riskiness of the bets. Whether it's a one-sided match or a toss-up, the draw is a moderate-probability outcome with similar variance. Yet the loss rates swing from 5% to 15%. This supports our idea that bettors aren't risk-lovers. They're just people who differ in their beliefs.

The Bottom Line on Draws

In balanced games, the draw is the best value bet. In mismatches, it is an awful bet. And the broader lesson is that our rational disagreement model isn't just capturing the impact of bets having different probabilities of success - it is also correctly predicting patterns that stem from how much people differ in their beliefs.

CHAPTER 17

Asian Handicap Football Bets

A central lesson of economics is that market structure shapes outcomes. We have seen that retail bookmakers set high profit margins and generally do not compete much on the odds they set. Here, we look at a market that works very differently - Asian handicap bets on football - and show that it gives different outcomes. In general, this is a pretty efficient market but no market is perfect. We document that Asian Handicap bettors often pick bets that give lower returns than others that are available.

What Is the Asian Handicap?

You may not have heard much about it, but by betting volume the Asian Handicap is the most popular way to bet on football worldwide. It began in Asia, where bookmakers wanted a way to balance matches between strong and weak teams. They called it *hang cheng* betting - a phrase that loosely meant the balance line.

These bets apply "handicaps" to the stronger team by subtracting a number from their score. You are no longer betting on the result of the actual match but rather the adjusted scoreline. The format caught on because many Asian customers disliked the draw being one of the options to bet on. When betting journalist Joe Saumarez Smith was asked to provide an English name in 1998, he chose "Asian Handicap", which stuck in the global betting industry.

The simplest case is when the handicap incorporates half a goal. Of course, a team can't score half a goal but if the handicap is -1.5 and you back the stronger team, they must win by at least two goals for you to win the bet.

Whole-number handicaps add another wrinkle. If you back the stronger team at -1, they need to win by two or more goals for you to collect. But if they win by exactly one, your stake is refunded.

Then there are the quarter-goal lines, written as -0.25, +0.75, and so on. These are hybrids, splitting your stake across two different handicaps. A bet on -0.25 places half your stake on -0.5 and half on 0. If the match is drawn, you lose the half-stake placed on the stronger team at the 0.5 handicap and get the zero handicap half-stake refunded. If the stronger team wins by one goal or more, both of your split bets win. The same logic applies to the other quarter-goal numbers: they split your stake across two neighbouring handicaps, which creates the possibility of half-wins, half-losses and half refunds.

As noted earlier, point spread bets are common in high-scoring US sports and, most of the time, the point spread is set so the two sides of the bet are equally likely to win. But football is a low-scoring sport and even with adjustments as small as quarter-goal increments, the adjusted bets are rarely seen as toss-ups, so the two sides of the bets typically have different odds.

Another difference from American sports is that the result exactly matching the spread - the Celtics winning by 10 points in the above example - rarely happens. But refunds (or half refunds) are common in Asian Handicap betting, typically happening about a quarter of the time. As we discuss below, this means you need to factor in the chance of a refund when assessing the probable return on these bets.

Who Places Asian Handicap Bets?

The Asian Handicap market is dominated by syndicates and professional bettors. These are groups whose betting is often guided by statistical models and who want to bet in very large volumes. Most forecasting models for football predict how many goals each side will score, so these groups are more comfortable with bets based on predicting the scoreline.

The popularity of Asian Handicap betting with sharp bookmakers has also been self-reinforcing. Higher volumes allow the competitive sharp bookmakers to set low margins per bet, knowing they can still make substantial profits by taking in a lot of bets. These low margins have further reinforced the attractiveness of Asian Handicap bets with knowledgeable bettors.

In recent years, retail European bookmakers have also offered Asian Handicap bets but they are a niche business compared with the 1X2 market. They mainly appeal to more serious price-sensitive bettors, not the casual weekend punter, and the retail bookmakers appear to largely copy sharp bookmakers' pricing of these bets, adding a slight additional margin.

Evidence on Margins

If Asian Handicap markets really are more competitive than the 1X2 markets, you would expect average loss rates on bets should be lower on handicap bets. Again, the www.football-data.co.uk dataset can be used to verify this.

Earlier we used a sample of 211,840 matches from this dataset. A slightly smaller sample of 154,269 European football matches across the same 20-year period has information on the average odds across a range of bookmakers for both 1X2 bets and the most commonly quoted Asian Handicap line for each match. As before, because we know the outcomes from these matches, we can figure out the average loss rate across all of the possible bets placed.

The table below reports the results. For the 1X2 market, the average loss rate across all bets was 8.7%. In contrast, the average loss rate on Asian handicap bets on the exact same set of matches was only 3.7%.

There is also a subset of the data with about 45,000 matches that has 1X2 and Asian Handicap odds from both Pinnacle, the world's leading sharp bookmaker, and Bet365, the biggest online British bookmaker. Bet365 loss rates were 7.1% on 1X2 but only 3.1% on the Asian Handicap. Average loss rates on bets with Pinnacle were, of course, lower: 4.8% on 1X2 and just 2.6% on the Asian Handicap.

These are big differences. They show how small changes in market design and structure can create large differences in outcomes. In particular, the big variations in profit margins for two different ways of betting on the same games – both available from the same app – show bookmakers know their markets and are well aware of how far they can push their pricing with each set of customers.

Loss rates on 1X2 and Asian handicap betting from the same samples of matches.

Dataset	*1X2 loss rate*	*Asian Handicap loss rate*
154,269 matches (average across bookmakers)	8.7%	3.7%
45,215 matches (Bet365)	7.1%	3.1%
45,215 matches (Pinnacle)	4.8%	2.6%

Favourite-Longshot Bias?

The size of the differences in margins between 1X2 and Asian Handicap bets might be a bit surprising, but it is hardly shocking that markets with more sophisticated bettors end up with lower margins. Our framework, however, makes a stronger prediction. If the Asian Handicap betting market is essentially competitive, then there should be no room for bookmakers to impose favourite-longshot bias – we should see similar loss rates on handicap bets no matter their probability of success.

Working out the probability of getting a full win – as opposed to getting a full or half refund – requires a few more calculations than the usual normalised probabilities. But Tadgh and I figured out that once you calculated the probability of refunds – and refund rates are pretty easy to predict – you can work out the probability that a bet will give a full win using a tweak on the normalised probability method.[60]

Before we did these calculations, we thought that the range of probabilities of full wins might be very narrow. In fact, we found that the probability of success of handicap bets typically ranged from as low as 25% to as high as 55%. This wide range reflects the limitations of the quarter-goal handicap increments - they rarely fully even up the teams - but also that some of the handicaps collected in the dataset do not seem to have been the most accurate predictor of the expected goal difference on the games.

To check for favourite-longshot bias, we again sorted both kinds of bets into five groups, this time according to their predicted probability of success. The results for 1X2 bets are just like those reported previously in Chapter 15 when we sorted bets by odds. Loss rates increase substantially as the probability of a bet winning declines.

In contrast, there is no evidence of loss rates on Asian Handicap bets depending on the probability of success. There is a weak pattern of both the highest and lowest probability bets having somewhat higher loss rates but overall, loss rates on these bets are low across the full range of probabilities of success. As predicted, this competitive market does not leave room for bookmakers to exploit the variation in elasticity of demand across these bets.

Average loss rates and probability of bet success on 1X2 & Asian Handicap bets on 154,269 Matches

1X2		*Asian Handicap*	
Probability of bet success	*Loss rate*	*Probability of bet success*	*Loss rate*
18%	15.8%	28%	4.9%
27%	10.1%	34%	3.6%
30%	6.8%	39%	3.3%
38%	6.7%	44%	3.3%
55%	4.1%	51%	4.2%

The Refund Anomaly

At first glance, Asian Handicap betting looks like a model of efficiency. Margins are low, there is no favourite-longshot bias, and the market is dominated by sophisticated players. But Tadgh and I also found a surprising inefficiency relating to how bets with refunds are priced.

Most bets lose on average. So, if you sometimes get a refund, that should improve your expected return. Not losing is doing better than average. In an efficient market, bookmakers should lower the odds on bets that come with refunds, so that average returns would be the same across no-refund, half-refund, and full-refund handicaps.

But that's not what we see. The table below reports the figures. In practice, bettors lose the most on the no-refund lines (±0.5). Losses are smaller on the half-refund lines (±0.25 and ±0.75). And they are lowest of all on the full-refund lines (integers like ±1 and ±2). The more chance of a refund there is, the better the expected return.

The differences in returns here are not trivial. On average, bets placed on half-goal handicaps lose almost 1% more than bets on integer handicaps. It takes a lot of hard work and insight to generate 1 percentage point worth of return and, here, it seems like people are just giving that up by betting on one handicap rather than another.[61]

Strikingly, the efficient market prediction about the odds - that they should differ according to how likely you are to get a refund - does not show up in the data at all. The average odds for each of the four handicap types are essentially identical.

Average loss rates on all bets, by Asian Handicap type

Handicap Type	*Integer*	*.25*	*.5*	*.75*
Loss rate	3.24%	3.61%	4.16%	3.57%
Average odds	1.924	1.924	1.923	1.923
Number of matches	23,730	29,250	20,762	10,488

One potential explanation that would be consistent with some form of rationality is that perhaps punters just don't like bets that incorporate potential refunds and they are willing to put up with inferior returns to take bets that rule them out. But that explanation is a bit too neat. There may be some "disutility" to picking a bet that can end in a refund. But it would be quite a coincidence for this disutility to take the specific values that end up with the average odds offered by bookmakers on all lines being the same.

Another possibility was that this result was just a quirk of the way the data were collected. Maybe half-goal handicaps were more popular with soft bookmakers with big margins and so more data were collected from them for those bets?

We tested this idea by acquiring a dataset with odds on multiple handicap options simultaneously on the same matches, all offered by Pinnacle. The pattern held: integer handicaps (with full refunds) consistently produced loss rates around 3%, while half-goal handicaps lost around 4-5%. For us, this was the most surprising finding of all: even in the sharpest corner of global betting, some bettors are systematically choosing the wrong options.

So what explains this? One possibility is psychological. Bettors place wagers hoping to win, maybe expecting to win. Perhaps the refund doesn't factor in to their thinking because they think it won't happen? But that's hardly a satisfactory explanation for how the sophisticated participants in this market think. You would imagine they are well aware that refunds happen fairly often and should be factored in.

Another possibility is that bettors assess bookmaker margins using the simple overround calculation, which doesn't apply once refunds enter the picture. The fact that average odds are the same across the different lines suggests that people may be doing the traditional calculation to assess whether the bets are good or bad value.

Whatever the explanation, these results show how a market can be both efficient and inefficient at the same time. Asian Handicap betting avoids the favourite-longshot bias because competition among bookmakers and sharp customers drives it out. Yet on the very same matches, even sharp bettors seem to consistently misjudge the value of refunds.

Practical Takeaway

If you're going to bet on football with bookmakers, the evidence shows Asian Handicaps provide better value than 1X2 bets. And among those, lines with full-goal handicaps offer the best returns – especially if you place them with a sharp bookmaker like Pinnacle.

Chapter 18

Insiders and Corruption

Have you ever seen a horse come out of nowhere to win at 50/1 or a tennis player retire suddenly from a match - and wonder if something fishy was going on? You wouldn't be alone.

When I tell people I'm researching sports betting, the most common question I get after "do you have a system for winning?" relates to people's suspicions that betting causes corruption in sports, with criminals bribing competitors or officials to produce rigged outcomes. A subtler worry is that betting markets are heavily influenced by a small fraction of people who have inside information even if no explicit corruption is involved.

This isn't just a concern expressed by members of the general public. There is a literature on this in the economics of sports betting, complete with theoretical models of how insiders affect odds and empirical estimates of the fraction of money being placed by them.

It sounds plausible until you take a close look. In this chapter, I show how neither the theory nor the evidence about insiders or corruption having a big effect on odds stands up to scrutiny. We'll start with the theory and then move to the evidence.

Professor Shin and the Insiders

Economists like to analyse data and sports betting provides lots of it, so there were plenty of papers on the topic over the years after Griffith's original study of pari-mutuel racing. But the literature paid little attention to how *bookmakers* might set odds until a young economist, Hyun Song Shin, published three papers on the subject in the early

1990s. Shin, then a lecturer at Oxford, later became a major figure in macroeconomics and finance, known for combining rigorous theory with exceptional communication skills.

His first paper was inspired by discussions among economists about inside information in horse racing.[62] Shin presented a model similar to our monopoly-plus-disagreement framework. It featured a monopoly bookmaker taking bets on an event with two possible outcomes. The bookie set odds to maximise expected profits. Potential bettors with differing beliefs took bets if they thought they had a positive expected profit.

There were two important differences, however, with our framework. The first was the presence of *insiders*. These bettors knew the outcome of the event and so would definitely be on the winning side. The bookmaker knew that a fraction of the potential money available to bet on the event was from these insiders but was not able to identify them and set odds understanding that insiders would always win. Shin showed the presence of insiders meant the bookmaker would set lower odds. Insiders don't care what the odds are. They know the winner and will bet at any odds that generate a profit. This reduced elasticity of demand and thus lowered the odds.

The second difference was what the model assumed about the beliefs of those who were not insiders. Shin assumed these bettors had beliefs about the probability of a team winning that were evenly distributed between 0 and 1, no matter what the true probability was. That meant the crowd wasn't wise at all – everyone was guessing at random. Given how much evidence there is that sports bettors collectively have lots of useful information, this wasn't a reasonable assumption.

What if you made a more realistic assumption about beliefs? For example, what if the average belief was correct, with modest levels of disagreement? We have seen this assumption provides a good match for the favourite-longshot bias pattern seen in the data. Well, it turns out that once the non-inside bettors have reasonable beliefs, then even a very small share of insiders leads to the market collapsing.

Plugging in the new beliefs and the fraction of insiders, you can still calculate the optimal odds. But if you check the bookmaker's profit at those odds, it is negative once the fraction of insider money goes above about 2%.[63] The optimal thing for a bookmaker to do in this case is to not open for business at all. Take away the assumption of a sea of clueless punters and the constant drain of even a small share of insiders would stop bookmakers from opening for business. Insiders may influence the occasional event but if they regularly played a role, no bookmaker would stay in business.

For years, Shin's model was cited as illustrating how insiders played a key role in shaping betting markets. But, in fact, reasonable versions of the model show the opposite: even a small fraction of insider money would make them collapse.

Measuring the Share of Insiders?

Shin also produced a different model that showed how you could use the odds to estimate the fraction of money placed by insiders.[64] This method was refined over the years by other economists so that you could take the odds for any contest and use them to get an estimate of the share of insiders for that specific event.

Several studies were published using this method, generally reporting that the share of money placed by insiders was somewhere between 3 and 5 percent across a range of different sports and times. These estimates implied that vast sums are being placed every day by people with privileged knowledge.

The problem with calculations of this type is that they are only as reliable as the assumptions they are based on. The crucial assumption in this case was that the bookmaker made zero profits. This meant that profits earned on the regular bettors were precisely offset by losses to insiders.

The published accounts of bookmakers show this zero-profit assumption is not at all accurate. For example, in its annual accounts, Flutter reports its gross profit margin for its UK and Ireland sports business: this measures how much more they take in bets than they pay out. In 2022, this margin was 10.7%, in 2023 it was 11.8% and in 2024 it was 13.8%.[65]

When I examined the evidence on insider share measures, I figured the underlying assumption would imply that when odds are relatively generous (with a low overround), the measure would report not many insiders, while the opposite would occur if the overround was high. Essentially, the method imputes the missing number (the share of insiders) from what we do see (the odds). If the odds are poor, so high profits are being made on non-insiders, then the zero-profit assumption points to there being lots of insiders.

Sure enough, if you apply this calculation to the football and tennis datasets we have discussed before, the insiders measure turns out to be 99% correlated with the overrounds.[66] It is very unlikely this research is really telling us anything about the importance of insiders.

Incredible Returns

It is also worth thinking about the returns that insiders would earn. Let's go back to the big football dataset with odds from 2005-2025. Applying the standard insider-measurement approach to this data, you get an estimate that 3.5% of the money placed is by insiders.

What kind of returns will these people earn? In the dataset, the average winning bet had decimal odds of 2.76 – meaning a profit of 176% of the stake when you win. At that rate of return, rolling over a £1 stake for just 25 bets would snowball into more than £1.3 million.

These are literally incredible returns. It is inconceivable that 3.5% of bettors have this kind of lucrative informational advantage.

It is possible, however, to re-interpret the model with a less extreme interpretation of the informational advantage of insiders. One version is that some bettors sometimes get a sure-fire tip while the rest of the time they pick bets with the average return. For example, you could interpret the 3.5% figure as coming from 35% of bettors having access to inside information one-tenth of the time. The football data shows that these bettors would earn an average return per bet of about 11%, which would be sufficient to generate huge profits over time. Remember there are tens of thousands of football matches to bet on every year.

This is an edge well above anything ever reported about even the most successful professional gamblers. Remember poor Spanky working hard to eke out a 1% to 2% edge on his bets? Who knew that one-third of football bettors were secretly outperforming this - and accumulating hidden millions? And remarkably, they were managing to get their bets placed, avoiding the stake limits or bans that are often imposed on even modest winners!

These figures show that, even taken on their own merits, the insider estimates reported by economists don't square with common sense.

Micro-Event Betting and Corruption

These arguments show the idea of regular insider trading amounting to a few percentage points of total betting volume is clearly not accurate. But that doesn't mean betting-related corruption never happens. In particular, modern bookmakers have introduced products that are almost designed to produce corruption, such as "next event" markets like "will the next pitch be a strike?" and "player prop" markets like "will this player shoot 15 points or more?"

A famous example of this was the "spot fixing" scandals in cricket in 2010/11. Players co-operated with bettors to manipulate discrete parts of a game (like a no-ball or a wide) that could be bet on in niche markets. Typically, the impact of these minor manipulations on a team's performance were small, so this kind of corruption was much easier to organise than actual match fixing.

More recently, special bets related to individual players - sometimes called proposition or prop bets - are more vulnerable to inside information. For example, cases have begun to emerge in American professional sports of players accused of disclosing information that can be used for placing player-specific prop bets. The information being supplied is generally harmless from a sporting perspective - a player might disclose their injury status to someone who can then bet on them scoring below a certain number of points. Similarly, coaches can leak that they don't plan to play specific players. In cases like this, the players or coaches may feel it is a "victimless crime" because they are not deliberately underperforming or undermining their team.

Bookmakers tend to make a pretty high profit margin on these bets, so they perhaps tolerate the odd case of insider trading or corruption. The greater concern has been for American sports bodies. These organisations have earned lots of money from their welcoming approach to sports betting but, the recent corruption stories have generated a lot of bad press. As a result, these organisations are seeking to shut down these markets and licensed American bookmakers are now placing severe limits on micro-betting options.

Point Shaving: A Smoking Gun?

One well known piece of evidence that there may be widespread corruption in sports is an interesting pattern in betting on college basketball in the US. Traditionally, people bet on basketball via a point spread. In 2006, Justin Wolfers published a striking paper. He showed that strong favourites in college basketball – those favoured to win by more than 12 points – tended to come up just short of "covering the spread" a suspicious amount of time. Comparing final points differentials with what you'd expect from a typical smooth Normal distribution, the data on outcomes showed too many "close misses" relative to the spread.[67]

One obvious explanation was "point shaving." Players on favoured teams wanted to win but they were willing to take money from gamblers to ease up on purpose, so the spread bet on their opponent would win. Their team still won and they earned some cash. Some point shaving scandals had been uncovered in the past, but Wolfers was showing systematic evidence, suggesting that the practice could be widespread.

The evidence presented by Wolfers has been replicated with updated studies. But the interpretation of the evidence has been disputed and, over time, alternative explanations to point shaving have been put forward.

For example, players that were caught point shaving had explained the easiest way to do this was to slacken up on defence, rather than chucking up bad shots, which looks more obvious. Economists Richard Borghesi and William Dare found, however, that strong favourites do not underperform defensively.[68] The anomaly is driven by them under-scoring relative to expectations.

Borghesi also showed strong favorites in the NBA and NFL also failed on average to cover.[69] But he argued point shaving was not the explanation. Instead, Borghesi pointed out that professional basketball and football players were much better paid than collegiate athletes and less willing to risk their careers for some kickbacks from gamblers.

The NFL results are a sort of reverse smoking gun in this case. Perhaps you can bribe enough players on a college basketball team to make a point shaving scheme work. But an NFL team? There are 53 guys on the active roster and lots of coaches and reserves. Good luck with getting enough of them to agree to win but be just short of the spread line and the rest of them (and the rest of the world) not finding out. So if this pattern shows up in the NFL, something other than point shaving probably explains it.

Borghesi explained why the best explanation lay with how sportsbooks priced point spread bets on strong favorites, rather than with anything the players were doing. He wrote *"Sports books intentionally inflate the lines of games in which a particularly strong team plays against a particularly weak team. This practice, called line shading, potentially maximizes sports book revenue ... This possibility is generated by a betting clientele that steadfastly prefers to bet on strong favorites, even if the spread is too large."*

In other words, if the public is just a bit too optimistic about strong favorites, then the optimal thing for the bookmaker to do is to let them bet into an unprofitable point spread. The truth about anything involving bookmakers' lines is that the explanation is almost always that it looks how it does because that is what maximises their profits.

Match-Fixing: More Myth Than Menace

Some might dismiss the arguments here as academic, unrooted in the tough reality of a crooked industry. So let me make a few more general points about corruption and modern betting.

First, time has moved on since Shin wrote his influential papers, when legal betting was dominated by horse racing. Racing stands out as a sport where true inside information available to those involved in training a horse can provide an edge – for example, information on horses that had never competed or were returning from injury.

But horse racing is relatively unimportant in modern online betting, with more popular sports like football seeing far larger volumes. And for most high-profile sports, there is almost no room for inside information because the form of the competitors can be well evaluated using publicly available information. By the time Liverpool line up to play Man United at 4.30pm on a Super Sunday, every last piece of useful information has been baked into the odds.

Of course, another source of inside information is corruption. This may take the form of competitors taking money from gamblers to deliberately lose or match officials being bribed to favour one of the teams.

The famous scandals – such as the 1919 World Series – are part of betting lore. But modern cases have been less dramatic. Two examples in football were the *Scommessopoli* scandal in Italian football in 2011 and the discovery of a gang of Croatian criminals in Bochum, Germany in 2010 who were rigging football games worldwide.

A key point about these scandals is that they were focused on fixing obscure events. *Scommessopoli* involved lower league matches. More recently, there have been controversies involving refereeing and betting in Turkish football, particularly in its lower leagues. The Croatians largely focused on minor league, often youth, games.

And the guys who ran these operations were not criminal masterminds making billions, but small-time hoodlums who didn't get away with it. Fixing matches requires a decent-sized circle of people, and the kind of people who think this is a good idea are rarely disciplined enough to keep pulling it off. Ante Sapina, the leader of the Bochum gang, was convicted of match fixing and sent to jail in both 2005 and 2011.

The truth is most bets are placed on events that are way beyond the influence of Croatian gangsters. Bookmakers don't share their volume data but publicly available data from the Betfair betting exchange give us a good idea of the true pattern. For football, for example, 47% of the total volume of bets on Betfair are placed on the matches with the highest 1% of volumes and 88% of it is placed on those in the top 10%. In other words, the vast majority of money is concentrated on the biggest games.

And the reality is that the stakes for competitors in high-profile events are huge and the career consequences associated with being caught taking bribes are severe. This makes it unlikely that this kind of corruption is commonplace in today's major sports. Even if corruption happens occasionally, bookmakers aren't building it into their odds for every event.

Monitoring and Detection

From the mid-2000s onwards, there was a concern among sporting bodies that the scale of online betting represented a major threat to sports integrity. From today's perspective, the picture looks different. If anything, it has become harder than ever before to fix sporting events and get away with it.

Bookmakers have always worried about being caught on the wrong side of inside information. That's why they are cautious when markets first open. Early on, stake limits are kept low and odds are adjusted quickly in response to the first waves of betting. Only once volumes build and the market feels normal do bookmakers open up and allow larger bets. They have never been the helpless "sitting ducks," easily exploited by insiders, that the Shin models suggested.

Modern monitoring tools also make unusual betting patterns easy to spot. A sudden surge of bets on one outcome in an obscure event will quickly trigger alarms.

Specialist firms such as Sportradar and Genius also now play a central role. They supply real-time data to bookmakers and sports federations, scanning hundreds of thousands of events each year for anything out of the ordinary. If something looks suspicious, the sport's governing body can be alerted within minutes.

The upshot is that sports bodies are far more on top of potential corruption than in the past. Fixing a match today means fooling not only bookmakers but also dedicated integrity units armed with algorithms and global data feeds. That is why the scandals seen in recent decades have mostly involved more obscure competitions. Still, with today's monitoring, it has never been harder to rig a match and get away with it. And even micro-betting scandals are becoming harder to pull off, with sports bodies getting tip offs on irregularities from bookmakers and other monitors.

As a bettor, corruption and inside information are largely things you can forget about as a relevant influence on the odds.

CHAPTER 19

Bigger Fields Mean Bigger Margins

Horse racing is the sport most commonly associated with insiders having an influence on odds. We start this chapter by documenting a pattern often considered evidence for the influence of insiders: Horse races with bigger fields have higher *implied margins* (which we showed how to calculate in Chapter 5). Here, we will report them in percentage terms so if $m = 0.05$, we call that a 5% implied margin.

You've heard my scepticism about insiders. Here, I show that this element is not needed to explain why implied margins rise with the number of horses in a race: our rational disagreement model also explains this pattern very well.

We then consider evidence on a wide range of different bets where the size of the field varies from small to big. These are what is known as *outright* bets. Who will win the Super Bowl? Who will win the Champions League? Who will win Wimbledon? I built a dataset of 137,402 price quotes on outright bets from SportsOddsHistory.com, often with odds collected over the course of a full season or after different rounds of a tournament. From this, I calculated 4,959 different implied margins corresponding to different points in time for various events.

This dataset has two nice features.

First, it has a huge range of field sizes. For example, every September, you can get odds quoted on about 300 different US college basketball teams to win the NCAA tournament the following April. A typical golf tournament will start with over 100 players, all with odds quoted. And as competitions proceed and competitors are knocked out, the number remaining that you can bet on declines. For example, for recent years, our data on Super Bowl betting starts each year with quotes on 32 teams, falls to 14 in January when the playoffs begin and ends up with quotes for just the two teams that made the Super Bowl.

Second, these are sports where private information is unlikely to matter much. Who has inside information about which team is going to win the Premier League or which golfer will win the Masters? And what are the chances that bookmakers are so worried about such hypothetical people that they adjust odds downwards across the board in response?

If margins also rise with field size for these bets, then the inside information story can't be the explanation. The data will show they do indeed display this pattern - and they again line up well with the rational disagreement model.

Field Size and Margins in Horse Racing

Let's return to our Kaggle dataset on over 400,000 horse races. It shows average implied margins rise with the number of horses competing: 7.5% for three-horse races, 11% for races with five runners, 17% for ten runners and 32% for twenty runners.

One explanation is that as the number of runners increases, it becomes more probable that one of them attracts bets from insiders who know the horse is going to run particularly well.

I don't think that's what lies behind this pattern. The argument in the previous chapter, about why betting markets will collapse if there are even a small fraction of insiders, still applies. And our rational disagreement approach provides a more reasonable alternative explanation. When we described the loss rates implied by our square root formula in Chapter 13, we discussed how the expected loss rate depends on the probability of winning, not on whether a competitor is the most likely to win. A horse favoured in a 20-horse race might only have a 20% chance of winning and be priced similarly to a rank outsider in tennis.

The table below shows how normalised probabilities change with field size. It tracks the ten (or fewer) horses with the lowest odds across races with different numbers of competitors. The results show a clear relationship. As we add more runners, the average probabilities of winning for each horse tend to fall. In a typical-sized horse race (the average number of runners in our sample is 11) *even the favourite is a longshot.*

Average normalised probabilities of the top 10 horses in races

	Number of Horses in the Race				
Horse Rank by Probability	*3*	*5*	*10*	*15*	*25*
1	56%	43%	29%	22%	17%
2	30%	25%	18%	14%	11%
3	14%	16%	13%	11%	8%
4		10%	10%	9%	6%
5		5%	8%	7%	6%
6			7%	6%	5%
7			5%	5%	4%
8			4%	5%	4%
9			3%	4%	4%
10			2%	4%	3%

We can plug these probabilities into the square-root formula from Chapter 13 to get predictions for the odds and thus the implied margin for any race. I again used a cost per unit bet for the bookmaker of $c = 0.03$. I chose $w = 0.045$, for the gap between the true probability and the most optimistic belief, because this value made the model's predictions most closely match those in the data.[70]

The first table below shows how the model does in explaining the evidence. It shows average implied margins for different groups of races, organised from those with the fewest runners to those with the most, and compares these with the model's predictions. The model's ability to explain the data is striking. We don't need inside information to explain why margins rise as the number of runners goes up. Almost every horse being a longshot is enough on its own.

But the predictions of the model go further. Remember that when there is a favourite-longshot bias pattern – and horse racing has it in spades – the average loss rate across all bets will be bigger than the margin implied by the overround. We can use the model to predict how big those losses will be and check them against the actual realized average losses across all bets.

The second table confirms the model's predictions that realized loss rates will be worse than the implied margins. This gap is typically about eight percentage points but widens even more for the races with the biggest fields. For races with over sixteen horses, realized average loss rates are 44%, compared with 34% predicted by the model. One explanation consistent with our approach is that perhaps the amount of disagreement about horses' chances of winning rise a bit for very large field sizes, leading to even bigger losses than if we assume the over-optimism parameter is fixed.

There are some pretty clear messages here. Don't bet on horses. And if you want to ignore that, then really don't bet on horses in races with big fields.

Average implied margins and the rational disagreement model's predictions (cost parameter $c = 0.03$, optimism parameter $w = 0.045$)

Number of Horses	*Implied Margin*	*Model Implied Margin*
2-6	10.8%	10.8%
7	13.2%	13.6%
8	14.8%	14.9%
9	15.8%	16.2%
10	16.8%	17.4%
11	17.9%	18.5%
12	19.0%	19.6%
13-14	21.0%	21.2%
15-16	23.9%	23.3%
Over 16	29.0%	26.7%

Average loss rates on bets and the rational disagreement model's predictions (cost parameter $c = 0.03$, optimism parameter $w = 0.045$)

Number of Horses	*Average Loss*	*Model Average Loss*
2-6	18.7%	17.2%
7	21.5%	20.6%
8	24.0%	22.2%
9	25.5%	23.8%
10	27.1%	25.4%
11	29.3%	26.8%
12	30.5%	28.1%
13-14	33.9%	29.6%
15-16	36.6%	31.2%
Over 16	44.4%	34.2%

The Dataset of Outright Bets

The table below summarises the dataset of outright bets.

For the four major professional American sports (baseball, basketball, football and hockey) we have a combined 44,233 quotes from various points during seasons on teams to either win the championship or their respective conferences, combining to give us 544 different margins from various points in time.

From NCAA college football and basketball, we have 31,304 quotes on teams to win the national championship and almost 700 distinct margins.

For football, we have 5,111 quotes on teams to win the English Premier League, Spain's La Liga and Italy's Serie A and an additional 1,539 quotes on teams to win the UEFA Champions League. Together, these give us 465 distinct margins.

Finally, we have men's golf and both men's and women's tennis, for which we have about 55,000 quotes on all players in the four major tournaments for each sport from 2000-2025, with quotes collected before each round is played. This gives us 1,265 distinct margins.

7 sports, 26 different competitions, 25 years, almost 5,000 implied margins. Let's see what the evidence shows.

Quotes on outright bets in the dataset

Sport	*Years*	*Quotes*	*Margins*
MLB (World Series, AL, NL)	2005-2024	9,177	604
NBA (Championship, West, East)	2009/10 to 2024/25	10,172	635
NFL (Super Bowl, AFC, NFC)	2008/09-2024/25	17,183	1,010
NHL (Championship, West, East)	2009/10 to 2024/25	7,917	492
NCAA College Basketball	2009/10 to 2024/25	17,412	190
NCAA College Football	2000-2024	13,892	298
Football Leagues (England, Spain, Italy)	2009/10 to 2024/25	5,111	373
UEFA Champions League	2009/10 to 2024/25	1,539	92
Tennis Grand Slams	2000-2025	24,915	970
Golf Majors	2000-2025	30,084	295

Margins and Field Size

Again, let's divide up these events into 10 roughly equally sized groups, going from those with the fewest competitors to those with the most, checking the average implied margins in the data against the prediction from our square root odds formula.

As with the horse racing example, I set the operational cost parameter to $c = 0.03$ and picked w (determining the belief of the most optimistic bettor) based on which value produced model predictions for margins that had the best correlation with the data. In these datasets, the probabilities are typically quite low, so it makes sense the best-fitting w parameters are lower than the $w = 0.06$ that worked well for individual football matches. The values that produced the best fits were typically about $w = 0.02$, so the maximum absolute difference in probability belief from the truth was 2 percentage points.

The table below compares the average implied margins in this multi-sport dataset with the predictions from the model. The model slightly under-predicts the average margins across the whole dataset but, overall, it does very well in explaining how margins increase as field size gets larger. Again, the realized average loss rates are greater than these margins and rise with the number of competitors.

Average implied margins and the profit-maximising bookmaker model's predictions

Number of Competitors	*Data*	*Model Implied Margin*
2-3	4.2%	3.5%
4-6	9.0%	5.8%
7-10	13.5%	8.8%
11-14	17.4%	12.7%
15	16.8%	14.6%
16	18.3%	14.8%
17-26	17.6%	13.7%
27-31	21.6%	22.1%
32-64	23.6%	22.4%
Over 64	34.5%	34.7%

How Outright Bet Margins Change During Seasons

Watching a pre-season NFL game? Fancy a flutter on the Super Bowl because the Broncos look good and the odds seem generous? Be aware that these bets have very high bookmakers' margins.

The tables below show average implied margins taken at various snapshots in the season for backing a team to win the Super Bowl, Champions League, World Series and NBA championship. Some of the figures are from snapshots taken in specific months, others are from before a specific round.

The common pattern is that margins start the season high, all over

20%. But then they drop persistently as the regular season goes on and the effective number of competitors falls. Bookmakers may still offer 1000/1 on teams that are clearly not going to win the Super Bowl but remember that the overround is the sum of the inverse of the decimal odds, so those bets will barely affect it.

Among the remaining teams who are still contenders and whose odds do affect the overrounds, their probabilities of winning tend to go up relative to the start of the season. The built-in margins on these teams come down and the overround declines. This is precisely what the rational disagreement model implies and, in this context, appealing to inside information as an important factor doesn't really make sense. Is there more inside information at the start of the season than the end?

Average implied margins for bets on who will win the World Series and NBA Championship at different points in the season

World Series Winner		*NBA Champions*	
December	22.4%	August	20.3%
April	24.4%	October	18.0%
May	20.8%	December	17.6%
June	19.7%	January	18.0%
All-Star Break	18.9%	February	17.2%
August	19.0%	March	17.1%
September	17.2%	April	15.7%
Wild Card	12.8%	Round 1	14.5%
Divisional Series	12.1%	Conference Semis	11.0%
League Championship	5.5%	Conference Finals	5.9%
World Series	3.5%	Finals	3.5%

Average implied margins for bets on who will win the Super Bowl and Champions League at different points in the season

Super Bowl Winner		*Champions League Winner*	
Week 1	20.8%	June	24.3%
Week 8	20.7%	August	22.7%
Week 12	20.3%	October	20.6%
Week 17	17.0%	Knockout Playoff	20.3%
Wild Card	13.6%	Round of 16	14.5%
Divisional Round	11.0%	Quarter Finals	10.7%
Conference Finals	5.9%	Semi Finals	8.0%
Super Bowl	3.7%	Final	5.4%

Favourites and Longshots Again

Let's take a quick look at the favourite-longshot bias for these markets. Beyond the pattern of rising margins with field size, the same principle we have seen before also applies to these bets: Expected payout rates get worse as a bet's chance of winning declines. And in this case, outright super-longshot bets do really badly.

The table below sorts all 137,402 bets in the outrights dataset into five groups, sorted from bottom to top by increasing normalised probability. The bottom row shows that the bets with the highest chance of winning (though not that high - the average probability for this group is 14%), lost 17% of their stakes.

Moving upwards, the next group, with normalised probabilities of between 1% and 4%, lost 49% on average. The group above that, with odds of winning from 0.4% to 1%, lost 73%. The next group, with probabilities of winning between 0.1% and 0.4%, lost an incredible 97%.

And then the final group, with probabilities below 0.1% - literally thousand-to-one shots or higher to win. These bets lost a mere 53%. Wow - that's not great at all but it's a lot better than the two groups above it. What's the explanation?

Two words: Leicester City. This dataset has 4 different quotes in this range that won. And all of them were on Leicester to win the Premier League in the 2015/16 season. Leicester could be backed at 5000/1 on August 1 and October 1, at 2000/1 on November 1 and 1000/1 on December 1.

I suspect bookmakers were thrilled that Leicester won the league. Hardly anyone would have taken up the incredible odds available early in the season and bookies got to win on all the bets placed on Arsenal, Manchester City and the other usual suspects.

Even more than that though, Leicester winning is just the kind of story to stick in the minds of punters. In the absence of any non-Leicester evidence that bets at thousands-to-one ever win, all you've got - cue *Arrested Development* meme - is "these bets never worked for other people but maybe they'll work for me." It's a fairytale come true story that encourages punters to take incredibly badly priced bets year after year.

Average loss rates on outright bets, sorted by normalised probability

Normalised probability range	*Loss rate*
Under 0.1%	53%
0.1% to 0.4%	97%
0.4% to 1.14%	73%
1.14% to 4.22%	49%
Over 4.22%	17%

A Caveat and An Alternative

We've seen that outright bets typically deliver large losses. There is one caveat worth noting. These markets tend to not be very active on a day-to-day basis, and they are often near the bottom of the priority list for bookmakers when updating odds. That means you are more likely to find stale mis-priced odds on some of the teams in these markets, perhaps enough to get positive expected profit bets. Still, the evidence suggests such bets are probably few and far between.

A final recommendation. If it is early in the season and you think a team is going to do better than expected, there is a simple low-margin alternative to betting on that team to win the title. Bookmakers also offer markets like "will this team get 80 points or more?" or "will this team make the playoffs?"

www.covers.com/SportsOddsHistory records odds and outcomes for these kinds of bets for the events we examined here. They typically have low implied margins of about 4.5%, consistent with what you see for individual matches between two teams in these sports. The reason for this is that there are only two possible outcomes: either the team achieves the goal in question or they don't. The bets are typically priced to have equal odds on both sides, so they are 50/50 toss-ups without any favourite-longshot bias.

These bets will lose a lot less money than outright bets to win titles, plus they have the advantage of offering the chance to make money if your insight is that a team is worse than others think, so you can take the under on wins or points.

CHAPTER 20

Margins Across Markets and Time

You're checking games to bet on this weekend. You've got some interesting information about a team playing in the Scottish Championship and check the odds. You calculate the overround and realise the implied margin is about 9%. The bigger the margin, the more wrong the bookmaker has to be for your bet to have a positive expected profit. So how confident are you really in Partick Thistle?

This is an example of a systematic pricing pattern by bookmakers: the lower and event's profile, the higher the implied margin. This chapter presents evidence on how bookmakers' margins differ systematically across markets and discusses what drives this pattern. It also presents some evidence on how margins in football betting change as matches approach kick-off.

European Football Leagues

The table below shows average implied margins from the 22 European football leagues in the www.football-data.co.uk data, sorting them from the lowest to the highest. They range from a low of 5.3% for the English Premier League to a high of 9.0% for the Scottish League 2.

Looking more closely, there is an obvious pattern. The lowest margins are clearly associated with the highest profile leagues – the "big five" leagues of England, Germany, Spain, Italy and France. As you go down the list, you see leagues that attract less attention. There is also a clear pattern of margins getting bigger as you move down the leagues within a country. For example, English Premier League (5.3%) → Championship (6.4%) → League 1 (7.1%) → League 2 (7.3%).

Average implied margins for 22 European leagues

League	*Implied Margins*
English Premier League	5.3%
Germany Bundesliga	5.7%
Spain La Liga	5.7%
Italy Serie A	5.9%
France Ligue 1	6.3%
English Championship	6.4%
Netherlands Eredivisie	7.0%
Scotland Premier League	7.0%
Portugal Primeira Liga	7.1%
Germany Bundesliga 2	7.1%
English League 1	7.1%
Turkey Super Lig	7.2%
English League 2	7.3%
Belgian First Division	7.4%
France Ligue 2	7.6%
Italy Serie B	7.8%
Spain La Liga 2	7.8%
Greece Super League	8.0%
English Conference	8.3%
Scotland Championship	8.5%
Scotland League 1	8.8%
Scotland League 2	9.0%

These margin calculations don't tell us how bettors performed when taking these bets. And if we look at realised outcomes, the average loss rate across all of the bets in each league sample is higher than the margins reported here. For example, while the Premier League's average implied margin is 5.3%, the average realised loss rate across all bets is 7.3%. We showed earlier, in Chapter 15, that this finding of average losses across bets being bigger than the implied margin, emerges when odds are set with a favourite-longshot bias.

So, the margin calculations don't tell us exactly how much bettors are losing. But the rankings of realised loss rates in our data line up well with these margins. When a league has relatively high implied margins, it also typically has high realised average losses across bets.

One way to measure the profile of a league is to get data on how much money is placed with bookmakers for each league. Bookmakers do not report these data but we have a useful alternative. Betfair Exchange, which matches people to take opposing positions on bets, provides detailed data on all matches. The next table reports average pre-match volumes on Betfair for the 22 European leagues, sorting the data from the highest average volume down to the lowest.

Average volume before kick-off on Betfair for 22 European leagues

League	*Average Volume*
English Premier League	£914,063
Italy Serie A	£417,729
Spain La Liga	£371,811
Germany Bundesliga	£247,742
France Ligue 1	£141,250
English Championship	£94,299
Turkey Super Lig	£70,733
Portugal Primeira Liga	£69,070
Scotland Premier League	£57,025
Netherlands Eredivisie	£46,734
Germany Bundesliga 2	£42,438
Belgian First Division	£30,283
Spain La Liga 2	£28,542
English League 1	£27,618
Italy Serie B	£24,810
Greece Super League	£23,700
English League 2	£18,274
France Ligue 2	£12,006
Scotland Championship	£6,025
English Conference	£5,819
Scotland League 1	£4,550
Scotland League 2	£3,228

As you would expect, the Premier League has by far the highest average volume per match of £914,000, more than twice the £417,000 average for Serie A games and 280 times the £3,228 for Scottish League 2. The positions in the margins table match very well with the positions in the average volume table, so we can say concretely that margins vary with the level of interest from the public.

Why Margins Depend on Volumes

A simple change to our model of profit-maximising odds can help explain why margins depend on betting volumes. We have assumed up to now that there is a proportional relationship between operational costs and volumes. If betting volumes double, then operational costs also double.

But the truth is more complicated. Some costs do indeed depend on the scale of bets taken. Banks and card companies take a small cut on every bet; running the app and website gets a little more expensive as more bets flow through; and many taxes are charged as a fraction of either stakes or winnings. You can bundle all of that into a simple "per-pound" rate, *c*. Double the amount staked and these costs roughly double.

But there are also costs that must be paid for every event you run a book on, no matter how many bets are placed. Economists call these *fixed costs*. A market has to be created in the system with clear rules about what counts as a result and where the official score comes from; opening prices and sensible limits have to be loaded; and someone has to check that the market is live and behaving as expected. Many retail bookmakers don't build the prices themselves – they buy them from specialist firms – and that service is paid for whether it's El Clasico or Grimsby versus Bristol Rovers. After the final whistle, the result has to be recorded and bets settled. Those tasks are required every time, so they amount to a fixed bill per match.

Put the two pieces together and the cost of taking a £1 bet has two components: a variable percentage c and a fixed amount F. If V is total volume and F is the per-match fixed bill, the unit cost is $c + F/V$. When V is big, the F/V term fades away and doesn't matter. But when volume is small, it matters a lot. With the cost figure c at, say, 3% and F at £500, a thin market with volume of £5,000 has a unit cost of 13% (because 0.03 + 500/5,000 = 0.13), while a market with volume of £50,000 has a unit cost of 4% (because 0.03 + 500/50,000 = 0.04).

These calculations are consistent with the spread in margins you see across football leagues. Higher unit costs lead bookmakers to set lower odds in less popular markets. They are aware this will reduce volumes, but profit maximisation requires that higher cost matches must have lower average payouts.

But Volumes Don't Explain Everything

When I began researching this issue, I was pretty sure that fixed costs explained why margins varied across leagues – differences in volumes provided the obvious explanation. But quick calculations are one thing, proper statistical evidence is another. My hunch was that once we accounted for volumes, there was no need to appeal to any other factor driving differences in margins across leagues. But the evidence did not confirm my hunch.

Simple statistical models using the year and the division the match was played in explain about 90% of the variation in margins in the football dataset. But when I lined up about 30,000 matches in the dataset with Betfair volumes, the total volume of bets placed on a match only explained about 50% of the variation.

I think some other factors are at work beyond differences in volumes.

Model Risk and Ambiguity

The Law of Large Numbers helps to make the business of bookmaking less risky than it might appear. They may lose on a particular match, knowing that over time they will come out ahead on average. But that doesn't mean they ignore risk altogether. One of their risks is that their odds may be wrong and they may get picked off by people with better models. For big sports, like the Premier League or the NBA, bookmakers can be pretty confident in their models, but they will be less confident about lower-profile sports where less data is available and their traders have more limited first-hand knowledge.

In practice, the probabilities we use to make judgements are not things we know. They are just our best estimates. The typical framework used for optimal decision making by economists says that's fine – just go ahead and use whatever you think is the average value.

For example, suppose you have a 50% chance of winning £100. The expected value of your gain is £50. Now suppose you don't really know that the probability of winning is 50%. It might be higher or lower but 50% is your average estimate. Your expected gain – averaged across all the possible outcomes – is still £50. The uncertainty about the probability didn't change your evaluation. This is how economists have applied expected utility theory going all the way back to Daniel Bernoulli.

But contrary to what the theory says, people seem to dislike taking decisions where the probabilities are more uncertain. The best-known example of this idea is the so-called *Ellsberg paradox*. You are offered two options, both giving a chance to win money. The first option allows you to pick a ball from a box that contains equal numbers of red and black balls. If you pick red, you win a prize. The second option allows you to win the same prize from picking red but there is a difference: this box also contains only red and black balls but you don't know how many of each.

Since there is nothing to distinguish between red and black, the correct subjective assessment should be to act like you are equally likely to draw a red or black ball, meaning you should be indifferent between the option where you know the mix of balls in the box and the one where you don't know. In practice, experiments have shown that people prefer the case with a known quantity of red and black balls. They don't just dislike risk, they also dislike *ambiguity* – situations where you don't even know precisely what the risks are.

Bookmakers face a similar issue. They feel confident in their estimates of the probabilities for a Premier League match. But they are far less sure about less prominent markets. They feel like these are "riskier" for them than the Premier League because they are not as sure about the probabilities.

You can see this approach with even the sharpest of bookmakers. For example, when Marco Blume, Pinnacle's long-time trading chief, was asked about pricing more obscure markets, he said: "*In the smaller leagues, we have zero information but so does everybody else. I mean, who really knows what's happening in Thailand's second division, right? We try to almost keep things on a level playing field by adjusting the margins.*" [71]

When asked about whether these bets were a weak point for Pinnacle's business, he said "*While we would take a tremendous amount of wagers on a La Liga game or NBA game or NFL game with a very low margin ... if you go down the tier leagues, the overround is increasing and the limits are reducing. So, it's to make up for that fact.*"

The higher margins that bookmakers set for more obscure events have clear implications for those looking to get an informational edge. Online betting discussions often focus on the idea that it's easier to get an edge when betting on more obscure sports where bookmakers have less sophisticated models - Swedish ice hockey perhaps. It probably is indeed easier to build a better model for these sports than the ones used by bookmakers. But they have already anticipated this issue and raised margins to protect themselves. If Paddy Power is running a book on a Swedish ice hockey match, you can be pretty sure they are confident they are earning a profit on this sport.

Margins Across Time

As well as varying across events, margins also vary systematically over time. As with debates about getting an edge by betting on more obscure events, you will find plenty of suggestions that the way to win is to bet early, when odds are more likely to be misaligned with fundamentals.

But, as we have already discussed, the odds formation process sees bookmakers starting out being more conservative, and more likely to set higher margins to protect themselves. Bookies may also figure that someone who is willing to bet two days early on a game must be super-confident in their pick and thus willing to take worse odds.

The table below shows average implied margins for four major European football leagues based on odds offered by UK bookmakers, again using data from The-Odds-API.com for seasons 2022/23 to 2024/25. Average margins fall by about 0.4 percentage points from two days before a football match up to the hour before kick-off. If you don't have a track record of winning by picking misaligned early odds, then most likely you are just giving 0.4% of your money away on each bet by going early.

Implied margins with UK bookmakers on four top European leagues from 2022/23 to 2024/25

Time to kick-off	*EPL*	*La Liga*	*Serie A*	*Bundesliga*
48 hours	5.9%	6.5%	6.6%	6.4%
24 hours	5.8%	6.3%	6.4%	6.3%
18 hours	5.7%	6.3%	6.3%	6.2%
12 hours	5.7%	6.2%	6.3%	6.3%
6 hours	5.6%	6.1%	6.2%	6.1%
1 hour	5.5%	6.1%	6.2%	6.1%
10 minutes	5.5%	6.1%	6.2%	6.0%
1 minute	5.5%	6.1%	6.2%	6.0%

VI. The Bookmaker’s Favourite Products

Our focus up to now has been on regular bets like backing a team to win a match. But you can now bet on almost anything that happens in sports, like whether individual players will score or how many corners there will be. There are also options to combine these bets into multi-leg single game "bet builders" similar to accumulators. Another important feature of modern betting markets is the widespread use of promotional free bets and odds boosts for customer acquisition and retention.

These products dominate bookmakers' advertising and marketing campaigns. One economic principle is useful for understanding this stuff: if bookmakers advertise a product heavily, you can be sure they are doing so because it generates higher profits for them.

We will also see that, when dealing with these more complicated products, we are pushing up against the limits of our rational disagreement approach. To understand the design of these products and their popularity with bettors, we will need to draw on behavioural economics and psychology.

CHAPTER 21

The Complexity Trap: Specials and Bet Builders

We previously discussed the prominence of brand advertising by bookmakers. But this accounts for a relatively small fraction of the industry's huge advertising budget. About three-quarters of TV ads – most of them aired during sporting events – focus on promoting specials (e.g. Declan Rice to be shown a yellow card) and multi-leg bets.[72] This chapter discusses the economics of these offers, which typically deliver terrible average returns. We discuss their popularity and why we need to go beyond our rational disagreement framework to understand it.

The Economics of Special Bets

Before the internet, sports betting was largely about picking a team to win or perhaps beat a point spread. Today, you can bet on almost everything that happens in sport: players to score, or get a yellow card, to be fouled at least twice or commit at least two fouls. You can bet on the margin of victory, the exact score, the number of goals, the number of corners and so on.

One explanation for this is simple. These bets are all priced with a profit margin for the bookmaker and the more options you give people, the more likely you are to get them to bet on something and so make more profits.

But there is a deeper reason. Bookmakers have always made more money on longshots than on favourites. Before the internet, by and large they just had to wait for suitable events to come along and hope to get some decent volume on the longshot. And even then, when these uneven matchups would happen, the big expected profits on the longshot would be partially offset by low expected profits on the favourite.

An alternative to just waiting for the sporting calendar to naturally provide longshot bets is to *manufacture* your own. Specials work perfectly for this purpose because they are typically longshots. In any given match, most football players don't score or assist; most players don't get a yellow or red card. All scoreline bets in football are longshots because even the most common scoreline (one-nil) happens in only 15% of games.

Bookmakers can post plenty of these offers on any event. And in most cases, they don't offer the favourite market. If Liverpool play Manchester United, a bookie is obliged to quote odds on all three possible outcomes of the match. But they can post odds on Dominik Szoboszlai to score without any obligation to offer odds on Dominik not to score. You can see this even for bet-types that would work well as simple over/unders. Take a look at the specials offered on football on a typical retail betting site. They tend to take the form "bet on 6 corners or more" but you usually can't bet on "less than 6 corners."

One reason for this is that if they post both options, you can calculate the overround-implied margin. But with only one outcome quoted, you have no way to even approximate what their underlying probability assumption is or what margin they have applied to it.

Another attraction of these bets for bookmakers is that they are considerably harder for bettors to figure out how likely they are to win. When deciding which team might win a match, there are a lot of easily available resources. You can consult the league table and recent form guides, check on injuries and historical results between the teams. Without being a genius, you can make a decent stab at estimating the likelihood of each outcome. But it's much harder to get information on individual players' records of getting yellow cards or to figure out probabilities for things like how many corners there are going to be. This increases the chance that the most optimistic bettors – the ones that matter most for pricing – are way off in their estimates, allowing bookmakers to make bigger profits.

Anytime Scorer Markets

We've had a lot of football in the previous few chapters so let's use a new sport. Bets on individual player performances, "player props" as they are known, are huge in the US. And nothing is bigger than the NFL. Let's take a look first at the most popular prop bet: "will this player score an offensive touchdown?"

I gathered 182,942 quotes from The-Odds-API.com covering 14 licensed US bookmakers on players to score an offensive touchdown over the 2023 to 2025 seasons, meaning they either rush the ball into the endzone or make a catch there. These quotes were matched to the NFL's official touchdown scorer statistics so we know whether they won or lost.

The results are ugly. On average, bets on a player to score a touchdown lost about 34% of their stakes. And, as seen in the table below, these bets have a huge favourite-longshot bias. Bets with odds in the lowest fifth of the sample lost 11%, with this rising gradually to 55% losses for the highest fifth.

These kinds of bets often come with special odds boost offers, but our results show these boosts need to be huge to turn them into profitable bets on average. Remember that we worked out in Chapter 5 bets with an average loss rate of one-third require a 50% odds boost to even reach breakeven. That's why specials are great candidates for boosts: bookmakers can offer very generous-looking boosts while still making profits on the bets.

You can add some caveats to this. We don't know if every one of these quotes was accepted as an actual bet. Many of the real longshots probably attracted little action. And the data show that the "big two" – FanDuel and DraftKings – don't offer as many of these extreme longshots. But even the lowest-odds bets here, which are probably the most popular, are losing a chunky 11%, which is well in excess of losses on NFL moneyline or spread bets. People might think calculating the probability a player scores a touchdown is easy enough but, in practice, those who take these bets seem to be far too optimistic.

And in case you are wondering whether this is just naïve American bettors falling victim to badly priced bets, the same calculations applied to the English Premier League "player to score" market show average losses of 23% across all bets over the 2024/25 season.

Average loss rates on "anytime touchdown" NFL prop bets over 2023-2025 seasons, from 182,942 bets.

	Loss rate
All bets	33.6%
Decimal odds range	
1.14 - 3.25	11.4%
3.30 - 5.50	21.6%
5.55 - 9.50	37.9%
9.75 - 20.00	39.0%
Over 20.00	55.2%

Over/Under Markets

As well as these largely "Yes only" markets like "Will Josh Allen score a touchdown?" American sportsbooks offer a wide variety of player props where people can take either the over or the under on a player doing better or worse than a specified line.

Again collecting odds from The-Odds-API, I gathered samples of prop bet quotes for two different kinds of over/under bets from the biggest three US sportsbooks (FanDuel, DraftKings and BetMGM). For the NFL, I have 25,655 quotes on rushing yard player props from the 2023 to 2025 seasons. For the NBA, I got 146,294 quotes on NBA player points scored bets offered on games between September 2023 and January 2026. All quotes were matched with official league statistics so we can figure out if they won or lost.

For customers to consider them reasonable, these bets have to be designed with credible lines. "Will Josh Allen run for 200 yards?" is not going to attract many bets no matter what the odds are. So, these bets generally have relatively even odds on either side. We know that markets with this feature, where the two sides tend to be evenly balanced, are less attractive for bookmakers and give better average outcomes for bettors. The evidence confirms this, but with a twist.

The average loss rate on NFL rushing under/over bets was 5.9%, a lot lower than for the anytime scorer markets. It's a bit higher than you see on US point spread bets, but the sportsbooks are hardly hiding this pricing. Odds on these bets are typically a bit worse than -110 and the average implied margin across the over and under odds is 5.8%. Even bettors who don't calculate overrounds can see the bookmakers are setting less favourable odds on these bets.

The twist is how that average loss rate is spread across bets. Average losses betting on over are 11% while average losses betting on under are below 1%. See the table below.

Our earlier discussion of the total goals scored market in football gives some indication of why you get this result: betting on someone not to have successful runs is pretty boring. But whereas soccer fans tend not to be too passionate about whether there will be at least 2.5 goals in a game, some NFL fans will probably have a strong belief that Josh Allen is going to rush for at least 60 yards. And bookmakers love people with strong beliefs.

The result is lines set so that over bets on rushing yards only win 47% of the time. This is what drives the difference in returns since odds offered on over and under tend to be pretty much the same.

Share of over wins and average loss rates on "over/under" NFL player prop rushing yards bets over 2023-2025 seasons, from 25,655 bets offered by FanDuel, DraftKings and BetMGM

Line	*Over Win Rate*	*Over Loss Rate*	*Under Loss Rate*
All	47.1%	11.1%	0.7%
Up to 12.5	46.8%	10.5%	1.9%
13.5 to 22.5	48.8%	8.2%	3.6%
23.5 to 40.5	45.5%	14.3%	-2.9%
41.5 to 58.5	47.1%	11.4%	0.3%
Over 58.5	47.4%	10.9%	0.5%

You can see a similar pattern in the table below for NBA points scored player props. Again, these are not 50/50 bets. Overs fall short of winning half the time by 1.3 percentage points. The average loss rate on money placed is 5.8%, precisely consistent with the implied margin, but over bets lose more - roughly 8% compared with 3.5% for unders.

Another interesting pattern that shows up for both types of bets, but particularly NBA, is that you generally see higher loss rates when betting on overs with higher lines. You are probably going to lose more money betting on a star NBA player to score a big points total than betting on a fringe player to come in and have a decent game.

This may reflect what psychologists term the *parasocial* relationship fans often have with celebrities. You don't just like Wemby. You love Wemby. You want nothing but the best for him. You're going to back him to beat that chunky 25.5 points line and celebrate with him along the way. Alas, the cost is a 12% average loss rate on those bets.

Share of over wins and average loss rates on "over/under" NBA player prop points scored bets over September 2023 to January 2026, from 146,294 bets offered by FanDuel, DraftKings and BetMGM

Line	*Over Win Rate*	*Over Loss Rate*	*Under Loss Rate*
All	48.7%	8.2%	3.5%
Up to 8.5	49.4%	7.1%	4.7%
9.5 to 11.5	50.3%	5.1%	6.5%
12.5 to 14.5	47.5%	10.3%	1.4%
15.5 to 19.5	49.2%	7.3%	4.2%
Over 19.5	46.6%	12.2%	-0.6%

Specials and the Attack Surface Analogy

We have discussed the possibility that bets on more obscure options might represent weak points for bookmakers. They respond by raising their margins on these bets, but someone with the right model might still be able to overcome those margins.

Specials provide a particularly interesting example of this idea. There are so many different special bets that it is hard to imagine bookmakers have the correct probabilities on all of them. Ed Miller and Matthew Davidow use an analogy from the world of computing. Protecting a computer network gets harder as the network grows and its "attack surface" expands.

Specials offer a bettors a huge attack surface, so maybe they provide greater room to beat bookmakers. But, if you are tempted to take up this approach, remember these bets typically have big average loss rates. Bookmakers are aware of potential weaknesses in their modelling, and more than make up for this with higher margins.

Bet Builders

We discussed the grim arithmetic behind Accas earlier. Accas are still the most popular multi-leg bets but there has been strong growth in recent years in bets involving multiple events in a single game: These are bets like *Haaland to score, City to win by 2 and the game to have over 11 corners*. In the UK, they are known as "bet builders"; in the US they are "same game parlays" (SGPs). Bookmakers advertise pre-packaged options, but you can also build your own single-game multiple by combining selections from a set of available options.

Bet builders make offering specials particularly attractive to bookmakers. As we've shown, specials are pretty profitable on a standalone basis but, packaged together, they are a product that very few people know how to value properly, making it all the more likely that those who take them are mistaken about their chances of success.

Unlike accumulators, which are priced off the original match odds that everyone can easily see, the component elements of bet builders are harder to track down on a standalone basis. And even if they are available, it is still tricky to figure out the correct price because, unlike the matches in an accumulator, the component events in these bets are not independent of each other.

When I bet on five matches in an accumulator, these are separate events. Winning my first leg does not make me more or less likely to win the other legs. If I have an estimated probability of winning each bet, I can calculate the chance of winning the Acca by multiplying these five probabilities together.

But City's chances of winning by two goals are correlated with whether Haaland scores. If they win by that many, then it's pretty likely their star striker scores. And if it's a very one-sided game with City having plenty of possession, then they will probably have a lot of corners. Figuring out the correct combined probability in this case is a lot harder than just getting three separate numbers and multiplying them. Bookmakers use computer models to come up with their own estimates of how likely these bets are to win.

Previously, we have argued that for most normal sporting events, it is reasonable to assume that the public are about right on average in their assessment of a bet's chance of winning. But when dealing with gambles like bet builders, where it is genuinely difficult to figure out the correct probability, that becomes less likely to be the case. And remember, all that matters for bookmakers is not whether people are right on average about a bet's chance of winning, just whether they can find enough people who are overly optimistic about it.

Bookmakers usually show some pre-packaged bet builder options as a starting point. These typically include outcomes that people will feel are probably going to happen. If a striker has been scoring a lot lately, they are likely to feature in a packaged multi-bet; if a defender has been getting a lot of yellow cards, you will see that option included. Each leg of the package seems like a decent bet, but the total package is priced with a huge profit margin. Bet builders that let you create your own combinations allow people with more extreme (and likely inaccurate) beliefs about certain players and teams to design bets that fit with those beliefs.

The idea that complexity of bets makes it harder for people to pick the right options has also been tested in controlled laboratory experiments. A recent Harvard Economics study asked participants to pick the best option among a set of lotteries of varying complexity. People were more likely to pick the options that had the highest expected payout rate but their ability to do this fell as the complexity of the lottery increased.[73] Figuring out fair odds on bet builders is probably beyond most people's computational abilities, even if you have significant knowledge about the sport. This makes these bets even more fertile ground for bookmakers than Accas.

Knowing that the complexity of bet builders could put some people off, sportsbooks are now rolling out AI assistants that will chat to you and help you build your own parlay – you can ask it "how has Mbappe been performing since his recent injury?" or "what's Real Madrid's away form been like since January?" But if you think those AI assistants are going to tell you the expected value of that bet, I have a bridge to sell you.

Evidence on Bookmaker Profits on Multi-Leg Bets

Once we move away from the world of pre-match bets on single events, it gets harder to find comprehensive evidence of how various kinds of bets perform. There is no equivalent of Joe Buchdahl's datasets for accumulators or bet builders. But there is still credible evidence that multi-leg bets deliver high loss rates for bettors.

First, reports published by US states provide explicit evidence on the profitability of multi-leg bets. For example, New Jersey reported that in 2025, parlays had a profit margin of 19.2%, compared with 4.9% for other bets, so parlay margins are four times higher than on regular bets. Parlays accounted for 65% of online sports betting profits in New Jersey, despite being only 32% of the bets placed.[74]

The other reason we know multi-leg bets are more profitable for bookmakers is because they say so. For example, Flutter CFO Rob Coldrake told investors in early 2025: "*it's the Parlay and the same game Parlay that helped compound up to why we've got the structural -- best structural margin in the sector.*" Kambi, a firm that provides "turnkey" betting products to bookmakers around the world, told investors in early 2025 that "*we continued to see strong engagement with our market-leading Bet Builder, which is a higher margin, lower staking product.*"

Indeed, away from the prying eyes of their customers, bookmakers are pretty cynical about the tactics they use to increase their margin or "hold percentage" by encouraging multi-leg bets. For example, in late 2023, DraftKings told investors about their plans to introduce "Progressive Parlays" on player-related proposition bets which would allow bettors to win even if some of the legs lost. These are a bit like the Acca insurance deals we described earlier but the small benefit for the expected payout from the insurance is offset by dramatically lower odds when all legs win.

This product didn't provide better value but DraftKings were confident that customers would be fooled and pick longer-leg parlays because of the new insurance element. CEO Jason Robins said "*We're excited about our Progressive Parlay offering and its potential to generate higher parlay mix and leg count, and thus higher hold percentage, as well as being a great win with customers who will be able to win money on their parlays even if they don't win every leg of their bet.*" The comment about a "great win" for customers was pure window dressing – his point was this product increased leg count and hold percentage, i.e., it extracted greater losses from customers.

Why Are Multi-Leg Bets So Popular?

Given the evidence that multi-leg bets have such bad returns, why are they so popular with bettors?

One possible answer comes from our rational disagreement theory. This assumes people take bets if they believe they generate a positive expected profit. There are plenty of things to bet on every weekend. Many people will think they can pick five bets that all have a positive expected profit. And if you think you have picks like that, then you would expect to win more by placing a multi-leg bet than by making five separate bets because your expected profits will compound. So, some people placing Accas or bet builders may be following our decision rule of accepting bets with positive expected profit.

Evidence from the Stanford study on US bettors sheds some light on this. It found bettors were more confident about their future returns from betting than was warranted by their historical record. It also reported that this "over-optimism" was most strongly present among those who placed more of their bets in the form of parlays.

However, this view of the popularity of multi-leg bets fits only partially with our earlier arguments about bettors as essentially normal risk-averse rational people. One aspect of these bets that is inconsistent with our earlier arguments is the amount of risk being taken. I argued that small average bet sizes were consistent with bettors being risk averse: Even if they believe the bet is a winner, risk aversion prevents them from wagering more than a small amount.

But bets like Accas involve a willingness to take much bigger risks. For example, someone who places a £5 bet on a five-leg Acca with each leg having decimal odds of 3 has effectively agreed to place £405 at risk on the final leg, should they get that far. This is far more money than most people would feel comfortable risking. We will also describe later how the best option for rational people with normal levels of risk aversion is to avoid multi-leg bets even if they believe each leg has a positive expected profit. And yet you see people placing bets of this sort all the time.

So the explanations for the popularity of multi-leg bets probably go beyond the rational expected utility maximising framework. One possibility is that the arithmetic underlying poor returns on multi-leg bets is not always understood. There is the pattern we discussed earlier of people extrapolating that their "near wins" indicate they are going to win soon. Some people may view an accumulator with boosted odds as perhaps having a higher expected value: I'm placing the same five bets but this time I'm getting better odds.

Others may know that their chance of winning an Acca or bet builder is low, and that they come with higher loss rates, without realising quite how bad the multiplicative maths behind these bets are.

Multi-leg bets may also feel a bit like mini-lotteries. Earlier, we described how the main reason people buy lottery tickets despite their terrible average returns is because they view the product as "buying a dream." Typical payouts on Accas and bet builders are not life changing but they are perhaps fun to think about winning when you place them on a Friday afternoon. The allure of the big win can tempt people into what are otherwise very poor bets.

Other characteristics emphasised by behavioural economists are also perhaps relevant. Loss aversion, for instance. Going back to our example in Chapter 6 where people placed £5 on a five-leg Acca with each bet having decimal odds of 3. This can win £1,215, with an effective bet of £405 being placed on the final leg. Most people would feel terrible if they risked £405 on a standalone bet and then lost it. However, nobody will be too upset about losing £5, so loss aversion doesn't stop someone betting that amount on an Acca.

Of course, if your first four legs of the bet win, then you really are placing £405 to win £1,215, which is precisely the kind of thing loss aversion predicts you shouldn't do. But people seem to treat this bet differently because they practice what Richard Thaler calls "mental accounting." Thaler pointed out that people will often treat separate financial decisions differently, based on the origins of the money or the purpose of the spending, resulting in decisions that a "rational maximiser" would not take.[75]

For example, someone may decide to save for a deposit on a home by placing £1,000 per month in a savings account earning 4%. With £40,000 in the account, they then take out a £20,000 loan at an interest rate of 8% to buy a car. The best financial option would have been to buy the car with the money in the savings account, but this account has been mentally "walled off" for a different purpose. In the same way, someone who makes a £5 Acca bet will often view the £405 bet on the final leg as a "free hit." It's "playing with house money" - if it loses, I didn't really lose £405, I only lost the original £5.

You can see this from decisions about whether to "cash out" a winning accumulator after a few legs. This is usually available (at a discount to the bet's expected value) but mostly ignored by bettors. There are two possible loss-aversion effects here: worry about regret from losing the £405 at risk if the final leg loses and worry about regretting a cash-out if the final leg wins and you miss out on the £1,215. The latter seems to win out, showing we are a long way from rational calculation at this point.

CHAPTER 22

Free Bets and Guaranteed Profits

Promotional offers to attract and retain customers are a key feature of modern sports betting. We've already discussed odds boosts and insurance for Accas. But the workhorse promotional tools are free bets and odds boosts on individual bets. It might seem strange to find these in a section called "the bookmaker's favourite products" since free bets cost money to give away and boosting odds also reduces their profits. But economics teaches us that if a firm is pursuing a strategy, it's because that strategy maximises profits. Bookmakers offer these promotions because they believe that, over the long run, doing so leads to higher profits.

This chapter focuses on the economics of promotional bets: how to value them, what the best strategy is for using them and why bookmakers are so keen to hand them out. We'll also explain how you can turn these bets into guaranteed money, including the bizarre "promo tourism" industry this has produced in the US.

The Surprising Maths of Free Bets

Free bets are everywhere in the world of sports betting. Let's look at what they are and what the best strategy is for using them.

A free £1 bet is clearly not the same thing as being given £1 in actual money because, by definition, you have to use it to place a bet. And that makes it worth less than £1. You may suspect what's coming next. I'm going to tell you that the expected payout on a £1 bet is worth $p \times D$ pounds which is less than £1. And then I'm going to tell you that $p \times D$ gets worse for longshots, so you should place your free bet on a strong favourite. Right?

Actually, no, I'm not going to say that. Free bets don't work like regular bets. In almost all cases, free bets offer you the chance to keep the *profits* when the bet wins, but the *stake* disappears just like it would if you'd lost the bet. If you get a £1 free bet at decimal odds of 5 and it wins, you will get £4 added to your account balance, not £5 – you keep the profit but not the original stake.

This means a one-unit free bet is not worth $p \times D$. It is worth $p \times (D\text{-}1)$ which is the same as $(p \times D) - p$. Remembering that the expected payout rate on a regular bet, $p \times D$, is just $1\text{-}m$, this means your one-unit free bet is worth $1\text{-}m\text{-}p$. The higher the probability of winning is, the lower the expected payoff. This is precisely *the opposite* of what happens with normal bets. The best thing you can do to maximise your expected payoff is to bet on the most extreme longshot you can find. I reckon you didn't expect me to recommend that!

It may seem unintuitive but, once you work through an example, it becomes clearer. Man City play Barnsley in the FA Cup and bookies reckon City are almost sure to win. Their decimal odds are 1.01. Use your free £1 bet to back City and they win, all you get back is 1p. If you are going to make any money from the free bet, you need to pick a higher odds option.

With your free bet having an expected value of $1\text{-}m\text{-}p$, margins rising as p falls might soften the recommendation to pick an extreme longshot with your free bet, but you certainly don't want to pick a favourite. If you calculate margins from our huge 20-year football dataset discussed earlier, it suggests expected payout rates on free bets keep rising as the odds go up until you reach decimal odds of about 8, which is pretty long odds for a football bet.

All of this means that if you get a free bet, ignore all my earlier advice about longshots. If you want to maximise its expected value, choose high odds – a serious outsider but not a completely wild one.

Guaranteed Money from Free Bets

Free bets are not free money – you have to place them on a bet and if your bet loses, there's no money for you. And the more you try to make them "safe" by putting them on sure-fire favourites, the smaller the amount you get back when they do win.

But there is a clever way to turn free bets into actual guaranteed money. It is called *matched betting* and it works as follows. Let's again consider Arsenal versus Chelsea. You place your £1 free bet on Arsenal at odds of D_A. You then place a *hedging bet* with another bookmaker on Chelsea, sized to produce the same final payout. For a unit bet on Arsenal, the correct size hedging bet is $(D_A - 1)/D_C$. This guarantees the same payout, whichever team wins.

Why do you place the hedging bet with a different bookmaker? Well, you could place it with the same firm but they can then see what you're doing and that your plan is to earn some free money rather than stick around to be a long-term loser. Indeed, in their terms and conditions, bookmakers often describe any strategy in which you can guarantee a profit as a "prohibited practice" or "promotion abuse". So, there is a good chance they will limit or ban you or at least cancel your promotional offers.

If the bets were priced at fair odds, then this strategy locks in a risk-free profit equal to the expected profit for your free bet. In the case of fair odds, that is 1-p, where p is the probability Arsenal win. The bookmakers having profit margins on the two bets means the actual risk-free profit is lower than this.

To illustrate, again assume Arsenal are a 70% chance to win and bookmakers price both bets with a 5% margin, giving odds of D_A = 1.36 and D_C = 3.17. First consider putting the free £10 bet on Arsenal at 1.36. The right hedge stake is

$$\frac{D_A - 1}{D_C} \times 10 = \frac{1.36 - 1}{3.17} \times 10 \approx £1.14$$

so you place £1.14 on Chelsea. Now look at the two possible outcomes.

- If Arsenal win, the free bet gets you £3.60 profit (£10 × 1.36 =

£13.60, minus the £10 stake you don't get back = £3.60) but you lose £1.14 on Chelsea. Net gain: £2.46.
- If Chelsea win, the free bet is worthless, but your £1.14 at 3.17 brings back a profit of £2.46.

You've turned the £10 free bet into a guaranteed profit of £2.46. If there was no margin in the odds, the expected profit from using a £10 free bet on a 70% shot would be £3; the margin on both legs eating into payoffs has dragged that down a bit.

Now flip it around and put the free bet on Chelsea instead at 3.17. This time you hedge by backing Arsenal at 1.36. The hedge stake is

$$\frac{D_C - 1}{D_A} \times 10 = \frac{3.17 - 1}{1.36} \times 10 \approx £15.96$$

so you place a £15.96 bet on Arsenal.

Again, check both outcomes.

- If Chelsea win, the free bet gets you £21.70 profit, but you lose £15.96 on Arsenal. Net gain: £5.74.
- If Arsenal win, the free bet is worthless, but your £15.96 at 1.36 brings in a profit of £5.74.

So with the free bet used on the favourite, you could lock in a profit of £2.46. With the same free bet used on the underdog, you can lock in a profit of £5.74. In both cases, margins on the two prices drag you below the "fair" expected profits (£3 and £7) but the pattern is clear: using a free bet on a longer-odds option generates a higher guaranteed profit than using it on a short-odds favourite.

You can see that the guaranteed profit in this case was bigger from placing the bet on the underdog rather than the favourite. But there is a limit to that. When you work through the maths (which I will spare you) you find that the value of the guaranteed profit equals the expected profit $1\text{-}m\text{-}p$ times a "hedging discount." This discount is small for high values of p but gets bigger as p falls. This means the guaranteed money eventually falls as you use the free bet on bigger long-shots.

I worked out a fun result on this. If the margin is m on both your free and hedging bets, you can use calculus to show that you maximise the guaranteed profit by picking a free bet with probability of winning of ... drumroll ... $\sqrt{m(1-m)}$, which looks super scientific![76] For example, with $m = 0.05$, this implies a bet with a 22% chance of winning. That will give a guaranteed profit of £5.94 on your £10 free bet.

Now some practical issues. Some sports have more than two options to bet on, so you can back a competitor but there isn't a simple bet available to back them not winning. One approach is to use betting exchanges, where it is possible to place a bet *against* something happening rather than for it. That can allow you to use your free bet on football if you really want to. But there are plenty of two-option bets out there, with tennis providing examples most days of the year, so you can back with one bookmaker and hedge with another. Tennis also works well because there are plenty of bets in the best odds range to place your free bet on.

We have also assumed the margins are the same on both sides of your bet, which is an extreme version of strong betting market efficiency: not only does each bookmaker price both sides with the same margin but each bookmaker uses the same margin.

Because that's unlikely to exactly hold in the real world, I checked the "square root" prediction with data. From The-Odds-API, I got about 28,000 tennis odds quotes from Ladbrokes and Paddy Power, calculating for each bet what the guaranteed profit was from taking the hedging bet with the other bookmaker. The average calculated margin was 5.8%, implying the best win probability for your free bet was 23% and the best decimal odds for it were about 4.

Sure enough, the best average guaranteed profits, of about £5.60 for every £10 in free bets offered, came from placing free bets with decimal odds of about 4, right in line with what the calculations above predicted. Tennis betting markets are not typically strongly efficient but it's a close enough assumption to correctly predict the best thing you can do to turn free bets into guaranteed profits.

Guaranteed Money from Odds Boosts

We discussed odds boosts in Chapters 5 and 15, showing how to calculate whether the boosted bets had positive expected profits. But if odds boosts are generous enough, sometimes they can also be turned into guaranteed money, though typically with a lower average profit per unit of the promotional bet staked than free bets.

As before, the size of the hedge bet is set so that you get the same payout you would on your original bet, thus guaranteeing the same return in both cases. For a unit bet on Arsenal, a hedge bet of size D_A/D_C on Chelsea gets you a guaranteed profit of $D_A - D_A/D_C - 1$. Again, the hedging does not translate the uncertain average profit one-for-one into guaranteed profits. In fact, this can be negative, even if the boosted bet on Arsenal has a positive expected profit.

Sometimes you get to pick which bet to apply your boost to. In that case, which option gets you the highest guaranteed return? I'm not going to work through any algebra here but the answer is that you should place the boosted bet on the shortest odds favourite that you can find (or will be allowed to bet on – sometimes bookmakers place restrictions on the use of odds boosts).[77]

To illustrate, again assume Arsenal are a 70% chance to win and that all bets are priced with a 5% margin, meaning odds of $D_A = 1.36$ and $D_C = 3.17$. Suppose you are offered a 33% odds boost. If you place a £10 bet on Arsenal with boosted odds of $D_A = 1.81$, your hedging bet on Chelsea would be of size £5.70 and your guaranteed profit would be £2.40 (because 1.81 – 1 – 0.57 = 0.24).

In contrast, if you placed a £10 bet on Chelsea with boosted odds of $D_C = 4.21$, your hedging bet on Arsenal would be of size £31 and your guaranteed profit would be £1.1 (because 4.21 – 1 – 3.10 = 0.11).

In this example, using the boosted odds bet on the favourite gives you a guaranteed return that is over twice what you would get from using the boost on a high-odds bet, though you can see the returns are smaller than for free bets. Again, checking these predictions using data for bets on 28,000 tennis matches with Paddy Power and Ladbrokes confirms that average guaranteed profits rise steadily as the boosted bet is placed on stronger favourites.

Free But Not Hassle-Free

There you have it. Finally, some risk-free money tips. In fact, this thing is so safe, you can even find threads about it on Mumsnet.

Why have I been holding out so long on this free money? Well, for starters, it's a limited amount of money. There are only so many bookmakers and there's a limit to how many initial free bets you can get. Once you've used up all the initial promos, you're not getting more of them, particularly if the only non-free bets they see you place are hedging bets during your initial promo spree. If you're very aggressive in opening all possible accounts, you might earn a couple of thousand pounds.

And then there's the hassle. You have to go through the verification processes, providing email addresses, phone number, ID, perhaps bills for proof of address. Then you have to find your bets and go place your hedging bets, hoping the odds haven't moved to make the maths work against you or that you don't make a mistake and bet on the same team twice. It takes time. It's almost like a job.

A 2018 article in Vice on matched betting by Hayden Vernon summed the process up well.[78] His first discovery was that "*Matched. Betting. Is. Extremely. Tedious.*" After a month, he had made £540, but he had spent 30 hours at it, for an hourly "wage rate" of £18. And that's the first month. It only gets less lucrative after that, once the most attractive first set of promos are gone.

Look, I'm not knocking matched betting. It might be a way to raise a modest-sized fixed sum for a specified purpose, without leaving your own home. And bookmakers offering free money bets can hardly be surprised if people exploit them. But it's not clear that the hourly rate for all this effort beats delivering pizza.

Promo Tourism in the US

If something strange exists in betting, you can usually rely on the United States to produce a version of it that's several times stranger.

American sportsbooks are expanding very aggressively and offering extremely generous initial promotions – often hundreds or even thousands of dollars in free bets. They're confident that gaining market share in a huge country with plenty of unsophisticated sports bettors will make these initial investments pay off. The combination of fragmented state-by-state laws, aggressive marketing budgets and a national talent for turning anything into a side-hustle has created behaviours you don't see anywhere else.

Take "promo tourism." Sports betting is legal in some American states but not others, and the apps use strict geolocation: you can only bet if your phone or laptop is physically inside a legal state. But you don't need to have an address in that state to bet there. That odd geometry, combined with much bigger sign-up bonuses than in the rest of the world, has created some weird incentives.

The basic model goes like this. Suppose you live in California, a state with no legal sportsbooks. You drive to Arizona, which has plenty of them, and check into an Airbnb after you've crossed the state line. You spend two days glued to your phone or laptop, open accounts with every local sportsbook, claim each sign-up bonus and place a sequence of longshot bets and their hedges. When it's over, you cash out and drive home. There are even "arb consultants" that will help you execute this plan, for a fee, giving you a list of sportsbooks and bets to place.

On paper, this can add up to a few thousand dollars of "risk-free" gain; in practice, once you subtract travel and accommodation costs, time and errors (you might back the same team twice at both books by accident), many people are probably just about covering the cost of the trip. Still, from their point of view, a weekend away where the sportsbooks effectively pay for your mini-holiday beats paying for it yourself. From an economist's point of view, it's an example of how regulation and incentives can produce some very strange outcomes: a whole subculture of people travelling around the country to sit in hotel rooms harvesting free bets.

Subscription Services and a Simple Alternative

There are firms that sell services that help you lock in guaranteed returns but, honestly, with monthly fees of about £40 in the UK, they're probably not worth it. The matched betting services say their fees "pay off multiple times over" but that's because they're counting the money you can make yourself anyway and dividing it by their cost.

These firms emphasise how complicated the calculations are and offer to help with that and with picking bets. But if you've bought this book and made it this far, I think you can convert fractional odds into decimal and divide one number by another.

Also, the bets are not hard to find, and you can use the patterns noted here without doing any maths. Use free bets on a tennis underdog at decimal odds of about 4 and then hedge on the favourite. And use boosts on the most extreme favourites you can find and hedge on the longshots. That minimises research time and will work out just about as well as if you sweated it, trying to maximise your profit.

If you really want to be more precise than that, I have provided some code on my website at www.karlwhelan.com/sports-betting/matched-betting that can suggest which are the best games to use free bets and bet boosts on. You sign up for a free-level subscription to The-Odds-API.com and can run the Python codes available on my site to get a list of the best guaranteed profits available from free bets.[79] In other words, install some simple free software and you can get a list of the best matched betting options (and the size of the hedging bet) without paying any monthly fees.

Why Promos Exist: Habits and Mental Accounting

So why are bookmakers so fond of offering promotional bets?

First, new customers are valuable. It is worth giving away some money as long as enough of them hang around to become profit centres – that is, long-term losers. US sportsbooks in particular are very open about their willingness to spend big on "customer acquisition costs" via marketing and free bets. The same logic applies to lapsed customers who have stopped betting with you: a free bet may be enough to get them betting again or to tempt them back from a rival.

Second, promotional bets push people towards longshots. As we have seen, the expected value of a stake-not-returned free bet increases when you use it on a higher odds option. It is not clear that most new bettors understand this. A recent experiment by Irish researchers found that only about half of participants realised that free bets did not return the stake, only the winnings - suggesting many bettors significantly overvalue these promotions.[80] But to the extent that people do understand how the offers work, bookmakers will hope they develop a taste for longshots and keep placing those bets even when they go back to using their own money.

Third, promotional offers are sometimes tied to the products with the highest expected losses. Free bets and odds boosts are often restricted to accumulators, bet builders or, even worse, virtual casino games. These are precisely the kinds of bets where the house edge is biggest. If the free bets encourage you to keep picking these options after the free bets are finished, then the bookmakers will probably win back more than they have given away.

Fourth, there is the role of "loyalty" bonuses for the most valuable customers. Evidence shows that bookmakers earn a large fraction of their profits from a small slice of customers. Keeping those people feeling appreciated is a key part of a profit-maximising strategy. They like being given free bets and VIP perks, and in aggregate they pay many times over for these treats via their regular, sizable losses.

Finally, Thaler's idea of mental accounting matters again. On average, bettors lose. That means there are more deposits than withdrawals, so people get used to making occasional deposits.

Consider someone who deposits £500 and then keeps betting until it's gone and then makes another deposit. £100 in free bets may feel like a windfall sitting in a separate mental account, so they are less careful about how much they are losing. If they respond to the free bets by playing more than they otherwise would, they may just end up losing £600 over the same period instead of £500. If this is how you use them, the value of your free bet isn't $p \times (D\text{-}1)$, it's zero.

The bottom line is that bookmakers are confident that, on average, they will win back the money they give away in free bets, and more besides. The promotions are carefully designed tools for acquiring customers, nudging them towards high-margin products and encouraging them to bet more often.

VII. When the Game Starts

In-play betting has exploded in recent years. Here, we will discuss the economics of this kind of betting and present some new evidence. We show that odds worsen as soon as the game starts and explain why. Then, we document a remarkable pattern of increasingly awful returns to longshot bets as matches play out. We also discuss the economics of cash out offers and some of the darker sides of in-play betting. Again, we will see patterns that are hard to reconcile with our earlier "rational disagreement" approach.

CHAPTER 23

Betting, Fast and Slow

So far, we have only examined bets that are placed before an event starts. However, in-play betting has grown spectacularly in recent years. In fact, industry estimates suggest that in-play now accounts for a majority of total sports betting in Europe. This chapter focuses on the economics of in-play betting and explains why it produces higher loss rates for bettors. We use rich "real time" data on odds on major sports to show the most dramatic favourite-longshot bias yet.

The Economics of Live Odds

As soon as events go in-play, the odds worsen. The first explanation is that operating in-play betting markets is more expensive. And this starts with the data.

Before a game starts, bookmakers can put together excellent models to forecast match outcomes. They buy data from providers like Opta and combine it with information in betting flows and from scanning news on injuries, suspensions and the like. This can be done at a pretty low cost relative to the amounts being staked.

Once games start, however, the data collection exercise becomes much more complex. The first problem is that information can leave the pitch before your price updates because people at the venue - "courtsiders" or "pitchsiders" - can place a bet or transmit information to a betting syndicate in a fraction of a second. If your odds move after the TV shows the goal rather than right after the goal is scored – a delay of several seconds – sharp bettors will happily take your stale price and on average will win money against you.

To counter this vulnerability, bookmakers must integrate specialised, high-frequency data. This isn't just in-match statistics, like how many goals or yellow cards there have been; it's a continuous, high-frequency stream of granular events captured by advanced optical tracking technology. For a sport like football, these systems use arrays of high-resolution stadium cameras and optical tracking systems that record the ball and every player up to 50 times per second. If you are offering live odds on Bukayo Saka to score the next goal, it's helpful to know whether he's defending a corner or running down the right wing.

Sporting bodies are well aware of the value of these data feeds to bookmakers. The rights to real-time collection of information from inside stadiums are owned by the sports organisations and, typically, they sell monopoly rights to provide the data in an auction to the highest bidding firm.

A recent court case provides insight into how this business works. In 2019, the British football leagues sold exclusive in-stadium data rights for the Premier League, EFL and SPFL to Genius Sports for over £70 million per year. Another firm that had been selling in-play data to bookmakers, Sportradar, did not secure the official data rights but continued to provide information using spotters in the stands, tapping events like goals, cards and subs into phones to beat the TV delay. Genius and the leagues sued over misuse of confidential live data. Sportradar settled – agreeing to stop in-stadium scouting. Today, if you go to a match and appear to be recording lots of information, there is a good chance the stewards will escort you out.

The costs of in-play offerings for bookmakers don't end once they have acquired the data. For some, turning the live data into odds is too complex. They will instead make additional payments to Genius or some other "B2B" firm to provide them with real-time odds for a menu of in-play bets.

Other larger bookmakers will use the data to offer their own selection of bets. This is resource intensive. The data need to be plugged into complex models: increasingly, bookmakers or their B2B suppliers use AI to process the hundreds of different inputs that influence real-time odds. And the software needs to make sure prices remain consistent across markets, so an update on one set of bets doesn't create a free-money bet somewhere else.

But the bookmakers can't just rely on computers. They also need a trading desk on shift when the games are on. In addition to the official fast feeds, you need to run video so traders can sanity-check big moments. Traders need to occasionally suspend and reopen markets and adjust limits. And they have to recover cleanly when scores are ruled out or a red card becomes yellow after a VAR review.

All of this makes in-play betting more expensive to run and higher costs mean lower odds for customers.

Evidence on Odds Worsening as Games Start

To illustrate how odds worsen as the game starts, I collected real-time odds quotes on 1X2 English Premier League bets offered by the UK bookmakers as well as odds on NBA and NFL "Moneyline" (win/lose) offered by a range of licensed US bookmakers. The data come from The-Odds-API. They cover three full seasons for each league, from 2022/23 to 2024/25 seasons for EPL (1,112 games) and NBA (3,669 games) and the 2023 to 2025 NFL seasons (1,088 games).

I gathered odds from an hour before the games start, about 5 minutes before the start and 5 and 30 minutes after the start, using the most recently available timestamped quotes. For each game, there are about 15 different bookmakers quoting odds: I calculated the average overround-implied margin from the quotes, as well as the average realised loss across the three different 1X2 options for the EPL and the two options (home/away) for the NBA and NFL bets.

The table below shows that margins jump as soon as games go in-play. Going from the last quotes before play starts (typically about 5 minutes before start time) to the first quotes after play starts (typically about 5 minutes after the start), the EPL margin goes up by 1.5 percentage points. The average NBA moneyline margin increases by 0.8 percentage points and the average NFL margin jumps by 0.9 percentage points. The NBA and NFL moneyline margins rise by another 0.6

percentage points by 30 minutes after the game starts.

Not reported in the table, but you see the same pattern for NBA and NFL point spread bets, with average margins going from about 4.5% just before game time for both to about 5.3% at about 5 minutes in and 6.3% after 30 minutes.

Average implied margins and loss rate across moneyline bets before and after games start in the EPL and NBA (2022/23 to 2024/25 seasons) and NFL (2023, 2024 and 2025 seasons)

	EPL 1X2		*NBA*		*NFL*	
	Margin	*Loss Rate*	*Margin*	*Loss Rate*	*Margin*	*Loss Rate*
One hour before	5.9%	7.8%	4.0%	3.8%	4.1%	6.0%
5 minutes before	5.8%	7.7%	4.0%	3.8%	4.1%	6.0%
5 minutes after	7.4%	9.6%	4.8%	4.6%	5.0%	7.1%
30 minutes after	7.4%	10.8%	5.5%	6.9%	5.7%	7.9%

The margins implied by the overround don't always map perfectly to actual outcomes, but we can see here that average losses jump from just before start time to just after. In fact, actual losses increase by slightly more than the jumps in the margins. This shows that pricing genuinely worsens as soon as the game goes in-play. And the amounts are not trivial. An additional margin of 1.5% as a game goes in play requires a lot of extra edge to offset.

Favourite-Longshot Bias on Steroids

We have shown plenty of examples of favourite-longshot bias but wait until you see what comes next. For EPL and NBA, I obtained odds for a set of in-play timestamps. The timestamps represent the actual passage of time, not game time, so for football 90 minutes here typically means about 20 minutes plus second-half stoppage time remaining.

I also collected the final odds quotes from the data provider. Sample coverage falls a bit as the games near the end. Almost all EPL games have these very late quotes but from fewer bookmakers, while US bookmakers tend to only provide very late (later than two hours after tip-off) quotes for about one-third of the NBA games.

For each time stamp, I sorted all the quoted bets by their normalised probabilities. The four tables below show loss rates for each group for the Premier League for different timestamps. The results are striking.

There is a clear favourite-longshot bias pattern in pre-match odds, similar in size to what we documented earlier. As the game goes on, average loss rates for longshots get bigger and bigger. The one-fifth of bets with the lowest normalised probabilities lose 14% if placed just before kick-off, 23% if placed 30 minutes after, 46% if placed 90 minutes after and a whopping 78% if you take up the very final longshot offers. Yes, you read that correctly. People who bet on very late in-play longshots lose almost four-fifths of their money.

Two things are driving these catastrophic results. The first is that the normalised probabilities of winning for late longshots are far lower than for even the biggest pre-match underdogs. A team might not be fancied to win before a ball is kicked but everyone's got a puncher's chance. One-nil down going into added time isn't a puncher's chance of winning; it's basically no chance. Even if the pre-game pattern of favourite-longshot bias prevailed, these bets would have very poor returns because the bias accelerates fast as probabilities fall to very low values. But when we compare pre-game patterns for specific low probabilities against the in-game ones, the evidence still shows a stronger bias than prior to the game. Bookmakers are adjusting their pricing of longshots to make greater in-play profits.

And, again, you could not tell this pattern from calculating overrounds. After their initial jump at kick-off, in-play implied margins stabilise and even decline a bit late in the game. The worst offers often hide behind pricing that looks perfectly fair.

Average loss rate on Premier League bets sorted by average normalised probabilities: 5 minutes before game

Normalised probability	*Loss rate*
0.14	14%
0.23	10%
0.28	8%
0.39	5%
0.63	1%

Average loss rate on Premier League bets sorted by average normalised probabilities: 30 minutes after game starts

Normalised probability	*Loss rate*
0.10	23%
0.21	14%
0.28	4%
0.39	9%
0.68	4%

Average loss rate on Premier League bets sorted by average normalised probabilities: 90 minutes after game starts

Normalised probability	*Loss rate*
0.03	46%
0.12	9%
0.25	6%
0.45	5%
0.81	5%

Average loss rate on Premier League bets sorted by average normalised probabilities: Final odds quotes

Normalised probability	*Loss rate*
0.004	78%
0.03	50%
0.07	42%
0.62	11%
0.95	2%

The NBA results, shown in the four tables below, are even more interesting. We showed before that US sportsbooks don't apply a favourite-longshot bias to pre-game NBA bets. But in-play? They absolutely do. NBA games have 48 minutes of clock time but there are lots of stoppages for time outs, commercials and quarter breaks. The sixty-minute snapshot here is typically about half-time in the games.

At one hour after tip-off, we can already see pricing moving against longshots, with the bottom fifth of bets by normalised probability losing 13%. NBA games typically last between 2 hours 15 minutes and 2 hours 30 minutes. At 2 hours, the bottom fifth of longshot bets are losing 46%. Where final quotes are available after that, outcomes are disastrous, with 95% loss rates on very late longshot bets.

Average loss rate on NBA bets sorted by average normalised probabilities: 5 minutes before game

Normalised probability	*Loss rate*
0.22	4%
0.38	4%
0.50	4%
0.62	4%
0.78	4%

Average loss rate on NBA bets sorted by average normalised probabilities: 60 minutes after game starts

Normalised probability	*Loss rate*
0.14	13%
0.32	12%
0.50	6%
0.68	3%
0.86	5%

Average loss rate on NBA bets sorted by average normalised probabilities: 120 minutes after game starts

Normalised probability	*Loss rate*
0.08	46%
0.26	11%
0.50	6%
0.74	3%
0.92	1%

Average loss rate on NBA bets sorted by average normalised probabilities: Final odds quotes

Normalised probability	*Loss rate*
0.05	95%
0.16	71%
0.50	17%
0.84	-6%
0.95	-1%

Why would bookmakers who are highly competitive in making low-margin offers across all pre-game NBA bets start penalising long-shots when the game begins? And why does this pattern become more extreme as the game goes on?

From a US sportsbook's perspective, one reason is that pre-game NBA odds are easily checked and widely compared across various websites. As discussed earlier, if you are looking to add customers, you do not want to post bad odds on these games and turn away high-volume NBA fans.

But in-play markets are different. These prices are not advertised all over the internet. They are only seen by your existing customers and most bettors only have a small number of accounts. And with the odds constantly changing, you're not scanning the real-time odds available from your different accounts. You're focused on one app on the phone in your hands. Bookmakers know this and it means they can price like they are a monopoly, so you get terrible odds.

From Slow Thinking to Fast

One of the themes of this book has been that favourite-longshot bias can emerge without assuming irrational behaviour but, in the case of in-play betting, we need to rely more on the tools of behavioural economics to understand what is going on.

For starters, we have generally assumed the public is good at figuring out probabilities of different outcomes. But some problems are too tricky for this to still be a good assumption. We described earlier how it was trickier to work out probabilities for specials like prop bets on the performance of individual players than to figure out the chance of a team winning a football match. The same applies to in-play markets.

Consider simple 1X2 football bets. Football is a low-scoring sport and as the game goes on, the current score becomes more likely to be the final outcome. For this reason, real-time odds constantly drift during the match, with the outcome given by the current score shown as becoming more likely. Until something happens.

Suppose Chelsea are playing Fulham and are the favourites to win.

Suppose Fulham score after twenty minutes. Are Chelsea still favourites? Probably, but what are the right odds now? To answer that, you would probably need a huge database to help you work out the typical outcome after a well-favoured team falls behind after 20 minutes. But what if we also told you Chelsea had 85% possession and 1.5 XG to Fulham's 0.1 XG (their goal is a long shot that deflects off a defender)? You'd probably want to factor that information in as well.

Bookmakers use all of this information to constantly update their live odds in line with their estimates of probabilities, while also factoring in a high profit margin. If an in-play bet looks attractive to you, there's a good chance you just haven't factored in all the relevant information, even if you're watching the game.

Indeed, it seems that, for most people, the decision-making process behind placing an in-play bet differs from betting before a game has started. Daniel Kahneman's best-selling 2011 book *Thinking, Fast and Slow* describes how people's actions are driven by two "systems" that work completely differently. System 1 (the fast one) is how we make quick intuitive decisions. It's how we come up with immediate answers to questions like: Is it safe to cross the road? Does this person look friendly? What is 4+4? System 2, on the other hand, is the slow one. It is how we approach questions like: What is 17 times 41? How should I invest my money? Are Chelsea a good bet at odds of 1.4 after Fulham have scored early?

Importantly, Kahneman argues that System 1 is particularly bad at statistical judgement. He gives the example of telling people that Steve is shy and withdrawn and then asking whether he is a librarian or a farmer. Most people's quick response is Steve is a librarian because these are characteristics we associate with that profession. But data show there are many more farmers than librarians. Even if farmers are less likely to be shy than librarians, the correct answer is that Steve is most likely a farmer.

People approach their betting in different ways and undoubtedly there are some who use their inner System 2 when making in-play bets. But in-play is designed more to appeal to System 1. Odds are constantly changing and the underlying probabilities are shifting as every second goes by. For most people, placing an in-play bet is a matter of "trusting your gut."

The flashing buttons, the sense of urgency – everything about the interface cries out for quick taps and the instant judgement of System 1. But this task – judging probabilities – rewards slow thinking and the use of System 2. With people letting their System 1 take over the decision-making, it is no surprise that bookmakers earn higher profits on in-play betting.

Late Game Longshot Disasters

What lies behind the extreme losses on late longshots? Why do people place bets that have such terrible returns? Again, behavioural factors that we did not need to explain pre-event betting probably play an important role.

The first is that the "System 1" process becomes even more important as the game goes on – if you think the losing team is about to stage a big comeback, then you might figure you need to get your money on quickly before they start turning it around and the long odds on offer disappear.

The second is misjudging small probabilities. People may just have no idea how bad these bets are. Extreme longshot bets placed in the final few minutes of a match are often priced at odds of about 100, so their breakeven win rate is about 1%. In practice, they might win about 0.5% of the time – half as often as needed – so they lose 50% of the amounts staked on average. People placing them expect them to lose but imagine that every so often they will win big to make up for that. They probably don't keep a record of how they have been performing with these kinds of bets.

The third explanation is that people approach these bets with a "lottery ticket" or "buying a dream" attitude. You know the bet is unlikely to win, so you're not too disappointed when it loses. But the rare occasion they win, and you can show off to your mates that you picked Villa to win from two goals down. Priceless, right?

The stakes placed on these bets are typically small and most people view them as a bit of fun. But it is useful to know that you are largely burning your money by taking them.

CHAPTER 24

Cash Out and the Dark Side of In-Play

We have seen that once a game starts, the odds get worse: margins rise and late longshot bets become especially poor value. Despite that, in-play betting has grown spectacularly, and one of the reasons is that bookmakers have bundled it with a feature that feels helpful to customers: the cash out option.

Using cash out looks like sensible risk management: your bet is winning, the bookmaker offers you a guaranteed return, and you can lock in a profit rather than sweat the last few minutes. The catch is that the offer is rarely fair. Cash out is just another transaction priced with a margin, so taking it reduces your expected return. After explaining how cash out pricing works, I turn to the darker side of in-play betting: its appeal to problem gamblers, and the grim "always-on" ecosystem that has grown up to feed demand for 24/7 action.

Cashing In By Cashing Out?

There are ten minutes left in the match and your bet is winning. The bookmaker is offering you a cash out payment that is a bit less than you would get if you hung on to the end and won, but there is the risk that the score turns around and your bet loses.

Cashing out in this situation is tempting. It seems like a safe and sensible option. It eliminates risk and guarantees that you have made a profit – and surely any profit you make is a good outcome? I noted earlier that the popularity of cash out was one way to see that bettors were not typically risk lovers. They will take cash outs as a way to avoid risk. Their System 1 mode of thinking also looks at the cash out offer and screams "take it" rather than stepping back and doing a careful evaluation of the merits of the offer.

Loss aversion is again a probable influence. Winning feels good and losing feels awful – the cash out guarantees you win on this bet. Also, if you don't take the cash out and then your bet loses, you will feel like you lost not just the original bet but also the extra cash out amounts that you decided to turn down.

This kind of reasoning seems sensible but the reality is that regularly taking the cash out option just increases your losses. To see this, consider the following simple scenario. You placed a £1 bet with a 50% chance of winning at decimal odds of 1.9, so your expected payout is 95p, a loss of 5%.

Now consider a simplified scenario where your 50% chance of winning can happen in two different ways.

- **Good start scenario**: The game starts well for your team and you have an 80% chance of winning and a 20% chance of losing.
- **Bad start scenario**: The game starts badly for your team and you have a 20% chance of winning and an 80% chance of losing.

Assume these two scenarios are equally likely. Your 50% chance of winning comes from winning the 40% of the time that the game starts well for your team and ends well, and an additional 10% of the time that the game starts badly for them but they turn it around.

Now assume a cash out option is available to you after you find out whether you are in the good or bad scenario. Suppose you decide to hang in there in the bad scenario, but you are interested in cashing out when things have started well. In the good scenario, you have an 80% chance of getting a payout of £1.9. The expected payout from hanging on to the bet is thus $0.8 \times £1.9 = £1.52$.

Suppose the bookmaker offers you this expected value of £1.52 for your cash out. If your approach is to always stick with your bet in the bad scenario and cash out in the good one, then your expected payout rate when you place the bet is

$$(0.5 \times 0.2 \times 1.9) + (0.5 \times 1.52) = 0.95.$$

The expected payout from this strategy is the same as if you always hang on to the end. And you will probably feel more relaxed during the good scenario now that you don't have to worry about your team throwing away its lead. Seems like cash out is a great option.

But unfortunately, that's not how cash out works. Bookmakers seek to make profits from all transactions and cash outs are just another transaction. So, in this example, they will not offer you 80% of £1.9. Instead, they will offer you less than the fair value. For example, they might offer you 75% of 1.9, which is £1.43. In that case, the expected payout rate from your strategy of sticking with your bet in the bad scenario and cashing out in the good one is

$$(0.5 \times 0.2 \times 1.9) + (0.5 \times 1.43) = 0.90$$

On average, you will now lose 10% of your money instead of 5%. Cashing in the win is tempting and winning feels good but at odds of 1.9, you need to get the full 1.9 payment half the time to limit your losses to 5%. If instead, you settle for a bit less than that when things are going well, your overall performance is going to be worse than losing 5%.

The key point is that your original bet probably had a positive expected loss. Adding to that by taking cash outs that are less than the bet's expected value adds to that expected loss. You are better off to sit tight and do nothing.

Manual Hedging

If you really want to close out a position, locking in some winnings or limiting your loss, there is a better alternative to taking the cash out offered by the bookmakers.

We saw in Chapter 22 how you could lock in a guaranteed profit if you had boosted odds on one side of a two-outcome bet. Indeed, while most people think of cashing out as just the bookmaker giving you some money back on your original bet, effectively you are placing a real-time hedging bet against your original outcome.

With two outcomes, we saw that the way to do this was to place a hedging bet sized to give you the same payout you would get if your original bet won. To give a concrete example, suppose again the two teams are Arsenal and Chelsea and you placed £1 to back Arsenal at decimal odds of 1.9. Now assume the good scenario occurs and Arsenal take the lead. Assume the bookmaker continues to price all bets with a margin of 5%. Chelsea's chances of winning are now 20%, so their odds drift out to 4.75. Placing a hedging bet on Chelsea of 40p will now also get you a payoff of £1.9.

This means whichever team wins, your profit will be 50p: the guaranteed £1.9 payoff minus the £1 placed on Arsenal minus the 40p placed on Chelsea. Note that this is better than the 43p cash out profit discussed above. It may not have been obvious, but that offer involved the bookmaker sneaking in an extra slice of profit margin, over and above what they would have earned from just offering you the hedging bet. Effectively, accepting the bookmaker's cash out means you are giving up a bit of profit to save having to work out how much to place on the hedging bet.

The logic of how to lock in a guaranteed return is the same if there are three outcomes. You place hedging bets on both other outcomes. If your team is ahead near the end of the game, the draw may still be priced as a reasonable possibility but your team losing is a serious longshot. Still, being fully hedged involves placing a small bet on your team to lose.

Manual hedges reduce your loss rates relative to accepting the bookie's cash out option but they still increase losses relative to placing bets and walking away. In our example, getting a certain payout of £1.5 in the good scenario and hanging on in the bad one gives you an expected payout of

$$(0.5 \times 0.2 \times 1.9) + (0.5 \times 1.5) = 0.94$$

so you are losing 6% on average instead of the 5% you would lose by not cashing out.

Which Cash Out Is Worse? Winners or Losers?

The examples above focused on cashing out on winners and hanging on to losers because that's how most people use cash out. And it's tempting to think that's the big mistake with cash out - accepting lower odds than you originally agreed to when things are going well means you don't win enough in those positive cases to offset the losses when things start badly.

But, in fact, accepting bookmakers' cash out offers on losing bets is even worse. The discount relative to expected value that bookmakers apply to bets that are likely to lose is bigger than for bets that are likely to win. This is because bookmakers set cash out offers on these bets based on what the value of an equivalent bet is for someone taking it during the match. We know from earlier that bookmakers price late longshot bets with big profit margins. So you want to cash in your late longshot? They check the current in-play price for that bet and offer you that or perhaps worse.

Data on cash out offers are hard to find but industry discussions about the product confirm that this is how it works. For example, GR8Tech, a B2B provider of "turnkey" services to bookmakers has described its cash out product as offering a bigger discount for bets that are losing than for bets likely to win.[81]

Popularity of Cash Outs

Cash outs have been a great success for bookmakers. Unlike other betting products that encourage people to take risks, cash out appeals to people's risk aversion. Recent experimental research shows that those with lower risk of gambling-related harm tend to cash out more frequently than those who displayed more signs of gambling-related impulsiveness.[82]

So cash out is popular with customers and increases profits, but it has another hidden benefit for bookies. Research has shown that the availability of cash out encourages people to make larger bets.[83] People think "I can either bet £5 on Aston Villa or else £10 but keep tabs on the game and, if it's going badly, I can cash out." This means cash out not only directly increases bookmaker profit rates, it also boosts the volumes placed with them.

From a bettor's perspective, your best option for long-run returns is to avoid in-play and cash outs. If you're going to bet, place it before the match, walk away, act like Jacob Bernoulli and come back later to see how it did.

The Darker Side of In-Play Betting

There is a darker reason why in-play betting is so popular despite the bad returns it delivers. Some people become addicted to gambling. That small twinge of excitement that we've referred to previously becomes the principal point of their betting. As soon as one bet is finished, problem gamblers want to get another hit of the rush they experience. Or perhaps having lost money, they are determined to quickly win it back.

In-play betting attracts addicts because it offers so many quick gambling hits. Bet on Bruno Fernandes to score the first goal? But then he doesn't. Well maybe he'll score the second goal. Bet on United to keep a clean sheet but they've already let a goal in and look leaky at the back? Well maybe switch sides and bet on them to let another one in and win your lost money back. Several studies have shown that problem gamblers are significantly more likely to bet in play than those who gamble without experiencing serious harm.[84]

And Even Darker: Sports Farms

The exploding demand for in-play betting has a darker side. Consider 1xBet. Founded in Russia, it now operates out of Cyprus and takes bets from all around the world, even though it only has licences to operate in a limited number of countries. Its UK licence was revoked in 2019 after the Sunday Times uncovered 1xBet was providing a wide range of unsavoury products too racy to describe here.

With the availability of in-play action limited by the sporting calendar and the daily rotation of the planet, 1xBet came up with a way to allow people to bet on live sport 24/7/365. They provide live footage from a series of "sports farms", apparently mainly located in Russia, where people, many of them teenagers, are paid low wages to play football, basketball and other sports, all to provide fuel for online betting. The footage available on YouTube is grim. A bunch of exhausted players in huge warehouses who don't even celebrate when they score.[85]

Surely not many people will be up at night betting on the Red team at the sports farm to beat the Blue team? But one key aspect of always-available sports betting is to funnel customers to their even more lucrative online casinos. Attracted by the sports farm betting but finding it a bit dull, you will probably be offered "free plays" at things like online slots. These are deliberately rigged games with higher profit margins for bookmakers and quick-hit always-on designs that foster gambling addiction in a way that a simple pre-match wager does not.

You might imagine this kind of thing would be damaging to 1xBet's reputation. But, as of 2026, 1xBet is an official betting partner of Barcelona football club. And also of Paris Saint-Germain, even though they are not even licensed to take bets in France.

VIII. Betting Exchanges

You don't need bookmakers to bet. On a betting exchange, you place bets against other people and the platform matches you up. Bookmakers build an unseen margin into their odds. Exchanges don't set prices at all: they run the marketplace and charge a transparent fee. And those fees tend to be low, making exchanges generally the best value option available to bettors.

And yet most bettors ignore exchanges because they find them complicated. I fully get this. When I became interested in this topic, I struggled to understand how they worked and focused my initial research on bookmakers' odds. Over time, though, I became interested in exchanges, particularly because they make detailed data available. Analysing trade-level data on over 200,000 football matches allowed me to build up a detailed picture of how these markets work.

This part of the book has two chapters. The first explains how betting exchanges work in practice and why they are generally a better option than betting with bookmakers. The second focuses on what our rational disagreement approach implies for exchanges: who decides to take each kind of bet and what this means for odds and returns.

CHAPTER 25

How Betting Exchanges Work

Betting exchanges are the purest form of agreeing to disagree. People have been betting against each other for thousands of years, but the internet added something new: a peer-to-peer marketplace where two ordinary bettors can take opposite sides of the same wager.

This chapter introduces betting exchanges and explains how they work. Exchanges don't quite "cut out the middleman" - they charge fees - but they are, on average, a better option than bookmakers.

The Economics of Market Platforms

The story of how the current market structure of betting exchanges emerged is an interesting example of the economics of information-driven markets. As we discussed earlier, markets that rely heavily on the use of information do not always work well. The internet age has shown that getting the platform design right is crucial for an online market to function properly.

Today, Betfair is the dominant exchange around the world, but it was not the first firm to bring this idea to market and, at first, it was not very well funded. It launched in June 2000, a month later than a firm called Flutter, which had significant backing from venture capital investors. But Betfair ended up winning out because their platform design worked well and Flutter's did not.

Flutter based their platform on eBay. People could propose whatever bets they wanted and someone else could accept it. If you offered a £100 bet, someone had to be willing to place £100 to take it. The menu of bets created in this fashion was driven by customers.

In contrast, Betfair modelled its platform on stock exchanges. People backing a team were like buyers of a stock and people "laying" a team (betting on it not to win) were like sellers. Betfair itself decided which markets to run and, crucially, orders could be filled by multiple counterparties. For example, someone who offered to accept bets of £100 for Manchester United to win a match at specific odds could be matched with £10 from one bettor, £70 from another and £20 from a third.

Betfair's platform design allowed those who wanted to act as "market makers" to make large offers without worrying about finding one specific person to match with. This attracted more money into the market and Betfair's higher liquidity made the platform work better than Flutter's. Bettors on both sides of any trade found it easier to execute their preferred bets in markets with high volume.

Within about a year, Flutter was taken over by Betfair. Later, Betfair was taken over by Paddy Power and the Flutter brand was revived to be the brand name of the conglomerate that includes Paddy, FanDuel and other businesses. Betfair has become the dominant betting exchange around the world, operating in about 50 different countries and aggregating the offers into a single globally integrated marketplace. Other smaller betting exchanges, such as Smarkets, BetDaq and Matchbook, offer competition, but their platform designs are essentially identical.

How To Bet on an Exchange

Let's go through how to place bets on an exchange. The table below illustrates what exchange interfaces look like, using real-world numbers from Betfair for a match between England and Serbia in November 2025, taken a few hours before kick-off.

There are several differences between how exchanges and bookmakers display odds. Two important ones are that exchanges always use decimal odds (yay!) and that they are explicit about how much money can be placed at each value of the odds.

There are a lot of numbers here so we will go through it carefully. There are four different ways that you can place a bet on an exchange. Let's take them in turn.

Betfair Interface for England versus Serbia, November 2025

	100.8%		*Back All*	*Lay All*		*99.4%*
England	1.27	1.28	1.29	1.30	1.31	1.32
	£43,459	£34,877	£15,759	£20,472	£18,663	£8,236
Serbia	13.00	13.50	14.00	14.50	15.00	15.50
	£773	£548	£567	£827	£365	£1,167
The Draw	5.90	6.00	6.20	6.40	6.60	6.80
	£207	£6,126	£1,727	£1,051	£3,223	£4,311

1. Accepting an Offer to Back

This is the easiest option to understand and it's all you need if you just want to use an exchange as a better-priced alternative to bookmakers. The numbers along the left-hand side show odds that are available for backing each option. The interface shows the three best odds that have been offered.

You want to accept the best-available odds. These are listed under "Back All" and shaded in blue on the Betfair interface. So, if you wanted to back England, you could do so at 1.29. You could back Serbia at 14 and the draw at 6.2. You click on the bet you want, decide how much to stake, hit accept and you're sorted.

The 100.8% number listed in the top row towards the left is the overround based on the best available back odds. This is an exceptionally low overround, indicating an expected loss rate of below 1%, far lower than you see with typical bookmakers' margins.

But this figure is slightly misleading. Exchanges are not charities and they need revenue to cover costs and make a profit. The typical approach is to charge a fee to the winner of the bet equal to a percentage of winnings. The standard commission on winnings on Betfair and other UK exchanges in recent years is 2%. So, you are not really getting decimal odds of 1.29 because if you win, you will have to share 2% of the 0.29 in winnings per pound staked with Betfair. So, the effective odds on England are really 1 + 0.98 × (1.29-1) = 1.284. Applying the same adjustment to each of the odds, the true effective overround is 1.016, consistent with an expected loss rate of 1.6%.

This is still exceptionally low. A comparison with the odds offered by bookmakers on the same match illustrates the differences. See the table below. The odds offered by bookmakers on England, the favourite, are pretty similar to those available on Betfair. The average was 1.28, almost exactly equal to the post-fee Betfair odds and indeed some bookmakers offered higher odds. But the bookmakers' odds on the draw and, in particular, on Serbia (the longshot option) were much worse. The average odds on the draw were 5.4 compared with effective post-commission odds on Betfair of 6.1 and average odds on Serbia of 10.25 compared with effective odds of 13.7 on Betfair.

Even the lowest implied margin offered by a bookmaker is three times that consistent with the post-fee odds available on Betfair.

Odds offered by bookmakers on England vs Serbia, November 2025

Bookmaker	*England*	*Draw*	*Serbia*	*Margin*
Ladbrokes	1.29	5.75	10.0	4.7%
bet365	1.29	5.50	10.0	5.3%
Betfred	1.25	5.50	12.0	6.1%
William Hill	1.30	4.80	9.0	8.2%
Betway	1.29	5.00	8.50	8.5%
Unibet	1.23	6.00	12.0	5.9%

This example is typical of pricing on exchanges relative to bookmakers. Odds on exchanges are higher, particularly for longshots, because there is no bookmaker applying a favourite-longshot bias to maximise profits. Even if you don't want to learn any more about exchanges, there is a useful lesson here: For most bets, but especially longshots, you will generally get better odds at Betfair than bookmakers.

The odds available on exchanges come from people making offers to take a specific amount of money at specific odds. Going back to the

Betfair interface table, the numbers below the odds show the amount of money available for backing at those prices.

The match highlighted here was a high-profile one, so most people wouldn't be constrained by these volumes. You could get the best-available odds as long as you were betting less than £15,759 on England, £567 on Serbia and £1,727 on the draw. If you placed a £10 bet, the amounts displayed as available would fall by £10.

---

2. Accepting an Offer to Lay

The second way to bet is one that you generally don't find with retail bookmakers. Instead of backing an outcome, you can "lay" it, placing a bet that it won't happen. So, as well as being able to bet that England will win, you can also bet that England will not win.

The simplest way to place a lay bet is to accept an offer to do so. These offers show up on the right-hand side of the interface. The odds are quoted from the perspective of someone backing England, so it works as follows. The three lay bet odds on England displayed are 1.30, 1.31 and 1.32. You can see there is £20,472 on offer for people to place lay bets.

This works as follows. If you clicked on 1.30 and agreed to accept a £1 bet from the other side, then you would win that £1 minus commission if England don't win. The amount available for lay bets would fall to £20,471. If England win, you would lose 30p: the person you are matched with gets their £1 back and you also have to fork over 30p.

If you decided to accept a £1 offer to lay Serbia at 14.5, then you would win £1 minus commission if Serbia lost but you'd lose £13.5 if Serbia won. That might seem a bit steep. For this reason, Betfair allows you to size your lay bets so there is a specified potential loss. Instead of accepting a £1 bet, you could accept a smaller bet so that the total potential loss to you is £1 – in this case, this would be accepting a bet of only 1/13.5 = 7.4p. Lay bets against longshots work like this – you win small amounts most of the time but occasionally lose larger sums.

When agreeing to a lay bet of this type, you want the back odds to be as low as possible. At this snapshot, 1.30 is the best option for lay bettors. Betfair's interface lists the best available offers for lay bettors under "Lay All" with these entries shaded in pink.

---

3. Backing by Making an Offer to Lay Bettors

We have shown you how to back a competitor and how to lay them. Surely that's it, no? Well, think for a minute: When you accept an offer to back England at 1.29, where did that offer come from? Betfair? Nope. They don't make offers, they just match people up. Those offers came from other people on Betfair. These are "market makers" - rather than taking up offers to back and lay made by others, they make their own offers.

This works as follows. You'd like to back England but you're not happy with odds of 1.29. You'd like to get a bit more. You can do this as follows. You click on the 1.29 but instead of placing a bet at these odds, the interface gives you the option to toggle a button and move the odds up to 1.30. You select how much money you want to bet at those odds and that money is added to the existing £20,472 potential England backers seeking to get matched at 1.30. In fact, if you think the bet is only worthwhile at better odds, you can make offers to back England at 1.31 or higher.

One technical thing to note about this process. Exchanges don't allow you to seek any possible odds - you can't ask for 1.303. Allowing offers like this would confuse customers because there would be many different prices and the liquidity would be spread thinly across them. On Betfair, the minimum "tick size" - the minimum increment you can make when offering odds - is 0.01 and this tick size gets bigger as the odds rise. In fact, in our example case, each of the gaps between the best back odds available to accept and the next highest odds sought equals the minimum tick size. The gaps between the blue back and the pink lay odds are the smallest amount that someone could toggle up from the best-available-to-back odds to ask for more.

The gap between these two odds - for example the gap between 14 and 14.5 for Serbia - is sometimes called a "bid-ask" spread. This is a term from stock markets referring to how stockbrokers quote a lower price to someone selling a share than to someone buying it. The broker earns profits off the spread in this "buy low, sell high" strategy. But in this case, there is no central broker. The gap emerges naturally from the exchange's customers seeking the best odds.

Acting as a Maker has one clear advantage. If your offer is successfully matched, then you get better odds than you would have obtained from clicking on the best available offer to back. In this case, you would have obtained odds to back England of 1.30 instead of 1.29.

The disadvantage is that you might not get matched. Offers from Makers at each price are filled sequentially based on who made the offers first. So, seeking odds of 1.30 to bet on England would place your offer behind £20,472 in offers from others. In a high-volume market like this one, your offer may eventually rise to the top of the queue and get matched, but it might not. And odds might change so that this is no longer the best price available to lay bettors. Also, the more ambitious you are on the odds you seek, the less likely you are to get matched.

Finally, going back to accepting offers to back, there is one subtle element. You may sometimes accept an offer to back at the best odds but seek to place more than is available. For example, if there was only £30 available on England at 1.29 and you placed a £50 bet on England, then £30 would be matched at 1.29. Rather than move you down to 1.28, Betfair move the other £20 to be an unmatched offer to lay bettors to match with you at 1.29. The blue button changes to 1.28 (the number shown to the left as the next best option available) and the pink button changes to be your 1.29 offer.

In this case, you clicked as a Taker but also ended up with a Maker offer. Betfair interpret your click on 1.29 as "I accept 1.29 but not less" and protect you against market dynamics forcing a worse price on you.

---

4. Laying by Making an Offer to Back Bettors

This is just being a market maker as a lay bettor. Instead of accepting the offer to lay England by agreeing to give the other side odds of 1.30, you ask if someone will accept 1.29. This puts you behind the £15,759 in offers already made at this price.

Which brings us back to where we started. For those coming into Betfair to back England, they see the offer to place that bet at 1.29 – and that offer comes from you and the others who picked this option.

Automated Trading

I have described trading on exchanges as people accepting or making offers through the web or phone interfaces. But much of the activity on exchanges comes from automated trading with orders placed via the Application Programming Interface (API) rather than the web page.

This trading is executed by "bots" that place offers based on certain conditions being met. For example, someone could run a bot designed to place bets 10 minutes before kick-off on the home team if the odds meet certain criteria. These orders typically come from people who operate as market makers rather than takers. The bots can interact with the API using software like BFBotManager or special libraries for Python programming.

API-driven trading is crucially important for Betfair to maintain its high liquidity levels. A serious market maker might want to offer bets across 50 different football matches kicking off at 3pm on Saturday. Manually monitoring and adjusting odds across that many markets simultaneously through the web interface would be impossible. The API allows one person with the right software to provide liquidity across hundreds of markets at once. Anecdotal evidence suggests there are many traders placing millions of pounds of bets a year as market makers on Betfair. These traders are crucial to making Betfair the high-volume fast-moving exchange that attracts people who come on the platform to accept offers.

Supply, Demand and Prices

Exchanges are an incredibly powerful way of translating the beliefs of bettors into odds. Let's go back to England vs Serbia. Suppose the team-sheet drops an hour before kick-off and it turns out Harry Kane and Declan Rice aren't playing because they have minor injuries.

Suddenly, money comes in backing Serbia because it looks more attractive at the current prices. Going back to our table, we can see that the first £567 of bets get odds of 14 and the next £548 will get odds of 13.5 and so on. The best available odds will move down mechanically as those offers are accepted. In fact, this might happen without that £1,115 being placed on Serbia. Unmatched offers can be cancelled, so some of those offers at 14 and 13.5 will disappear when the team-sheet drops.

Suppose that by the time this wave of new money has been matched, the best available offer to back Serbia is down to 12. Traders interested in seeking better odds to back Serbia will now come in and look for 12.5, which becomes the new number in the pink box under "Lay All". Within seconds, all the listed odds on Serbia have shortened, as the extra demand for betting on them has moved the odds down. In the same way, money will come in laying England at odds of 1.30 and these odds will move upwards.

This shows how, without bookmakers being involved, the judgement of the public translates new information rapidly into odds. Just as stock markets operate on supply and demand, with prices going up when more people want to buy than sell, odds on betting exchanges are driven by the balance of people who want to back versus those who want to lay.

Real-Time Trading and Cash Outs

There is another way to view the analogy between betting exchanges and stock exchanges. Going back for a moment to our discussion of cash out options with bookmakers, consider again our simple two-way market where either Arsenal or Chelsea will win. If you back Arsenal and it's going well, the bookmaker will offer you a cash out. But remember that this is effectively you placing an offsetting bet on Chelsea, and it is more cost-effective to do this yourself.

On an exchange, you can place this hedging cash out without even having to do the maths. Exchanges automate this procedure by offering you a cash out option and placing the correctly sized hedging bet, to save you the mental arithmetic.

So, just like stock markets, if you "pick a winner" and it goes up in value, then you can lock in a profit by selling it. The offsetting hedge locks in a guaranteed profit. And in this case, there is no bookmaker adding a substantial new margin to reduce the value of your cash out. In fact, exchanges only charge commission on your net winnings across your original and hedging bet – they subtract your losses on the losing bet from your winnings before they apply the commission. This means cash outs are far better value on exchanges than with bookmakers.

Some people build their strategies around this kind of exchange trading. They recommend backing or laying outcomes if you see a good price and automating a hedging trade to give you a guaranteed profit once prices have moved in your favour. This is known as "scalping."

Perhaps some people make a profit this way but there is no magic formula. Given that Betfair's low commission and high volumes are well known to attract many skilled bettors, why do you think you can spot a "bad" price that others are accepting? And it is not obvious that a strategy of cashing out on your winners is the most profitable approach. The odds may have moved in your favour for good reasons, with the market seeing your bet as being better than originally priced. You might be better off to hang on.

CHAPTER 26

Makers, Takers and Returns

We've explained how betting exchanges work. In this chapter, we show what determines odds and outcomes. We use our rational disagreement framework to discuss why some people post offers (Makers) while others accept them (Takers) and what these choices mean for returns on bets. We then assess the framework's predictions using both pre-game and in-play odds from a huge dataset from Betfair.

Commissions and Odds

Let's start with why commissions are important. If there were no commissions, exchanges would just be people swapping money so by definition the average return on a bet would be zero. You might expect half the bettors to win money and half to lose, depending on their skill. Once you add commissions, then the average return to bettors is negative: they are not just swapping money because the exchange is keeping some of their stakes. The higher the commission, the more skilled you will have to be to earn a positive average return. In this sense, commissions act as a hurdle for winning at betting in the same way as bookmakers' margins do. But they have the advantage of being completely transparent.

We will use the rational disagreement framework to figure out how commissions interact with people having differing beliefs. But, let's start with a simpler approach. Assume the Maker market is highly competitive and they expect to only break even, after accounting for commissions. Assume also they are correct in their assessment of probabilities.

For example, suppose a Maker offers odds on a bet that they think has a 50% chance of winning. Without a commission, the break-even decimal odds they would offer would be $D = 2$. But with a commission, if they offer to take a £1 bet, they will win 98p after commission half the time. To break even on that bet on average, they need to offer $D = 1.98$, so when they lose, it costs them 98p.

What happens to the Taker that accepts this bet? If the Maker is right that the bet wins half the time, then the Taker will lose £1 half the time. The other half, they will win 98p but they will pay a 2% commission on this, so effectively they will only win 96p. Averaging across these two outcomes – equal chances of losing £1 and winning 96p – the Taker loses 2p on average, meaning a loss rate of 2%.

The commission affects the Taker twice. It causes the Makers to offer lower odds and then it cuts the Taker's profit when they win. If you repeat the calculation for a bet with a much smaller chance of winning, the Taker's average loss rises towards about 4%. That's because Makers, who expect to pay commission when they win, move the odds down further on those bets. Even so, a 4% loss rate on longshots is far better than you will get for these bets with a bookmaker.

You can figure out a similar pattern for odds offered to lay bettors. Where the 50/50 back bet gets offered at 1.98, the 50/50 lay bet gets offered at 2.02. Note that the average of the back and lay odds here – the average of 1.98 and 2.02 – will precisely equal the fair odds of 2. This explains the pattern you see on exchanges. Typically, back odds are a bit less than fair while lay odds are a bit higher than fair. But, if the market for making offers is competitive, then the average trade – which will be a mix of people accepting back offers and lay offers – will be roughly at fair odds.

Overrounds and Returns for Takers

Consider an event with two outcomes, each equally likely to happen. We have just worked out that a Maker that expects to break even will offer back odds of 1.98 on both sides. The overround can be calculated as $1/1.98 + 1/1.98 = 1.01$. Similarly, lay bets involve the backers getting odds on both sides of 2.02, implying an overround of $1/2.02 +$

1/2.02 = 0.99.

You can get different overrounds from plugging in different scenarios – e.g. if you have three equally likely outcomes, the same calculations give you a back overround of 1.013 and a lay overround of 0.987. But the general point is the same. Makers breaking even on average and factoring in the commission when setting odds leads to reported overrounds of about 101% for back odds and 99% for lay odds.

This simple model explains the pattern that you see in most high-volume markets on Betfair. Typical overrounds for back bets are in the region of 101% and typical lay overrounds are about 99%.

But note again that you can't map these overrounds, even the versions adjusted for commission, into expected loss rates. This is because the assumption we have made here is not consistent with strong betting market efficiency because it implies not all bets are created equal. Makers break even while Takers lose. And the amount the Takers lose increases as their probability of winning falls.

How Disagreement Drives Decisions

The model with Makers expecting to break even is a useful shorthand for how exchange pricing works in high-volume markets. But it does not describe what is actually happening. Many market makers put in a lot of effort, including setting up complex bots to place offers via the API. They may enjoy betting and might even enjoy the technical challenge of building a bot but nobody puts in time and effort like that unless they expect to win.

Similarly, the "Maker breaks even" model doesn't explain why Takers just accept the offers that are available, even when the odds suggest that they will lose money.

So, let's think a bit deeper. The framework of rational disagreement again helps to explain how this market operates.

Let's start with thinking about who decides to be a Maker and who decides to be a Taker. One explanation is that these are just two different groups, with Makers being more sophisticated than Takers. There probably is something to that. For new participants, accepting offers to back by clicking on the blue buttons is the simplest option, followed by accepting offers to lay by clicking on the pink buttons.

However, while market making is less intuitive for new participants, anyone who uses exchanges for a while gets to grips with the four options available for any bet. We will not base our views on who becomes a Maker or a Taker based on differences in intelligence but on differences in *beliefs*.

Go back to the England vs Serbia example in the previous chapter. I am thinking of backing the draw and I can accept an offer to back at 6.2 or I could seek better odds of 6.4. Which option do I pick?

Let's leave aside commission for now and assume I believe the probability of a draw is $p > 1/6.2$. This means that backing at 6.2 is attractive but getting matched at 6.4 is even more so. The downside of seeking 6.4 is that I might not get matched.

Suppose I've used Betfair enough to know there's an 80% chance I will get matched. Which strategy has the best expected return? Consider the expected payoff from a £1 bet. If I accept 6.2, my expected payoff is $p \times 6.2$. If I seek 6.4, there is an 80% chance my bet gets matched and a 20% chance I get my £1 returned to my account unmatched. In that case, my expected payoff is $(0.8 \times p \times 6.4) + (0.2 \times 1)$

Accepting the offer to back at 6.2 has a higher expected payoff if

$$p \times 6.2 > (0.8 \times p \times 6.4) + (0.2 \times 1)$$

A quick calculation shows this will hold if $p > 0.185$. And the other option to get matched on the draw at 6.4? That will only be considered profitable if $p \times 6.4 > 1$, meaning $p > 0.156$.

This gives us a model for how people approach betting on exchanges. We have figured out how everyone will approach the possibility of backing the draw at these odds.

- Those with $p > 0.185$ will accept the offer to back at 6.2.
- Those with $0.156 < p \leq 0.185$ will seek to back at 6.4.
- Those with $p \leq 0.156$ will not back the draw.

More generally, for any potential outcome, we can divide people into five different categories, ranking them from high values of p to low.

- **High-conviction backers**: Confident enough the outcome will happen to accept the back odds offered.

- **Low-conviction backers**: Less confident the outcome will happen but believe it is worth backing at the odds offered to lay bettors.
- **Fence-sitters**: Neither confident enough that the outcome will or won't happen to either back or lay.
- **Low-conviction layers**: Think the event is worth betting against at the current odds offered to backers.
- **High-conviction layers**: Confident enough the outcome will not happen to accept the lay odds offered.

The four groups that don't sit on the fence interact with each other. High-conviction backers accept offers from low-conviction layers and high-conviction layers accept offers from low-conviction backers. What makes this all work, however, is that those who make offers are not certain of getting matched. This means the market produces odds that result in there being more low-conviction bettors posting offers than high-conviction bettors taking them.

Odds Under Disagreement

Like pari-mutuel markets, exchange odds are determined by prices and volumes interacting with each other. An "equilibrium" on an exchange is a set of odds and volumes so that everyone is happy with their choice to take one of the five possible decisions.

Figuring out the right odds and decisions taken by bettors in this equilibrium is tricky but, for each value of the matching probability, you can solve it on a computer. Previously, we assumed a uniform distribution of beliefs, where the same number of people had each belief within a certain range. But this is probably not the most realistic assumption, and since this model needs a computer to solve anyway, I assume beliefs have a Normal bell-shaped distribution with a standard deviation of 0.03, meaning 95% of people have beliefs within 0.06 of the average.

The results from this model allow us to understand exchanges without having to break people into arbitrary Maker vs Taker social castes. Depending on their beliefs, some people will decide to be Makers on a bet, and some will decide to be Takers but they may switch roles for other bets. We can assume that everyone is just trying to maximise their own subjective expected return.[86]

While this model is more sophisticated, its predictions justify using the "Maker breaks even" idea as a useful shorthand for what happens on exchanges. Suppose, for example, that the match rate for offers is 60%. Then with a 2% commission on winnings, consider an outcome for which the average belief is that it has a 50% chance of happening. The rational disagreement model predicts the back odds for this outcome will be 1.98 and the lay odds will be 2.02. This is precisely what the "Maker breaks even" approach predicts even though both Makers and Takers in this model believe they are going to earn a profit.

As the probability of the bet winning worsens, however, the model predicts slightly worse outcomes for Takers than the "Makers break even" model. Consider a bet where the average belief is that it has a 10% chance of happening. The model predicts the back odds for this bet will be 9.62. If this average belief is correct, the Taker will lose 5.4% on average, worse than the 4% lower bound described above. It predicts Makers will make a very small profit (0.2% on average) after commission.

The model predicts that, if the public is correct in its average belief, then high-conviction bettors have less accurate beliefs than low-conviction ones. That bet with a 10% chance of winning and odds of 9.62? Those who accept it on average believe its probability of winning is 13%, while those who have made the offer believe, on average, that it is 9%. Both sides are wrong in their beliefs but those backing the longshot are more wrong and this leads them to accept a bet that allows the other side to make a small profit.

The model predicts that, most of the time, Makers just about break even or perhaps make a tiny profit after commission but there is an interesting exception. It predicts Makers can make non-negligible profits if they are the ones placing an extreme longshot bet, one with less than a 10% chance of succeeding. Those accepting the offers that have an over 90% chance of succeeding are overconfident relative to Makers and this means they come out of the transaction doing worse.

For example, an event with a 90% chance of happening could be priced with a breakeven rate of 91% for the Taker and 9% for the Maker. That 1% price discrepancy allows the Maker to make a nice profit. Winning 10% of the time on a bet priced to break even if it wins 9% of the time earns an average pre-commission return of 11.1%. After commission, that would be a return of 9.1%.

Thick and Thin Markets

Not all exchange markets are alike. Markets for big events like Premier League matches attract very large amounts of money. This means that matching rates for offers tend to be high. For this reason, Makers don't need as large an inducement in terms of better odds to be willing to make an offer. This is why the typical bid-ask spread in large-volume "thick" markets tends to equal the minimum tick size.

In contrast, more obscure contests attract less money. In these "thin" markets, Makers will have less confidence that their offers will be matched and so they seek higher odds. For this reason, thinner markets typically have higher bid-ask spreads.

This means the odds offered to Takers on lower-volume markets are less competitive, with back overrounds often above 103% and lay overrounds below 97%. Of course, as we've shown previously, odds on low-volume markets with bookmakers also show higher overrounds, so exchanges will still usually offer the best odds.

This difference between thick and thin markets also likely explains why Betfair has remained so dominant in the exchange sector, retaining over 80% of the volume despite the existence of competitor exchanges such as BetDaq, Matchbook and Smarkets which offer essentially the same model. High liquidity is a crucial ingredient in making an exchange successful. The high volumes on Betfair mean Makers are willing to offer higher odds and these higher odds attract more Takers.

Exchanges As Aggregators of Information

We have explained why the average odds on an exchange should provide a good proxy for the average beliefs of the participants. The argument is not that exchanges satisfy strong betting market efficiency. Neither the back odds nor the lay odds will perfectly satisfy this property. But we have seen that when Makers roughly break even, the average of the back and lay odds will reflect their assessment of the underlying probabilities.

Are these probability estimates likely to be good ones? Before we show some evidence, there are clear arguments suggesting they should be. There are no bookmakers setting odds to exploit disagreement among bettors.

And exchanges are designed to attract highly skilled bettors. Their commissions on winnings translate into lower effective margins than you get from betting with most bookmakers. There is no bookmaker profiling them and throwing them out for winning too much. Betfair's high volume markets and API system allow serious participants to place large amounts of money. And since Betfair makes money from volumes, these bettors are welcomed rather than discouraged.

These factors point to average odds on Betfair as likely to be better predictors of outcomes than the odds posted by bookmakers. Various studies have confirmed this but here I will describe my own evidence, based on a more comprehensive dataset than any used in other academic studies.

Unlike bookmakers, Betfair is incredibly open in providing data about its business. This includes making full historical data available for individual events, with files showing the size and price of all trades from when the market opened to when it closed.

I will describe evidence from a dataset of just over 200,000 football matches on Betfair from 2022 to 2024.[87] The first thing I did was assess whether the odds on Betfair were good predictors of match outcomes. I started by looking at the last traded prices before a match. For each match, I calculated normalised probabilities from these last traded prices. Sometimes, these last traded prices were at back odds and sometimes they were at lay odds, but we would expect the average implied probabilities to be good predictors of outcomes.

The results are remarkable. The matches had over 600,000 different outcomes (home, away, draw) that you could bet on. I sorted the bets into ten groups by the average predicted probability of winning according to the Betfair odds and then checked how often these bets actually won. The results are shown in the table below. The accuracy of the Betfair odds is striking. The predicted probabilities are all extremely close to the actual win rates. There is no evidence of the favourite-longshot bias that you see in odds set by bookmakers.

Betfair implied probability of winning and actual win rate for bets on home/away/draw in football from 2022-2024.

Betfair implied probability of winning	*Average win rate*
0.0934	0.0936
0.1771	0.1794
0.2223	0.2238
0.2536	0.2530
0.2797	0.2819
0.3076	0.3101
0.3484	0.3457
0.4201	0.4175
0.5203	0.5179
0.7110	0.7106

Pre-Match Returns for Makers and Takers

Once you know about the type of people who use Betfair, it perhaps isn't surprising that its odds provide excellent estimates of the underlying probabilities. You could get that prediction from a wide range of models of how exchanges might work.

Our rational disagreement model, however, made some more specific predictions about how Makers and Takers would perform. It predicted that Takers would lose money after commission, with losses getting worse as the probability of their bet winning falls. In particular, it predicted that the biggest longshot bets accepted by Takers would lose more than the "Maker breaks even prediction" of twice the commission rate, meaning 4%.

For Makers, the model suggested they would largely just break even after commission, with the exception of bets where the Taker has a very high chance of winning (so the Maker is placing an extreme longshot bet).

Figuring out which side of these historical bets was taken by the Maker or Taker requires some work. To give an example, going back to the England-Serbia game in the previous chapter, for the snapshot that we recorded, the data file would have information showing that the best available odds for backing England at that moment was 1.29 while the best available to lay was 1.30. This means that if the data showed a bet just after this moment and its odds are 1.29, then we know the Taker accepted an offer to back and if it is 1.30, then the Taker accepted an offer to lay.

Using this method, I was able to identify which side of bets on home, away or draw had been taken by Makers and Takers and calculate normalised probabilities that the Taker's bet would win for about 150,000 matches just prior to kick-off. The table below shows evidence on the returns to Makers and Takers on these bets after accounting for commissions. Just as the rational disagreement model predicts, losses for Takers worsen as their chances of winning fall, with the biggest longshots losing almost 6% on average – worse than predicted by the simple "Maker breaks even" rule. And Makers generally come close to breaking even, though there is some evidence that they earn profits on their own longshot bets.

Average returns for Takers and Makers, sorted by the estimated probability for home/away/draw football bets from 2022-2024: Bets placed just prior to kick-off

	Returns	
Average probability that Taker wins	*Takers*	*Makers*
0.186	-5.7%	0.5%
0.316	-2.5%	-0.1%
0.500	-2.1%	0.3%
0.685	-1.6%	1.0%
0.814	-0.8%	1.3%

Returns in the Total Goals Scored Market

I also collected data from the Total Goals Scored markets, from over/under 0.5 goals to over/under 5.5 goals. The table below shows returns for Makers and Takers for just over 2 million different bets on these markets.

Again, we see Takers doing worse on average as the probability of their winning falls, though these results look more like the case where the Maker breaks even on average. At the bottom of the table, however, we see a striking result. The model had predicted Makers could make significant profits when they were placing extreme long-shot bets. The total goals market includes options like over-under 0.5 goals or over-under 5.5 goals, which offer plenty of opportunities to make extreme longshot offers. And the data show that when Takers have an average chance of winning of 89%, so Makers have an average probability of winning of about 11%, they made a remarkable average return per bet of 7.4%.

Yes, I have checked these figures. Multiple times. Did I discover a secret way after all this research to make lots of money? No. These results are true and also, in a sense, too good to be true. Read the next chapter to find out why.

Average returns for Takers and Makers, sorted by the estimated probability for total goals bets from 2022-2024: Bets placed just prior to kick-off

	Returns	
Average probability that Taker wins	*Takers*	*Makers*
0.108	-3.8%	-0.1%
0.306	-2.3%	-0.1%
0.500	-2.1%	0.9%
0.694	-1.8%	1.8%
0.892	-1.0%	7.4%

In-Play Evidence

Finally, and briefly, I want to describe some evidence from in-play betting on home-away-draw outcomes. I suggested earlier that one reason in-play betting was so popular with bookmakers is that the rational disagreement model was less likely to apply because people move from the "Slow" mode of thinking to the "Fast" mode, which is less good at statistical problems.

Perhaps the bettors on Betfair are more sensible than those who take up really bad late-game longshot offers from bookmakers? Alas no. The favourite-longshot bias is also evident in the late-game transactions on Betfair.

The two tables below show average returns to Makers and Takers, again sorted by the average probability that the Taker will win, for two different in-play snapshots: 90 minutes after kick-off and 105 minutes after kick-off. This is measured in normal clock time, not the game clock, so 90 minutes means the match has 15 minutes left plus whatever time was added for stoppages in the two halves. 105 minutes would typically mean the match was a couple of minutes away from going into added time.

The results show that Takers do very badly when making these longshot bets, but Makers also perform badly when they are on the longshot side. And these patterns are more evident at 105 minutes than at 90 minutes. Average losses for the bottom group of Takers go from 36% at 90 minutes to 66% at 105 minutes. Similar losses for Makers backing the most extreme longshots go from 20% at 90 minutes to 47% at 105 minutes. The evidence shows this pattern begins after 15 minutes into matches, and it gets more extreme as games progress.

This evidence provides useful information because one weakness of the earlier evidence on late-game quotes from bookmakers is we can't be sure anyone accepted those quotes. To be honest, we can be pretty sure – if nobody is biting on a quote, bookmakers will adjust the prices. But this Betfair dataset only includes actual trades, so we know for sure that people placed these terrible longshot bets.

The tables again suggest some chances of winning on average by taking the other side of late longshot bets but it is worth knowing that the variance associated with these offers is extreme. It is not clear that this represents a risk-free strategy for long-term profits. But we can offer a very concrete piece of advice. Don't place longshot in-play bets, even on betting exchanges.

Average Returns for Takers and Makers, sorted by the estimated probability for home/away/draw football bets from 2022-2024: 90 minutes after kick-off

	Returns	
Average probability that Taker wins	*Takers*	*Makers*
0.038	-36.1%	1.1%
0.209	-10.3%	2.5%
0.500	1.9%	0.1%
0.791	3.1%	-7.7%
0.962	0.1%	-19.8%

Average Returns for Takers and Makers, sorted by the estimated probability for home/away/draw football bets from 2022-2024: 105 minutes after kick-off

	Returns	
Average probability that Taker wins	*Takers*	*Makers*
0.015	-65.9%	1.3%
0.122	-21.0%	2.9%
0.500	4.2%	-1.2%
0.879	2.8%	-13.8%
0.985	0.5%	-46.6%

The Bottom Line on Exchanges

Exchanges aren't perfect. On average, bettors lose and the exchange earns its commission. Commission fees are low in the UK but less so elsewhere – for example, in Australia there is a 6% commission on winnings because of taxes and fees charged by sporting bodies.

Once you move away from high-profile events, volumes are often low and pricing can be poor. Even for high-volume events, there are no guarantees of getting offers matched at the current best available market rates. And while pre-event odds are exceptionally accurate indicators of the underlying probabilities, strange things can happen with in-play betting.

Exchanges also have a complexity problem. Many people find their interfaces difficult and struggle to understand what all the different numbers on the screen mean. The irony is that people stick with bookmakers, who hide a lot of complexity behind what looks like a simple product, while on an exchange the pricing is transparent and the act of placing a bet is often just clicking the blue Back button.

But the bottom line is that, for most bets, the odds on exchanges are generally higher than you get from betting with bookmakers. The percentage of money Takers lose is well below the rates from betting with bookmakers. And acting as a Maker generally gives you the best chance you can get of breaking even or making a profit if you can identify even a small edge. Exchanges also won't throw you out for being successful. So, while exchanges take a bit of getting used to, for most bettors they represent a far better option than bookmakers.

Personally, I find it a bit sad that the leading global exchange, Betfair, is part of a conglomerate that has no strategic interest in exchanges replacing bookmakers as the dominant way for people to bet. If you are going to use exchanges, consider supporting some of its scrappy competitors. But obviously not at the expense of taking inferior odds. Never take bad odds on purpose.

IX. Betting With An Edge

So far, we've been realistic about the prospects of winning money from betting. Most bettors don't have an edge: bookmakers make money, exchanges take commission, and the typical bettor loses on average. But edges do exist. Some professionals win consistently and a few non-professionals are savvy enough to come out ahead more years than not.

In the next two chapters, we look at where an edge might come from and then ask the natural follow-up question: if you do have an edge, how much should you bet?

CHAPTER 27

Where Could Your Edge Come From?

Profiting from betting over time is only possible if you have an edge. Your bets need to have $p \times D > 1$.

Where would you get an edge of this sort? Again, it's worth remembering that I'm writing this from rainy Dublin where I make my money teaching economics, not from my villa in Saint-Tropez overseeing my professional betting operation. Despite spending lots of time analysing betting markets, I don't have an edge.

So, no secrets, but this chapter will focus on ways you might get an edge, arguing that most of the widely discussed methods are not much use for regular bettors. But I will also discuss the idea that perhaps, with careful analysis, you could use historical data from Betfair Exchange to implement strategies that make money. Even then, however, the caveats and difficulties will take up most of our discussion.

Knowing Your Teams

Many people hope they get an edge from what they know about sports. You know your team and their close rivals inside out, watch all their games and keep up with line-ups and injuries. It is natural to think this gives you an advantage when you focus on a few matches each weekend and try to spot where the bookies have "got it wrong." You have a subjective probability in your head and, if $p \times D > 1$ according to that belief, it is perfectly rational for you to bet.

But there are thousands of people like you, and many of them are feeding their views into models or betting syndicates. The odds on Premier League matches already embed the opinions of devoted fans, full-time analysts and traders who watch just as much football as you do and have access to far more data. So the fact that you follow your club closely should not, on its own, give you much reason to think your p is closer to the truth than the market's p.

There is also the problem that you may care a bit too much. When your favourite team loses a few games, it is tempting to decide they are "rubbish" and downgrade their chances. But short runs of results in football are heavily influenced by luck: a team can "win on xG" and still lose on the scoreboard if a few shots hit the post or the opposing goalkeeper has a great day. Strong feelings about a club can make you overreact to recent results, so your carefully thought-out p can still be distorted by emotion and randomness.

A simple reality check here is to ask whether you have a track record of winning on average from this kind of betting. Not over a lucky fortnight, but over hundreds of bets on the sort of matches where you feel you "know the teams." If, once you add everything up, your returns are negative, then whatever information edge you thought you had is not showing up in the numbers. In that case, it is better to accept that your information is not giving you a reliable profitable edge.

Tipsters

Maybe you can buy an edge? There are businesses that promise to give you tips on profitable bets. Maybe a small subscription fee is worth paying to get access to regular winning tips?

Well, there is no evidence that tipster sheets will help you profit from betting. You certainly can't trust any that don't have a long and credible track record available showing which bets they recommend and the returns you would have got from placing them.[88] But even those that appear to have a successful track record should be considered carefully.

Again, there is a useful analogy in finance. Investment funds that beat the market tend to attract money from investors; those that don't tend to be shut down or merged with successful ones. This creates a "survivorship bias" so that most existing funds appear to be "better than average." A financial firm could start out with 16 funds and then even if their returns were completely normal, they can expect to have 8 of them beat the market in the first year, 4 in the second year, 2 in the third year and 1 in the fourth year. That last fund can honestly advertise its persistent success, but it is just luck. Research, including a famous paper by Gene Fama, shows that returns for investment funds tend to be pretty random.[89]

Similar points apply with tipster sheets. Joseph Buchdahl, source of much of the data used in this book, has done a forensic analysis of tipster services, showing that they are generally not worth paying for and highlighting sharp practices like launching multiple services and closing the less successful ones.[90]

Again, basic economics points to these services not working. If these guys really had a workable profitable edge, they could turn that into millions with carefully placed bets with sharp bookmakers and on exchanges. Why would they dilute that edge by encouraging others to crowd the same picks in return for small monthly fees? It's almost like they don't really have that edge after all.

Courtsiding

We discussed "courtsiders" before in the context of in-play betting. There are videos online pitching this as a near "risk-free" way to profit: if you're in the stadium you see the point, goal, or basket before it appears on TV, you bet in that gap before the odds update.

What those videos leave out is that this has become much harder than it once was. The biggest in-play markets are explicitly designed to prevent these kinds of "latency" edges: odds are driven by fast official feeds and automated pricing, and the most vulnerable moments are protected by bet delays and market suspensions.

And even if you occasionally beat the clock, it is not scalable for ordinary bettors. To make serious money you need to repeat the edge at meaningful stakes, but bookmakers can spot these timing patterns and will limit or ban accounts that look like they are exploiting latency. On exchanges, you face a different constraint: many of the micro-markets in which courtsiders hope to make their money either don't exist on exchanges, or else they exist but do not have much liquidity, so there often isn't enough money sitting there at the stale price to scale up.

Then there's the unglamorous question the videos never ask: how much does it cost you to travel, buy tickets, and spend your time hopping between events? Add in the fact that courtsiding is usually against venue terms and increasingly policed in the stadiums, and it's not a viable strategy for the vast majority of bettors.

Statistical Modelling

Edges are real. As we have discussed before, professional bettors who earn a living from betting do exist. And, going back to Benter and Woods at the Hong Kong track in the 1990s, the most common method they use for generating an edge is statistical modelling.

These models are a long way from "stick some numbers in a spreadsheet and see what pops out." Even the Hong Kong operation from the 1990s - well behind the current technological frontiers - involved teams collecting and cleaning data, specifying and re-estimating models, and carefully back-testing them. Modern professional syndicates use code, databases and simulation in a way that is closer to running a small quantitative hedge fund than filling out a weekend accumulator. If you are anything like most bettors, it's unlikely that you have an advantage at this stuff.

As we discussed earlier, you probably have a bit more chance of beating the bookmakers' own models if you focus on more obscure sports (think NCAA lacrosse) but bookmakers price these markets with a big margin so even if your model does a better job than the bookmaker at predicting winners, the extra few percentage points you gain will often be eaten up by worse odds. And eventually, the bookmakers will spot your superior performance on this obscure sport and it's bye-bye lacrosse betting for you. A lot of wasted effort for not much return.

Exchanges are not much help here either. The more obscure the event, the less money is available to back and lay, and the wider the gap between the best back and lay odds. You may be able to place the occasional bet that looks attractive according to your model, but it will be hard to get any meaningful volume placed without moving the price against yourself.

Again, the analogy with financial markets is useful. Investment funds devote lots of money to finding small pricing errors but generally don't deliver risk-adjusted returns much better than a simple stock-market index once you factor in their staff costs, the fees they charge and the risks they take. Modern betting markets are similarly competitive. After all the database building and statistical modelling, we don't really know whether professional bettors make superior risk-adjusted returns. They may be better off placing their money on the stock market.

So statistical modelling is the right place to look if you are serious about finding an edge but, in practice, it is a demanding, technical route. If you can combine incredible coding and data management skills with extremely strong sports intelligence then you may have a chance but for most people, this approach is time consuming and unlikely to produce reliable profits.

Getting an Edge with AI?

What about AI? If it is changing everything else, why not betting? Maybe you don't need to be a statistical genius anymore because you can harness the power of AI to figure out what to bet on.

Sure enough, there are now videos and articles about how you can use AI to build "bookmaker crushing" models that tell you which bets to place. They tell you to sign up for sites with monthly fees to gather odds and team information and to run this information through one or more AI agents to come up with recommendations that will give you an edge over bookmakers.

Again, it's worth thinking through the economics. Bookmakers have far more at stake than you do and thus far more incentive to invest in quantitative models. In fact, bookmakers have been using AI models for years, back when it used to be called "machine learning" and anything you can do on the quantitative modelling front, they can almost certainly do better.

These systems are usually fed the same publicly available data – team statistics, recent results and, crucially, the bookmaker odds themselves. Running this through one or more AI models does not create new information. It just produces another way of processing what is already factored into the odds.

Some of the more elaborate versions of these systems use multiple AI models and even have them "debate" each other before arriving at a consensus pick. But these models are not independent sources of information. They are trained on similar data and given the same inputs, so asking them to agree with each other is unlikely to uncover anything the market has missed.

And even if you managed to build a system that matched the bookmaker's ability to estimate probabilities – which is already a very high bar – you would still lose money on average because of the margin built into the odds.

Betfair Strategies

I've been a bit dismissive of all the strategies so far, so let me finish with one that is perhaps more promising. Betfair makes enormous amounts of historical data available, albeit most of it for a charge. For example, the football data I have described here costs £700 for a full year of data. At the time of writing, older data from 2016 and 2020 are available free but you may not want to base your strategies on such old data.

So, at a cost, you can get data showing second-by-second trading information, including odds and volumes for executed trades as well as continuously updated information on available-to-back and available-to-lay offers.

These data can be used on their own or combined with external data. For example, for football, data on the recent performances of the teams, Elo scores, rolling XG differences and so on. You could also incorporate match-level information such as when goals were scored. From the Betfair data alone, you can assess historical returns to accepting various offers that are available. For example, you can assess what the average return would be from backing the away teams ten minutes into a game. Incorporating detailed match data, you could assess the return to backing away teams that are 1-0 down after ten minutes.

I don't have a sure-fire winning strategy to offer – it's pretty much all caveats from here on – but we have seen enough to know that markets do not always price complex bets correctly. And we have seen that in-play markets are full of strange pricing. We also know from Betfair's discussions around its expert fee that there are traders who make large profits from their exchange bets. Given the huge number of possible strategies you can assess with historical data, there are almost certainly strategies that the data will show to be profitable.

Now, the caveats. First, the flip side of there being thousands of strategies to test is that some will look brilliant just by chance, even if there is no real edge there, so impressive historical results always need to be treated with suspicion.

Second, if you plan a strategy involving placing bets once certain conditions are satisfied, you need to set up a bot of some sort. I have used BFBotManager and it can execute simple strategies, including those that depend on the current scoreline but it's not good at doing anything complex. For that, you need to learn to code Python and run your own scripts. And BFBotManager costs money (currently about £150 per year) while writing Python scripts costs valuable time.

Third, the easiest historical strategies to assess are those that involve being a Taker. You can see which bets were offered and what would have happened if you had taken them. But you need to be careful about the scale of betting you have in mind. If the data show £5 was available to back at odds of 4 and £20 at odds of 3.9, then if your strategy involves taking £15 bets, your historical calculations should assume you got £5 placed at 4 and the rest placed at 3.9. And just because bets were available at a certain price at a certain time, that doesn't mean you would always have been able to execute those trades given the inevitable delay between your bot recognising the conditions for the strategy hold and actually making the order. Ultimately, you can only assess a strategy by implementing it in reality.

Fourth, profitable strategies are most likely to involve acting as a Maker. Here, the historical data are even less useful because you don't know if your offers would have been accepted. Actually knowing whether your hypothetical Maker order would have been accepted is impossibly complicated. Which is to say, I tried to figure this out with the historical Betfair data and failed! Either way, the caveat emptor of relying on historical performance based on all your offers being matched is even stronger for Maker bets.

Which brings us back to the story I told you was coming in this chapter.

The Story of a Failed Bot

In the previous chapter, we showed how Makers had a 7.4% average return per pre-match bet on the total goals scored market when the Taker had a very high chance of succeeding. In practice, these bets were almost all from the under/over 0.5 goals and the under/over 5.5 goals markets, so the Maker was backing a scoreless draw or else six goals or more.

I decided to investigate the 0.5 goals market, in particular whether backing the under at the current offered prices was profitable. The historical data suggested making offers to others to back the over at the current best-available back odds was a highly profitable approach. So, I set up a bot to execute this strategy.

Despite the evidence from the historical data, I was conscious of some of the caveats above and didn't want to risk too much money, so I set the standard bet size to €1. The bot then attempted to place tens of thousands of bets. After a few months, the verdict was in. Instead of making a substantial profit, the bot had just about broken even. Visions of the villa in Saint-Tropez disappeared and all I was left with was this goddamned anecdote for my book.

What went wrong? First, the match rate for these offers was very low, about 20%. So, most of my tens of thousands of offers went ignored. And the ones that were matched didn't have the fantastic returns the historical data had promised.

After a while, I realised my strategy had fallen victim to not one but two different asymmetric information problems. Remember how health insurers don't want too many sick customers? On Betfair, your "customers" are the people who accept your offers, and many of them are sharp. Those are not the customers you want. And on Betfair, your competitors are the other Makers, and even more of them are sharp. These are not the competitors you want either.

Historical data that assumes you will always be matched may tell you a whole class of bets looks good, but the reality is that some of these will be good bets and some will be bad. The average return doesn't matter once you're not getting matched all the time. And sharp bettors can often tell which of any group of bets is a good one and which is a bad one.

The result was that my bot's offers to make bad bets were the ones most likely to be gobbled up, while its offers to make good bets (where the supposed edge actually was) sat unmatched in the queue behind others running similar strategies. Checking the Betfair interface, I could regularly see that my offer had no chance of getting matched. Beyond this particular strategy, you see these dynamics all across Betfair's markets: lopsided queues, obvious crowding at certain prices, automated strategies competing for the same trades.

So, a word of advice. If you try this at all, start small — £1 stakes — and gather data on how your bets actually get matched. Even if the edge survives at tiny size, don't assume it scales. At larger stakes, you may find your worst bets filled in full, while your best ones only get partially matched.

With the right strategy, it is almost certainly possible to make money with automated trading on Betfair, but you need a greater quantitative edge than just some historical data showing a particular type of offer worked on average in the past.

Checking That You Have an Edge

How would you know you have an edge? Ultimately, your account balance will give you the right answer. Jacob Bernoulli's Law of Large Numbers will reveal the truth.

But what if after years of losing, you've adopted a new strategy over the past three months and you have been winning. Does that mean you have an edge now? Maybe, maybe not.

This isn't a statistics book, but what I can say is that the sample size you need to be pretty sure your underlying win rate on toss-up bets is, for example, 53% rather than 50% — sufficient to beat most bookmakers' margins — is annoyingly large. And if your strategy involves placing some bets on extreme longshots and your profitability has relied on some of these winning, well then you could be waiting a very long time before the data offer a definitive judgement. I recommend Joseph Buchdahl's book *Monte Carlo or Bust* as a good introduction to the kind of tools you need to use to figure this stuff out.

One thing you can do, while you are waiting for enough data to accumulate, is to check the win rate on your bets against their predicted values from Betfair's closing prices. These are pretty close to unbiased predictors. So, for example, if Betfair-implied probabilities suggest you should have won 20% of your bets but you actually won 21% of them, then that may be a better indicator that you have some skill than actually making a profit over the same period, since outcomes are innately "noisy."

But the same arithmetic applies that we have discussed all along. You don't just need to win more often than the true probability. You need to win more often than the true probability so that you beat the bookmaker's margin or the exchange commission. You can be a skilled gambler and still lose. Equally, a few months of profits do not necessarily mean you are skilled.

Edges are Complex and Fleeting

In this chapter, we've looked at a range of ways to potentially get a consistent and reliable edge: knowing your teams, paying for tips, beating the bookie's feed, building models and even running a Betfair bot.

A key conclusion is that getting an edge is hard. It requires a combination of insight and expertise that is difficult to explain in simple terms. And this complexity is a defining feature of edges: If the strategy you had that gave you an edge was simple, then others would probably discover it too and the weight of money being placed on the bets you have picked would change the odds and the profits would disappear. Even if you are pretty sure you have had an edge in the past, it is worth running the checks just suggested to see whether or not it is holding up over time.

Again, there is a useful analogy to financial markets. Investors are always looking for a secret trick that gives them better risk-adjusted returns and, over the years, the pages of academic finance journals have been filled with strategies that seemed to beat the market. Indeed, Richard Thaler's first few *Anomalies* columns covered unusual patterns in returns like "The January Effect", the tendency for stocks to perform well in January. The statistical evidence for these effects has generally weakened over time because once investors knew about them, they adapted their strategies.[91]

In the same way, a simple betting strategy that generates systematic profits is unlikely to continue working forever, not least because bookmakers will spot it and re-price the relevant bets accordingly. And on betting exchanges, even the strategies that look good in historical data, like my own failed bot, can be undermined by the way markets adapt and by who you end up trading with. Making money systematically on betting is a lot of hard work, which may or may not be worth the effort you put into it.

CHAPTER 28

Risk, Ruin and the Kelly Criterion

You probably don't have an edge for most bets you place, but let's just assume for this chapter that you do for some of them. How much should you bet in those cases? The story of the answer to this question is an interesting one. Before getting into it, I will note that we are assuming here that you can actually bet as much as you want - perhaps at an exchange or with a sharp bookmaker - leaving aside the always-tricky question of how people with an edge can place large bets with retail bookmakers.

Maximising Expected Wealth

You have a probability p of winning a bet that gives you a payout of D if you risk one unit and zero otherwise. You have an edge, so the expected payout rate from this bet is $p \times D > 1$. If your stake is W, your expected payout will be $p \times D \times W$. This means your expected profit gets bigger as you bet more. If you want to maximise the expected value of your wealth, you should put all your money into this bet.

But that seems a bit extreme, doesn't it? There is a probability $1-p$ that you won't win and then you'd lose all of your wealth. If you were in any way risk averse, you would not be willing to do that.

This strategy gets even crazier if you think about how you would approach having a sequence of bets of this type. If you start with a stake of W and then keep rolling over any winnings you have, always betting the lot, your expected wealth after N bets will be $(p \times D)^N \times W$. As N gets larger, this gets bigger and bigger. No matter how much money you placed on the original bet, your expected wealth spirals towards infinity. You are going to be rich, super rich ... on average across all possible outcomes.

But you are also almost certainly going to be broke. Because a single loss wipes out all your money, the chance of losing everything with this strategy is $1 - p^N$, which heads inexorably towards 1 as N gets bigger.

How can you be unimaginably rich on average while still almost certain to go bankrupt? The explanation is that there is one incredibly unlikely winning streak that you could go on but almost certainly won't. The riches you earn from that one case overwhelm all the other times you lose all your money when it comes to calculating the average.

So while it's fun to imagine an edge making you infinitely wealthy, in the real world, nobody would ever try this strategy.

Fixed Stakes: The Gambler's Ruin

The "bet everything" strategy invariably ends in ruin even though you had an edge. One obvious problem with the strategy was that as you got richer, you kept increasing the amount that you risked. A more sensible approach might be to have a fixed bet size.

Consider then the following scenario. Rather than assume you have an edge, let's start by assuming you play a repeated set of coin toss games with a 50% chance of success. You start with wealth of W, stake one unit on each round and stop when either your wealth is gone or you reach a target level of wealth T. How likely are you to lose all your money? The best way to think about this question is to use Louis Bachelier's idea of a random walk.

When you are playing this game, you have an equal chance each round of your wealth moving upwards or downwards. It is a classic random walk. If you have wealth of W, the 50% chance of winning each round means you have an equal chance from there of either eventually doubling your wealth and getting to $2W$ or else eventually losing everything. More generally, the chance of losing all your money if you only stop when you reach a target of T is W/T, the ratio of your current wealth to your target. For example, if $T = 5W$, then you are only one-fifth of the way to your target – this makes it 80% likely you will lose your money and only 20% likely you will reach your target.

If you don't set a reasonable finite target – in other words, you just decide to keep playing no matter what – this is equivalent to setting T to some huge number. The result is that your chance of ruin is essentially one.

Notice what is happening here is not related to the typical admonition to not gamble because you have no edge. The odds in this game are fair. You're not losing all your money because the game is rigged against you. But even in a fair game, randomness will conspire to eventually ruin you if you don't set a reasonable target for walking away from betting.

The story gets a little bit better if you do have an edge but not as good as you might think. Imagine for example that the coin is slightly weighted in your favour, so that your chance of winning one unit is 50.25%. That gives you an expected return of 0.5% on every bet. It might seem small but, over many bets, that could make you incredibly rich.

Figuring out how likely you are to avoid ruin is a bit more complicated in this case, but working through the maths shows that if you size your bets at one percent of your initial wealth, you still have a 37% chance of losing it all. If your edge jumps to an expected return of 1% on every bet, your chance of ruin falls to 13% but the point remains that even having an edge and betting a fixed bet size does not guarantee avoiding ruin.

These examples where you can gain or lose an equal amount are not how most bets on sports work. Often, you have less than a 50% chance of winning, but your potential win outweighs your potential loss. The maths required to figure out the chance of ruin with these bets are complex. But you can show that for a fixed edge, higher odds bets make it more probable that you will be ruined when betting a fixed amount. The higher variance associated with these bets increases the chances that an unlucky streak sees you lose all your money.[92] Absent a careful staking strategy, an edge on its own is not enough to guarantee you don't lose all your money.

John Kelly and the Garbled Wire

John Kelly was an engineer at Bell Labs in the 1950s, the research arm of the American telephone monopoly and one of the most important scientific institutions of the twentieth century. Kelly worked on how information could be transmitted over imperfect wires. A signal sent down a wire might be right or it might be corrupted, and Kelly was interested in how a receiver should act when they believed it had a specific probability of being accurate.

Kelly knew this was not an abstract problem. Sports results were being transmitted over wires, and early or more reliable information could be extremely valuable for betting – something bookmakers and gangsters like Bugsy Siegel understood very well. If you have information that gives you an edge, but it is not a sure thing, the question is not whether to bet but how much to bet.

Kelly knew that betting everything or even betting a fixed amount could end in ruin, so his starting point was you should bet a fixed fraction of your wealth or whatever bankroll you have made available for your betting activities.

But what was the right fraction of your wealth to bet? The next idea Kelly had was key. He described how your wealth changes over time according to

$$W_t = G_t W_{t-1}$$

so that whether your wealth increases or decreases after each bet depends on a growth factor G_t. If you win, the growth factor is greater than one and if you lose, it is less than one.

Kelly realised that betting everything maximised your wealth in the sense that it maximised the expected value across the two possible growth factors. But he suggested that a more sensible criterion was to maximise the expected *geometric* average of the growth factors. Let G_{win} be the growth factor when winning, G_{lose} be the growth factor when losing and assume you have a probability p of winning.

The geometric average is

$$(G_{win})^p (G_{lose})^{1-p}$$

Betting everything means G_{lose} is zero so the geometric average will be zero no matter how big the potential win is. Once there is any chance of losing, betting it all does not maximise the geometric average. And it turns out that, among all the possible criteria for picking fractions of your wealth to invest, Kelly's geometric average criterion is the best way to maximise expected wealth while avoiding losing all your money.

Kelly's Rule

Using our terminology, Kelly showed that you maximised the geometric average return by betting a share of your wealth equal to

$$s = \frac{(p \times D) - 1}{D - 1}$$

The upper part of the fraction is your expected rate of return on your bet - it makes sense that the more edge you have, the more you should bet. The lower part of the fraction is the decimal odds minus one, which is the traditional UK fractional odds. The formula has often been expressed as "edge over odds."

Kelly's rule is thus - "bet more if your edge is bigger but temper this if the odds are high." The latter part of the rule is where the risk aversion implicit in Kelly's approach comes in. You might have an edge on a 100/1 bet but it's only going to win slightly more than one times in a hundred and you might be broke by then if you have been risking a lot of money.

To give some concrete examples, suppose you think you have a 51% chance of winning a bet that has decimal odds of 2. Kelly recommends you bet 2% of your money on this bet. But if you think you have an 11% chance of winning a bet with decimal odds of 10, it recommends staking only 1.1% of your money. The expected payout rate is only 1.01 for the first bet and 1.1 for the second bet but the extra variance means Kelly recommends staking less.

After its publication, other researchers demonstrated various positive properties of the Kelly criterion. For example, if you had a target level of wealth but wanted to avoid losing all your money, Kelly's rule is on average the quickest way to use your edge to reach that target. The tales of gamblers and academics using Kelly's rule to try to get an edge at blackjack, unbalanced roulette tables and stock warrants became legendary – many of these are covered in William Poundstone's entertaining book, *Fortune's Formula*.

Samuelson's Critique

By the late 1960s, Paul Samuelson, godfather of the efficient markets theory, had heard of the Kelly criterion and he wasn't impressed. Kelly had pointed out that his approach of maximising the geometric average of growth factors was mathematically the same as maximising the expected logarithm of wealth. The two formulae look different but they give you the same answer about how much to bet.

Samuelson had promoted the mathematical method of describing people as maximising "utility functions" when making decisions. He pointed out that people whose utility function had a logarithmic form should follow the Kelly criterion; and nobody else should. Since the logarithmic form of utility was a very specific one, Samuelson reasoned that Kelly's rule was not suitable for most people. He wrote a series of increasingly irritated papers about this issue, concluding with his 1979 article "*Why We Should Not Make Mean Log of Wealth Big Though Years to Act Are Long*" which used almost entirely one-syllable words. He was saying "how can I spell this out as simply as possible?"

While Kelly advocates debated with Samuelson that surely people should adopt a strategy that ruled out ruin while maximising returns, the balance of logic lay on Samuelson's side. As an MIT economics PhD, I'm practically legally obligated to side with Samuelson. But leaving aside my institutional loyalties, his logic on the Kelly Criterion was inescapable. Logarithmic utility functions feature diminishing marginal utility but in a very specific way. Someone with a different pattern of diminishing marginal utility, because they are either less risk averse or more risk averse, should not pursue this rule.

And in fact, while the Kelly criterion is a regular topic on betting discussion sites around the world, one of the most common themes is that it seems way too aggressive. Samuelson would just say – "yep, that's because you don't have a log utility function." Indeed, there have been many studies by economists that have aimed at measuring how risk averse people are and those studies point to most people having higher levels of risk aversion than implied by log utility. So, if the Kelly criterion generates predictions that you are uncomfortable with, that's not you being irrational and there is no "scientific" result that says the best thing for you is to use this rule.

Online discussions often promote the idea of implementing a "fractional" version of Kelly. For example, you could risk half the amount suggested by the Kelly criterion. You can show that for simple even money bets, this kind of scaling works pretty well to give the best outcome for people with an edge who don't have log utility. But this result does not hold at all for the kind of long-odds bets people often place.[93] If Kelly is too aggressive for you, then you should bet less than it recommends, but that doesn't mean you should always bet a fixed fraction of what is recommended by Kelly.

Kelly and Accumulators

Some "expert" discussions of accumulator bets claim they become good bets once you have an edge. Suppose you have a set of bets with $p \times D$ greater than one. As we discussed earlier, an N-leg accumulator of these bets has an expected payout rate of $(p \times D)^N$ which gets bigger as N grows. Similar expert discussion will also often tell you to use the Kelly criterion to size your bets. But these two recommendations contradict each other.

You can plug p^N and D^N into the Kelly formula in place of p and D and figure out how much you should bet on an accumulator and what the geometric average return is. The results show that you should bet a lot less as the number of legs go up: the effect of compounding your edge is offset by the ever-higher variance.

And Kelly actually recommends you should pretty much never accept long-legged accumulators even if you have an edge. With realistic edges of one to five percent expected returns, for bets with an average chance of winning of about one half, the best outcome comes from a two-leg accumulator. For bets with an average chance of winning of one third (as in football, for example), Kelly actually tells you to ignore accumulators and just place single bets.[94] Kelly turns out to provide a good argument against placing accumulators, even if you are tolerant enough of risk to follow its advice.

Returns on Bets: Kelly versus Fixed Stakes

The logic behind the Kelly criterion is compelling. If you have an edge and want to grow your wealth over time, it tells you how much to bet. But in practice, the way Kelly performs in the betting records people keep can be surprisingly underwhelming.

This was discovered first by legendary blackjack gambler, Stanford Wong. His argument went like this.

Suppose you have a 50% chance of winning a bet at decimal odds of 2.2. That gives you a 10% edge: if you stake £1, your expected payout is £1.10. Kelly tells you to stake 8.33% of your bankroll. So if you start with £100, your first bet is £8.33.

Now suppose you win. You make a profit of £10, and your bankroll rises to £110. On the next bet, Kelly tells you to stake 8.33% of £110, which is £9.17. Suppose this bet loses. You are then left with £100.83. So after one win and one loss, you are ahead by £0.83.

How much did you stake? £8.33 on the first bet and £9.17 on the second, for a total of £17.50. Calculating 0.83/17.50, your return on bets is 4.8%.

Now compare this with a fixed-stakes bettor who stakes £8.33 on both bets and also wins one and loses one. The win earns £10, the loss costs £8.33, so they are ahead by £1.67 on total stakes of £16.66. That is a return on bets of 10%.

Two bettors with the same edge and the same results. But the Kelly bettor's return on bets is less than half as large.

The reason is subtle. After the win, the Kelly bettor increases their stake slightly, from £8.33 to £9.17. That doesn't look like much. But the extra 84p is large relative to the profits involved. The fixed-stakes bettor makes £1.67 across the two bets, so the increase in the Kelly stake on the bet they lost is about half of that entire profit. When the loss comes, it arrives on a slightly larger stake and eats into the gain.

This is not just bad luck in a short sequence of bets. There is a beautiful mathematical result that, when your edge is small and you place many bets, the return on bets from Kelly-staking tends to be about half the return from flat staking.[95]

In the end, of course, provided there really is an edge, the Kelly bettor will have more profits. But Kelly is designed to maximise the long-run growth rate of wealth, not the return on stakes. If you tracked your performance using return on bets - and let's face it return on investment risked is the standard criterion almost everyone uses to assess financial decisions - you might conclude that the fixed-stakes strategy is better.

The Real Reason Not to Use Kelly

If you want to consider using Kelly to size your bets, your starting point should be a pretty large data sample showing that you have a track record of making profits. At that point, you might want to start using Kelly as a reference point for how much to bet, but keep in mind that, for many people, it is far too aggressive.

But most people shouldn't use Kelly at all. You probably don't have an edge, so basing your betting decisions on the assumption that you do is starting from the wrong place. Your best approach to sizing your bets is probably to keep the stakes small so that losses over time are modest. You can enjoy the fun that comes with betting without risking your financial security.

X. What Should We Do?

We have covered lots of interesting ideas and evidence about how the world of sports betting works. However, we have only briefly covered "the dark side" – gambling addiction and its impact on society.

But just as economics can help us understand how bettors and bookmakers take decisions, it also provides a useful toolkit for thinking about how governments should tax and regulate complex products like sports betting that sometimes inflict harm. So, I want to finish the book with a brief discussion of the issues facing governments when dealing with the sports betting industry, before concluding with some practical takeaways for bettors.

CHAPTER 29

Sports Betting and Government Policy

We have largely focused on the economics of how the betting industry works and its implications for bettors. But this sector does not just matter for those who place or take bets. There are important questions for governments about how gambling should be regulated and taxed. Here, I will briefly discuss the evidence on the financial impact of betting and of problem gambling, before moving to policy debates.

Betting and Household Finances

Everybody knows that on average, bettors lose money and bookmakers make profits. But, until recently, you couldn't say much about the impact this had on the finances of those who bet. In the past few years, however, researchers have been able to obtain "big data" from banks that allow them to observe spending on betting and other financial transactions.

A study in *Nature Human Behaviour* used anonymised data from Lloyds Bank to go beyond the idea that betting just causes "financial harm" in the abstract.[96] It shows what gambling seems to *push out* in everyday life. When people devote a bigger share of their monthly outgoings to gambling, their spending falls on the sorts of things you'd normally associate with a reasonably healthy, balanced life: self-care, fitness (think gym memberships), hobbies, education, social activities and travel.

More concerningly, they construct a measure of spending between 1am and 5am, and it rises with gambling intensity: heavier gambling months are followed by more "nights awake". They show that a 10-percentage-point increase in gambling as a share of monthly spending is associated with an 11.5% increase in nights awake and a 9% reduction in outlays on social activities. Less ordinary social life, more late-night activity – these findings are consistent with gambling shifting for some people from a daytime hobby into something that eats into sleep and routine.

One argument against this evidence is that it doesn't necessarily prove that gambling *causes* these bad outcomes. Perhaps if gambling was made impossible, people would switch to day trading or crypto-currencies or other risky behaviours, so restricting gambling would have no impact.

The legalisation of sports betting in the US has provided a good way to check whether this objection is correct. Online sports betting rolled out at different times across US states after the Supreme Court struck down the federal ban. A recent research paper using anonymised bank account data compares each household's finances before and after legal online betting arrives in their state, relative to similar households in states where it has not arrived yet.[97]

What the authors found was not a harmless reshuffle of spending. After legalisation, households where people opened sports betting accounts saved and invested less. In particular, net deposits into investment accounts fell by about 14% relative to the comparison group that lived in states where sports betting was still illegal.

And the impact was not evenly spread. The effects were larger for poorer households. For those low-savings households, opening a legal online betting account was followed by a clear deterioration in day-to-day finances: higher credit-card balances, lower repayments on debts and an increased likelihood of needing an overdraft. Taken together, this is hard to reconcile with the idea that "they would have taken some other set of risky decisions anyway." The evidence points to legal sports betting creating a new and persistent drain on household balance sheets, concentrated among the people least able to afford it.

Problem Gambling and Its Impact

The bank-account-based studies provide some signs that governments should perhaps be worried about the impact of sports betting. However, most people who bet are well aware that it is hard to win over the longer run but enjoy the fun from placing a few bets every week. Of course, it isn't good for their finances, but neither is spending money on alcohol or golfing or whatever else it is that people enjoy. Despite the concerning evidence in the *Nature* study, you could still argue that for most people, their betting habit is pretty harmless.

But it is not harmless for everyone. Some people become addicted to gambling and it takes over their lives. Estimating the prevalence of "problem gambling" is difficult because it is hard to come up with a precise measure of it and people will not always be honest when asked about it in surveys. Results from the UK Gambling Commission's 2024 national survey suggest about 3% of adults have a gambling problem and some researchers argue it may be higher.[98]

While that is a small percentage of people, the costs of problem gambling are not trivial. A UK study from the National Institute of Economic and Social Research placed the total fiscal cost associated with problem gambling at between £1.1 billion and £1.7 billion per year. These estimates combine costs to the health system with lost income tax and higher benefit costs from problem gamblers struggling to hold down a job. This is a significant fraction of the £3.3 billion the study estimated the UK government raises from betting and gaming duties.[99] And this is before we put a cost on the impact that problem gambling has on families, who also suffer serious financial and emotional consequences when their relatives become addicted to gambling.[100]

I am not at all a moralist about gambling. I believe it should be legal and that it generates a lot of fun for many people. But as a social scientist, I think any debate about public policy has to acknowledge the damage it can cause. The subject of this book – sports betting – actually features pretty low down the list of gambling activities that are typically associated with addiction. Problem gamblers tend to gravitate towards "always on" options like online slots or card games.

But, for many, opening an account with a bookmaker is the first step on a journey that ends up being devastating for them and their family.

Regulation

The extent of harm caused by problem gambling means there is a clear case for governments to consider what can be done to reduce it. This isn't a new thing. Governments have always been heavily involved in the legalised gambling industry, granting licences, setting conditions and raising taxes from it.

The UK has the longest history of having a fully-fledged online gambling industry. Its Gambling Act of 2005 introduced a highly deregulated environment with very few restrictions on how bets could be placed or how the industry could advertise. It is perhaps no surprise that, today, the UK is having a serious debate about whether regulation needs to be tighter. Indeed, unusually in this age of highly divided politics, there is broad cross-party acceptance that the current UK system is not working and stricter regulation is needed.

The Gambling Act largely relied on self-regulation by bookmakers, and over the years the industry has made various efforts to police itself and promote "responsible gambling". Recently, operators have agreed that one-fifth of television advertising will focus on safer-gambling messages. These initiatives are not meaningless, but it is hard to see them as a sufficient response to the scale of the problem.

Ultimately, self-regulation is not credible in this industry for a simple reason: problem gamblers are extremely valuable customers. Research by economists David Forrest and Ian McHale shows that about 85% of online gambling profits come from just 6% of bettors.[101] This figure certainly includes many wealthy "high rollers" who are able to bet heavily without experiencing serious financial harm. But it also certainly includes many problem gamblers and that creates an obvious tension. An industry that makes much of its money from a small group of vulnerable customers can't be expected to put their interests first without strong external constraints.

So where does this leave policy? I think there are three areas where progress can be made without disrupting normal people from their usual betting activities.

First, limits on advertising can be made stricter. These limits are not popular with sports authorities but there is significant precedent. Complete bans are in place in Italy and the Netherland and Australia has recently introduced a strict tightening of sports betting advertising, including a ban on logos being used on shirts and in stadiums.

Second, governments need to consider how to counter the way the sports betting industry constantly encourages bettors to make bad decisions. Richard Thaler wrote a famous book with Cass Sunstein, called *Nudge*, about how governments can design policies that gently encourage people to make good decisions about their finances. Psychologist Philip Newall has pointed out that online betting firms employ "dark nudges", pushing people towards bets with the highest loss rates.[102]

This suggests a role for countervailing government-designed nudges that push bettors towards making more informed decisions. Governments could consider requiring betting apps to include a short information module before customers are allowed to place their first bet. New users might be asked a few basic questions about odds and probabilities, with clear explanations whenever they get an answer wrong.

Another policy in this vein would be to require greater transparency from bookmakers about pricing. For example, we discussed earlier how some US states require bookmakers to provide separate reporting about stakes and profits on high-margin bets like parlays. Reporting like this is easy to implement and would give regulators and bettors a much clearer picture of where losses are really coming from. Another option would be to require advertisements for products like Accas to contain explicit warnings about their historical loss rates.

Third, there is a need for gambling companies to take stronger action to restrict problem gamblers. In the UK, steps are being taken towards checks being required on gamblers who lose large amounts of money. Currently, a net deposit of £150 over 30 days triggers checks in the public record for whether the person has serious debt problems. And there are active debates about whether or not large gambling losses should trigger concrete affordability checks, requiring gamblers to provide income statements.

Some object to such requirements as an invasion of privacy. Others argue, reasonably, that pubs don't have to check whether someone can afford to buy alcohol or has a track record as an alcoholic. But those arguments only go so far. There are relatively few licensed gambling operators in any country and that changes the logistics of what is possible. You can't stop every pub in the country serving alcoholics, but you can impose a "duty of care" requirement on a small number of licensed gambling operators. And this should include bookmakers needing to know whether someone who is losing large amounts of money with them is able to easily afford it or is in fact bankrupting themselves.

One problem with the current and proposed UK restrictions is that they only apply on a firm-by-firm basis. If you get cut off from gambling with one firm because your losses are too big, you can just move on to the next one. Or you can gamble with multiple operators right up to the point where the limits kick in. No single operator sees that the customer is experiencing very high losses across the firms.

The solution to this problem is the implementation of a "single customer view" system. This would require centralised data collection of each gambler's records across all operators. The single customer view would be administered by a separate body, so none of the firms would see the data from their competitors. Once a gambler has gone over a combined loss threshold across all operators, the firms would receive messages that would trigger stake restrictions or affordability checks.[103]

This sounds complicated but the UK already operates a nationwide self-exclusion scheme, GamStop, which allows customers to exclude themselves from all licensed online gambling sites at once. The UK's data protection regulator has confirmed that data protection law does not prevent implementation of a single customer view. If cross-operator coordination is feasible for self-exclusion, it is clearly feasible for monitoring customer losses. The technical infrastructure and regulatory framework are already in place.

Tax Policy Issues

The other big policy issue in relation to gambling is how it should be taxed. Indeed, the ability to raise tax revenue from gambling has been a key factor motivating governments to legalise and deregulate online gambling. They figure that banning it is impossible and people generally prefer to gamble with licensed operators, so you might as well legalise it and use it as a source of tax revenue.

But how should it be taxed? Economists have long thought about how best to tax products that can inflict harm. They talk about "Pigouvian taxes", named after Arthur Pigou, an early 20th century economist who promoted the idea that taxes could be used to discourage socially undesirable activities. Pigou believed that banning harmful activities was often not possible and so it was best to discourage them via taxation and perhaps use the revenue raised to offset the harm. Economists' favourite policy for addressing climate change – a carbon tax – is pure Pigou.

As just documented, gambling clearly generates some harm. But in most countries, its taxation is not Pigouvian at all. The most common approach is to tax Gross Gaming Revenue (GGR), which is total stakes minus total payouts. In other words, GGR is total losses from gamblers. Operators also pay normal corporate profit taxes on the profits they retain after the GGR tax.

Why do I say a GGR tax is not Pigouvian? Well, GGR is the main determinant of profits for bookmakers. They have other costs but they are typically small relative to the cost of payouts to winning bettors. So, at least at low rates, a GGR tax is like a tax on profits. And taxes on profits don't change prices or quantities. That might seem a surprising claim but think about it for a moment. Our monopoly model's predictions were all based on bookmakers choosing odds that maximised profits. Bookmakers may not like sharing profits with the government, but the same odds that maximise profits before tax will also maximise them after tax.

This suggests a GGR tax will do little to change odds and thus won't change the amount of gambling. Betting industry sources argue that higher GGR taxes will lead to worse odds for customers but the evidence from the US points against this. Each US state has its own GGR tax rate, ranging from about 10% at its lowest to a high of 51% in New York. States report the pre-tax profit margin made on bets (the "hold" percentage) and the data show there is effectively zero correlation between these margins and the GGR tax rate. Raising GGR rates does not seem to worsen the odds offered to customers and, in this sense, it doesn't discourage betting.

Beyond its lack of "Pigouvian" features, GGR taxes raise questions about the incentives of government. Effectively, they make government an "equity partner" with the bookmakers in sharing the losses that bettors incur. The more bettors lose, the more the government takes in tax. This hardly encourages governments to look after bettors' interests by promoting a more competitive market with lower margins.

There are alternatives. One option is to have a turnover tax, so bookmakers have to pay over a share of the total amount of money staked. In our model, that raises the c parameter and leads to lower odds and lower betting volumes even when raising the same amount of revenue. Another is to have bettors directly pay a duty on their stake, which was the system in the UK before 2001. In our model, this changes the rule for betting from "bet if $p \times D > 1$" to "bet if $p \times D > 1+t$" where t is the levy rate. Our model predicts this system would produce higher odds because bettors would become pickier about which bets they would accept, but the end result is also lower volumes while raising the same amount of revenue.

Bookmakers hate these tax proposals, arguing that they will put some of them out of business. But that is the point of a Pigouvian tax. After you apply it, you get less of the activity you taxed. It is pretty easy to use the rational disagreement model to show that either a turnover tax or a betting duty can raise the same amount of revenue as a GGR tax while having lower betting volumes. Operators argue that this means jobs would be lost in their sector. But – briefly putting my macroeconomist hat back on – people will spend the money on other things and other jobs will get created; at any point in time, you see some sectors expanding and some contracting. That's just how the economy works. It doesn't impact the total number of jobs.

Limits to Tax Policies

The theoretical case for switching to Pigouvian taxes is strong and you could also argue the case for relatively high values of these taxes to discourage betting. On closer inspection, however, there are likely to be serious limits to how far you could push such an approach.

One reason comes from the disagreement-based theory we have been using. Typically, the odds data could be explained with relatively small amounts of disagreement about probabilities. That means demand is pretty sensitive to the odds, so even modest increases in tax have a substantial effect in reducing betting volumes.

The idea that tax increases could actually cut tax revenue has been a conservative holy grail dating back to the famous *Laffer curve* in the 1970s.[104] In reality, for the vast majority of taxes on income and capital, the Laffer curve has failed to survive contact with reality. But betting markets may be an exception. Using realistic levels of disagreement, our model predicts Laffer curve effects will happen.[105] And indeed, the UK betting market of the early 2000s was a concrete example where the tax rate was halved and yet betting volumes doubled, so revenue did not fall.

So, even in theory, raising taxes on betting runs into limits pretty quickly, and this is a theory that assumes people can only bet with legal bookmakers. In truth, if you tax the legal sector enough, betting with unlicensed bookmakers becomes more attractive and you start to lose tax revenue even faster than theoretical models will predict. In the past, unlicensed bookmakers meant backstreet operations. Today, they take the form of offshore operators.

The Offshore Threat

Whenever governments propose tighter regulation of gambling or higher taxes on bookmakers, the industry reaches for the same argument. Push us too hard, they warn, and customers will drift to unlicensed offshore operators. Regulation will backfire, tax revenue will evaporate, and bettors will be exposed to firms that have no responsible gambling policies at all.

This argument is not invented out of thin air. Unlicensed online gambling is clearly sizeable in many countries. It would be naïve to think that regulation has no effect on where people choose to place their bets. But the threat is too often treated as a conversation-stopper rather than something to be actively tackled.

And the truth is that the approach of many governments to unlicensed operators is weak. You can particularly see this in the UK, where action has tended to be reactive and piecemeal. Regulators issue warnings, send cease-and-desist letters, and refer URLs for takedown. This activity is not meaningless, but it amounts to whack-a-mole rather than sustained pressure. Payment intermediaries and advertising channels are only intermittently targeted.

You can see the UK government's lack of seriousness on this issue in its approach to advertising. Betting companies targeting the Asian market have long been advertised on Premier League shirts and advertising boards. For a while, many of these companies were using a UK license owned by a company called TGP Europe. You brought up their site but under the hood it was all TGP. This arrangement ended in May 2025, when TGP left the market after the Gambling Commission found it had failed to do due diligence on money laundering or possible criminality of the ownership of these firms.[106]

Rather than shut down all advertising for these companies, who no longer had any UK license, in July 2025, the UK government decided that clubs could still enter into commercial partnerships with unlicensed operators provided they use geo-blocking to stop UK customers from betting with them. You know, the kind of geo-blocking you can get around with a cheap VPN.[107]

France shows that a very different approach is possible. In 2022, French law gave the gambling regulator the power to administratively block and delist illegal gambling sites, bypassing the slow court-based processes that had previously limited enforcement. The result was a significant increase in the speed and scale at which illegal sites could be disrupted. Over the first 18 months of this policy, as many sites were blocked as in the previous 12 years.[108] And France and other European countries are much stricter on advertising from unlicensed gambling firms at European football matches. The message to operators, payment providers and advertisers is clear: operating outside the licensing system involves constant friction.

This "full-court press" is labour-intensive. It requires technical capacity, legal authority and a willingness to annoy businesses that would prefer to be left alone. Moves by unlicensed operators toward crypto-based payments have already weakened the ability of regulators to use traditional banks as chokepoints. While these firms certainly have bank accounts, they are often tucked away in jurisdictions far beyond the reach of domestic law. For a government, the goal of the full-court press is not necessarily 100% elimination – it is about keeping the friction high enough that offshore betting remains a niche activity for those willing to seek it out rather than a mass-market alternative.

There is also a stronger reason for taking enforcement seriously that goes beyond the usual debates about tax and regulation. Unlicensed online gambling operations are often linked to wider criminal ecosystems. These include scam centres, payment laundering networks, and, in some cases, forced labour and human trafficking. Recent reporting has shown how online gambling brands, scam operations, and fraudulent investment schemes often share infrastructure, payment channels, and ownership structures. Tolerating large unlicensed gambling markets is providing cover and cash flow for organised crime.

My own, perhaps cynical, reading is that the current situation in most countries reflects an unfortunate "equilibrium." Licensed operators invoke the threat of unlicensed competition to oppose tighter regulation, affordability checks or higher taxes. Regulators and governments, for their part, emphasise the difficulty of policing offshore operators as a reason to move cautiously. Each side points to the same problem to justify inaction. The result is a system in which enforcement remains weak and regulation is inadequate.

Breaking out of this equilibrium requires treating unlicensed gambling not as an argument against reform, but as a separate policy problem that deserves serious attention in its own right.

CHAPTER 30

Takeaways for Bettors

1. Know Thyself

An ancient Greek proverb, it applies very well to sports betting. Self-delusion and sports betting go hand in hand. Research shows that even when confronted with hard evidence of their past losses, bettors still predict they will break even or win money in the future.

Don't be those guys. Check your record. How much have you staked and how much did you win? You can easily get this information from your accounts. You may have worked hard at it, checking video, factoring in the Expected Threat, figuring you might be the next laptop legend to crack the code of beating the bookmakers. But if the reality is that you tend to lose, for example, 8% on your bets, then Jacob Bernoulli wants to have a word. The Law of Large Numbers is telling you that your strategy is not a winning one.

If that's the case, consider two options. First, ask yourself: is it worth the money you are losing? Does the enjoyment you get from betting make it worthwhile? Maybe you could put that weekly amount aside and take a nice holiday or a few special dinners out? Think about it.

You've thought about it and you want to keep going? Cool. But consider transitioning from an unsuccessful laptop legend to a successful *margin minimiser*. Pick the bets that you know have the lowest margins. We have shown lots of evidence on what this means in practice: Don't bet on longshots and stick to higher-profile events.

This will slow your losses and make your money in the account last longer. Or even perhaps get you the odd year when you win more than you lose. As advice, it's not as sexy as "here's how to make a fortune beating the bookies" but it might be more valuable because it's something you can easily implement.

---

2. Test, Test and Test Again

You have an idea for an approach to betting that might work? Remember that a gut feeling is not a strategy. A good starting point is to check whether your idea would have worked in the past. The evidence in this book shows that it's pretty easy to obtain big datasets of odds and results from past sporting events. Many of the resources used here were free. Others, like The-Odds-API.com, can be obtained for low-cost subscriptions. Collecting odds and results and seeing how a strategy would have done historically isn't complicated coding and, these days, AI tools can help you with the tricky bits. Testing whether a strategy worked in the past can prevent you from finding out the hard way that it doesn't work.

If the evidence does show that it worked in the past, don't be sure that it works now. Other bettors are constantly looking for new strategies, and edges that can be discovered from past data don't necessarily still work. Track how the strategy would work with real-time results and only place real money when it confirms what the historical data showed. If you're using a "Maker" strategy on an exchange, just offer £1 bets and see how that goes before risking greater money.

---

3. Avoid Bookmakers

I know exchanges seem strange to many bettors but if you want to bet and get the best results, they are by far the best option. I've explained them here and even the length of the explanation shows that they are not simple. But you can start by accepting offers to back the team you want – the odds will typically be better than you can get from any bookmaker. And then you can figure out the other options by making small test bets.

You will generally do better by making offers to get your preferred bet at higher odds than those currently available for sure: being a

Maker, not a Taker. You won't always be matched but the data show that the alternative approach of accepting lower odds typically loses money. You pay for the certainty of execution. And remember that Betfair is not the only exchange - you may get better prices at some of its competitors.

---

4. If You Do Use Bookmakers, Avoid Advertised Bets

Maybe you don't want to follow my last recommendation and still want to bet with bookmakers. If you do so and want to lose as little money as possible, then use one simple rule: Do not bet on product lines that bookmakers advertise such as bet builders. Advertising costs money. They only promote these bets because punters lose more on them.

Accas, bet builders and specials are all designed to seem like fun but they carry brutally high margins, partly because the fun comes at a cost and partly because bettors find it hard to understand the underlying probabilities. Cash-out options appeal to people's sensible side - bank the win rather than risk getting nothing - but taking them also worsens your losses over time.

---

5. Be Particularly Careful About In-Play Betting

In-play betting is exciting, but it comes at a cost. The moment the game starts, the odds worsen. And the bad performance that we have documented for longshot bets throughout the book goes into overdrive near the end of games.

You can argue that the evidence we showed for awful performance on late-game longshots reflects a few people who get overly excited, and you can point out we don't know how many people actually took these bets. But the evidence from Betfair, which generally has more sophisticated bettors, shows plenty of real late-game longshot trades that typically deliver terrible losses. Listen to Danny Kahneman and let your System 2 take your betting decisions, slowly and calmly before the game starts.

6. When the Fun Stops, Stop

This is, by now, a cliché in the UK. It was the industry's flagship "safer gambling" message for years until it was discontinued in 2021. The campaign had many critics. Some pointed out the word FUN in the campaign materials had a much bigger font than the rest of the message. Others argued against "fun" being part of any message about problem gambling. The industry has moved on to messages like "Take Time to Think" as well as the generic Ray-Winstone-style "gamble responsibly" lines.

But actually, I think "When the Fun Stops, Stop" was the right message. Betting is a leisure activity. It should be fun. Losing money isn't fun but you can still find value in the activity if you accept that the excitement and distraction from everyday life that it brings makes your net losses worth it. But when it starts to take over your life. When you start chasing losses. When you switch to online casinos because you need the quick hit that gambling brings. That's not fun. And you should stop.

If you've gotten in too deep, it's ok to admit you have a problem. You are by no means alone and many others have gone through it and recovered. There are many resources available now to help. In the UK, you can sign up to GamStop and the betting companies will no longer take your bets. You can also get help by calling the free National Gambling Helpline (0808 8020 133). Similar resources are available in most countries. Even if you're not sure you need them, consider making contact if you have any concerns that you might need help.

Beyond Betting

I hope you can also take something from this book beyond sports betting. Economics might not seem like the obvious lens for understanding the world of betting. But it turns out that the whole sector basically runs on the insights of economics.

This is true when understanding many other things in life. In particular, keep those economics X-ray specs in mind when you make other financial decisions. Ask what you're paying, who sets the terms, and how they get paid.

In betting, the trick is to see how the pricing works, those fine margins that tip things in the bookmaker's favour. In other parts of life, an economist's viewpoint can help you spot how things like fees or unnecessary complexity work against you, helped along by flashy advertising that nudges you towards pricier options. The labels change, but the logic doesn't.

Additional Resources

If you'd like to dig further into the economics of betting markets, including seeing some of the more technical details that I kept out of the book, there are plenty of supporting materials on my website: www.karlwhelan.com. This includes research papers and blog posts with extra material not included in the book.

Lecture notes from a class I have taught on this topic are available at www.karlwhelan.com/BettingMarkets

If you're an instructor and are thinking of using this material for teaching, you can contact me at karl.whelan@ucd.ie.

Acknowledgements

I would like to thank Constantin Bürgi, Vincent Hogan and Bobby Treacy for their helpful suggestions for this book. Thanks also to Brian Woods for catching some errors in an earlier draft. And, of course, I am deeply grateful to Tadgh Hegarty for feedback and for getting me into this whole thing in the first place and to Chris Jepsen for setting us up as a research team.

Notes

[1] For an entertaining guide to the history of British gambling, I recommend Michael Atherton's *Gambling: A Story of Triumph and Disaster*

[2] Some bookies already offered telephone bet services but a click of a button is a lot easier and more anonymous than a phone call.

[3] David Paton, Donald Siegel and Leighton Vaughan Williams (2004). "Taxation and the Demand for Gambling: New Evidence from the United Kingdom," *National Tax Journal, Volume 57,* pages 847–861.

[4] Kit Chellel's article on Benter, *The Gambler Who Cracked the Horse-Racing Code,* is a fantastic read.
https://www.bloomberg.com/news/features/2018-05-03/the-gambler-who-cracked-the-horse-racing-code

[5] Michael Rothschild and Joseph Stiglitz (1976). "Equilibrium in Competitive Insurance Markets: An Essay on the Economics of Imperfect Information," *Quarterly Journal of Economics,* Volume 90, pages 629-649.

[6] Akerlof, George (1970). "The Market for 'Lemons': Quality Uncertainty and the Market Mechanism," *Quarterly Journal of Economics,* Volume 84, pages 488–500.

[7] Michael Spence (1973). "Job Market Signaling," *Quarterly Journal of Economics,* Volume 87, pages 355-379.

[8] Rob Davies's book *Jackpot: How Gambling Conquered Britain,* has a detailed discussion of how stake limits and bans work.

[9] Charles Clotfelter and P. J. Cook. (1991). "Lotteries in the Real World," *Journal of Risk and Uncertainty,* Volume 4, pages 227-232. Also, Sigrid Suetens, Claus Galbo-Jørgensen and Jean-Robert Tyran (2016). "Predicting Lotto Numbers: A Natural Experiment on the Gambler's Fallacy and the Hot-Hand Fallacy," *Journal of the European Economic Association,* Volume 14, pages 584–607.

[10] Matthew Brown, Nick Grasley and Mariana Guido (2025). Do Sports Bettors Need Consumer Protection? Evidence from a Field Experiment. Working paper, Stanford University.
https://papers.ssrn.com/sol3/papers.cfm?abstract_id=5191510

[11] Richard H. Thaler and William T. Ziemba (1988). "Parimutuel Betting Markets: Racetracks and Lotteries," *Journal of Economic Perspectives,* Volume 2, pages 161–174.

[12] Tadgh Hegarty and Karl Whelan (2025). "Estimating Expected Loss Rates in Betting Markets: Theory and Evidence," *Applied Economics.*

[13] You can find this interview at https://users.nber.org/~jwolfers/aboutme/HowJustinWolfersbecameabrightAussieexport.pdf

[14] David Hill (2019). Requiem for a Sports Bettor. https://www.theringer.com/2019/06/05/gambling/sports-betting-bettors-sharps-kicked-out-spanky-william-hill-new-jersey

[15] You calculate the variance of a series by subtracting the average from each number, calculating the square of the subsequent number and then calculating the average of the squares.

[16] This result was in a set of lectures Arrow gave in Helsinki in 1965. They are included in the not-online 1971 book *Essays in the Theory of Risk-Bearing.*

[17] Sarah Nelson, Timothy Edson, Eric Louderback, Matthew Tom, Alessandra Grossman and Debi LaPlante (2021). "Changes to the Playing Field: A Contemporary Study of Actual European Online Sports Betting," *Journal of Behavioral Addictions,* Volume 10, pages 396–411.

[18] Matthew Brown, Nick Grasley and Mariana Guido (2025). Do Sports Bettors Need Consumer Protection? Evidence from a Field Experiment. Working paper, Stanford University.

[19] Matthew Brown, Nick Grasley and Mariana Guido (2025). Do Sports Bettors Need Consumer Protection? Evidence from a Field Experiment. Working paper, Stanford University.

[20] https://www.gamblingcommission.gov.uk/news/article/2024-gambling-survey-for-great-britain-published

[21] This survey can be found at https://www.spotlightsportsgroup.com/sports-betting-news/who-is-the-legal-u-s-sports-bettor/

[22] Tversky had died of cancer in 1996 at the tragically young age of 59. Nobel Prizes are not awarded posthumously.

[23] Lisa Farrell, Edgar Morgenroth and Ian Walker (1999). "A Time-Series Analysis of U.K. Lottery Sales: Long and Short Run Price

Elasticities." *Oxford Bulletin of Economics and Statistics,* Volume 61, pages 513–26.

[24] Melissa Kearney (2005). "State Lotteries and Consumer Behavior" *Journal of Public Economics,* Volume 89, pages 2269–2299.

[25] David Forrest, Robert Simmons and Neil Chesters (2002). "Buying a Dream: Alternative Models of Demand for Lotto," *Economic Inquiry,* Volume 40, pages 485–496.

[26] Thomas Garrett and Russell Sobel (2004). "State Lottery Revenue: The Importance of Game Characteristics," *Public Finance Review,* Volume 32, pages 313-330.

[27] The person that bets on Chelsea with $p = 0.69$ has an expected payout rate that rounds to 1.00 at two digits but is actually slightly greater than 1.

[28] Richard Griffith (1949). "Odds Adjustments by American Horse-Race Bettors," *American Journal of Psychology,* Volume 62, pages 290-294.

[29] Thaler's book about his career, *Misbehaving: The Making of Behavioral Economics,* is an excellent read.

[30] Richard Quandt (1986). "Betting and Equilibrium," *Quarterly Journal of Economics,* Volume 101, pages 201-208.

[31] Mukhtar Ali (1977). "Probability and Utility Estimates for Racetrack Bettors," *Journal of Political Economy,* Volume 85, pages 803-815.

[32] This meant solving two equations for two variables to get the longshot odds and again to get the favourite odds. Anyone interested can consult the paper that does this algebra. It is available open access. Karl Whelan (2024). "Risk Aversion and Favourite-Longshot Bias in a Competitive Fixed-Odds Betting Market", *Economica,* Volume 91, pages 188-209.

[33] This interview is in Rob Miech's book *Sports Betting for Winners.*

[34] Steven Levitt (2004). ``Why Are Gambling Markets Organised So Differently From Financial Markets?," *Economic Journal,* Volume 114, pages 223-246.

[35] For some reason, Koleman's paper was never published in an academic journal.

[36] Raphael Flepp, Stephan Nüesch and Egon Franck (2014). "Does Bettor Sentiment Affect Bookmaker Pricing?" *Journal of Sports Economics,* Volume 17, pages 3-11.

[37] Sanford Grossman and Joseph Stiglitz (1980), "On the Impossibility of Informationally Efficient Markets," *American Economic Review,* Volume 70, pages 393-408.

[38] https://www.kambi.com/news-insights/price-right-or-least-it-should-be/

[39] The studies are Behavioural Insights Team (2021). Gambling Behaviour: What Can Bank Transaction Data Tell Us? A Feasibility Study. Available at https://www.bi.team/wp-content/uploads/2021/07/Patterns-of-Play-BIT-HSBC-report-final-June-4th-2021.pdf
and Kasra Ghaharian, Jay Peterson, Mana Azizsoltani, Richard J. Young & Eric R. Louderback (2025). "Across the Bettor-Verse: An Open Banking Perspective on Gambling in the United Kingdom," *Journal of Gambling Studies,* Volume 41, pages 1419-1436.

[40] The evidence on the average number of sportsbooks being two is an S&P Global study available at
https://www.spglobal.com/market-intelligence/en/news-insights/research/who-are-americas-sports-bettors
The evidence on only 31% of bettors shopping around for odds is a Pickswise/Beacon Research survey
https://www.spotlightsportsgroup.com/sports-betting-news/who-is-the-legal-u-s-sports-bettor/

[41] Maurizio Montone (2021). "Optimal Pricing in the Online Betting Market," *Journal of Economic Behavior and Organization,* Volume 186, pages 344-363.

[42] This formula is from Tadgh Hegarty and Karl Whelan (2026). "Market Structure and Prices in Online Betting Markets: Theory and Evidence", *Oxford Economic Papers,* Volume 78, pages 90-113.

[43] The uniform-distribution assumption for beliefs is, of course, a simplification of a more complicated reality. But you can solve the model with alternative specifications such as a Normal distribution and the results turn out to be very similar to those reported here.

[44] Sebastian Braun and Michael Kvasnicka (2013). "National Sentiment and Economic Behavior: Evidence From Online Betting on European Football," *Journal of Sports Economics,* Volume 14, pages 45-64.

[45] Vanessa Cashmore, Neil Coster, David Forrest, Ian McHale, Babatunde Buraimo (2022). "Female Jockeys - What Are the Odds?"

Journal of Economic Behavior and Organization, Volume 202, pages 703-713. Alasdair Brown and Fuyu Yang (2015). "Does Society Underestimate Women? Evidence from Performance of Female Jockeys in Horse Racing," *Journal of Economic Behavior and Organization,* Volume 111, pages 106-118.

[46] Deniz Igan, Marcelo Pinheiro and John Smith (2015). "A Study of a Market Anomaly: "White Men Can't Jump" but Would You Bet on It?" *Journal of Economic Behavior and Organization,* Volume 113, pages 13-25.

[47] Anyone interested in how this optimal takeout was derived can find it at https://www.karlwhelan.com/Papers/Optimal-PM.pdf

[48] Daniel Kahneman, Jack Knetsch and Richard Thaler (1986). "Fairness As a Constraint on Profits," *American Economic Review,* Volume 76, pages 728-741.

[49] This model can be found in an appendix to Tadgh Hegarty and Karl Whelan (2026). "Market Structure and Prices in Online Betting Markets: Theory and Evidence", *Oxford Economic Papers,* Volume 78, pages 90-113. An ungated version is available at https://www.karlwhelan.com/Papers/OEP.pdf

[50] Lyn Pankoff (1968). "Market Efficiency and Football Betting," *Journal of Business,* Volume 41, pages 203-214.

[51] Peter Pope and David Peel (1989). "Information, Prices and Efficiency in a Fixed-Odds Betting Market," *Economica,* Volume 56, pages 323-341.

[52] Patrick J. Ferguson and Matthew Pinnuck (2022). "Superstar Productivity and Pay: Evidence from the Australian Football League," *Economic Record,* Volume 98, pages 166-190.

[53] Marius Ötting, Christian Deutscher, Carl Singleton and Luca De Angelis (2025). "Betting on Momentum in Contests", *Economic Inquiry.*

[54] Tadgh Hegarty and Karl Whelan (2023). "The Wisdom of No Crowds: The Reaction of Betting Markets to Lockdown Football Games," *Journal of Prediction Markets,* Volume 17, pages 123-138.

[55] J. James Reade, Dominik Schreyer and Carl Singleton (2020). Echoes: what happens when football is played behind closed doors?

[56] Technically, The-Odds-API.com provide snapshots every 5 minutes. So, what we really have is the odds from the closest snapshot looking back from 10 minutes before the event starts. They

could be as early as 15 minutes before start time.

[57] This is shown in Tadgh Hegarty and Karl Whelan (2025). "Estimating Expected Loss Rates in Betting Markets: Theory and Evidence," *Applied Economics.*

[58] Being internally consistent requires acknowledging that we have already shown that normalised probabilities are flawed. But we did not come up with a simple way of fixing them. Also, all we are doing here is trying to roughly sort bets by their likelihood of winning. Actual win rates may not move one-for-one with normalised probabilities, but they do increase with them, so this kind of grouping exercise is fine.

[59] This research was described in detail in Tadgh Hegarty and Karl Whelan (2026). "Market Structure and Prices in Online Betting Markets: Theory and Evidence", *Oxford Economic Papers,* Volume 78, pages 90-113.

[60] Details can be found in Tadgh Hegarty and Karl Whelan (2025). "Forecasting Football Matches with Betting Odds: A Tale of Two Markets," *International Journal of Forecasting,* Volume 41, pages 803-820

[61] This research was published as Tadgh Hegarty and Karl Whelan (2024). "Returns on Complex Bets: Evidence from Asian Handicap Betting on Football," *Review of Behavioural Finance,* Volume 16, pages 904-924.

[62] Hyun Song Shin (1991). "Optimal Betting Odds Against Insider Traders," *Economic Journal,* Volume 101, pages 1179–1185.

[63] The research demonstrating this point is published as Karl Whelan (2025). "How Does Inside Information Affect Sports Betting Odds?" *Scottish Journal of Political Economy,* Volume 72, Issue 5.

[64] Hyun Song Shin (1992). "Measuring the Incidence of Insider Trading in a Market for State-Contingent Claims," *Economic Journal,* Volume 103, pages 1141-1153.

[65] https://flutter.com/media/s44lcmmb/flutter-uk-wrapper-10k_fnl.pdf

[66] This research was published as: Karl Whelan (2025). "On Estimates of Insider Trading in Sports Betting," *The Manchester School,* Volume 93, pages 217-229.

[67] Justin Wolfers (2006). "Point Shaving: Corruption in NCAA Basketball," *American Economic Review,* May, pages 279-283.

[68] Richard Borghesi and William Dare (2009). "A Test of the Widespread-Point-Shaving Theory," *Finance Research Letters,* Volume 6, pages 115-121.

[69] Richard Borghesi (2008). "Widespread Corruption in Sports Gambling: Fact or Fiction?" *Southern Economic Journal,* Volume 74, pages 1063-1069.

[70] Technically, I chose w to minimise the sum of squared errors from subtracting the actual implied margin for each race from the model's prediction.

[71] You can find the first part of this interview at https://www.youtube.com/watch?v=8VpaC-4qYQY

[72] Steve Sharman, Theodore Piper, Ellen McGrane and Philip W. S. Newall (2023): "Gambling Adverts in Live TV coverage of the Qatar 2022 FIFA Men's World Cup," *Addiction Research & Theory,* Volume 32.

[73] Benjamin Enke and Cassidy Shubatt (2024). Quantifying Lottery Choice Complexity. https://www.nber.org/papers/w31677

[74] These figures are available at https://www.nj.gov/oag/ge/docs/Financials/PressRelease2025/December2025.pdf

[75] Richard Thaler (1985). "Mental Accounting and Consumer Choice," *Marketing Science,* Vol. 4, pages 199-214.

[76] You can find my paper "The Economics of Free Bets" at www.karlwhelan.com/Papers/FreeBets.pdf

[77] The details are in my paper "The Economics of Odds Boosts" at https://www.karlwhelan.com/Papers/Boosts.pdf

[78] https://www.vice.com/en/article/i-tried-matched-betting-to-see-how-much-easy-money-i-could-make/

[79] This video is a short and simple guide to installing Python and Microsoft VS Code. That's all I needed to run this code. https://www.youtube.com/watch?v=6i3e-j3wSf0&t=24s

[80] Diarmaid O'Ceallaigh, Shane Timmons, Deirdre Robertson and Peter Lunn (2025). "Effects of Inducements on Sports Gambling and Decision-Errors: An Experimental Study," *Journal of Behavioral Addictions,* Volume 14, pages 959-971.

[81] https://gr8.tech/blog/cashout-in-betting-one-more-revenue-source-for-operators/

[82] Ong George Ngieng et al (2026). "Greater Impulsivity is Associated with a Reduced Propensity to Cash Out of Bets." *Addictive Behaviors Reports,* Volume 23.

[83] Daniel Bennett et al (2024). "People Place Larger Bets When Risky Choices Provide a Postbet Option to Cash Out," *Psychological Science,* Volume 35, pages 1231-1245.

[84] Elizabeth Killick and Mark Griffiths (2020). "Why Do Individuals Engage in In-Play Sports Betting? A Qualitative Interview Study," *Journal of Gambling Studies,* Volume 37, pages 221-240. Sally Melissa Gainsbury, Brett Abarbanel and Alex Blaszczynski (2020). "The Relationship Between In-Play Betting and Gambling Problems in an Australian Context of Prohibited Online In-Play Betting." *Frontiers in Psychology.*

[85] https://www.youtube.com/watch?v=_4f52yoExJE

[86] These results are from my paper "Agreeing to Disagree: The Economics of Betting Exchanges", available at https://www.ucd.ie/economics/t4media/WP2025_22.pdf

[87] I am grateful to Neil Thomas from Betfair for making this data available free for research purposes.

[88] The long track record requirement can perhaps be balanced against the public reputation of a tipster. For example, Ted Knutson, who founded Statsbomb, worked at Pinnacle and has been head of sports analytics for some well-known clubs, runs a tip service called Variance Betting. Pretty clearly, Ted has exceptional credibility as an expert on football and betting. And, at least at the time of writing, you would have made a profit from following his tips.

[89] Eugene Fama and Kenneth French (2010). "Luck versus Skill in the Cross-Section of Mutual Fund Returns," *Journal of Finance,* Volume 65, pages 1915-1947. Another nice paper on this topic is Keith Cuthbertson, Dirk Nitzsche and Niall O'Sullivan (2008). "UK Mutual Fund Performance: Skill or Luck?" *Journal of Empirical Finance,* Volume 15, pages 613-634.

[90] This evidence is in Joe's 2012 book, *How to Find a Black Cat in a Coal Cellar: The Truth About Sports Tipsters.*

[91] A good paper on this topic is Savva Shanaev and Binam Ghimire (2021). "Efficient Scholars: Academic Attention and the Disappearance of Anomalies," *European Journal of Finance,* Volume 27, pages 278-304

[92] You can find the calculations that show this in my paper Ruin Probabilities for Strategies with Asymmetric Risk, available at https://www.karlwhelan.com/Papers/Ruin.pdf

[93] I showed this is my 2025 paper "On Optimal Betting Strategies with Multiple Mutually Exclusive Outcomes," *Bulletin of Economic Research,* Volume 77, pages 67-85.

[94] You can find details on this in my paper "The Parlay Puzzle: Expected Utility and Multi-Leg Betting"
www.karlwhelan.com/Papers/Parlays.pdf

[95] The theorem was first proved in Stewart Ethier and Simon Tavaré (1983). "The Proportional Bettor's Return on Investment," *Journal of Applied Probability,* Volume 20, pages 563-573. This is a forbiddingly difficult paper, so I have worked out a less difficult proof in my paper Kelly Strategies and the Return on Capital Deployed, available at https://www.karlwhelan.com/Papers/KellyROI.pdf

[96] Naomi Muggleton et al (2021). "The Association Between Gambling and Financial, Social and Health Outcomes in Big Financial Data," *Nature Human Behavior,* Volume 5, pages 319-326.

[97] Scott Baker, Justin Balthrop, Mark Johnson, Jason Kotter and Kevin Pisciotta (2024). Gambling Away Stability: Sports Betting's Impact on Vulnerable Households.
https://www.nber.org/papers/w33108

[98] https://www.gamblingcommission.gov.uk/news/article/2024-gambling-survey-for-great-britain-published

[99] Arnab Bhattacharjee, Peter Dolton, Max Mosley and Adrian Pabst (2023). The Fiscal Costs and Benefits of Problem Gambling: Towards Better Estimates, NIESR.
https://niesr.ac.uk/publications/fiscal-costs-benefits-problem-gambling

[100] Rob Davies's book *Jackpot: How Gambling Conquered Britain,* has some excellent reporting on gambling addiction in the UK and how bookmakers design products that foster addiction.

[101] David Forrest and Ian McHale (2025). "The Dependence of Online Gambling Businesses on High-Spending Customers: Quantification and Implications," *Journal of Gambling Studies,* Volume 41, pages 693–714.

[102] Philip Newall (2018). "Dark Nudges in Gambling," *Addiction Research and Theory*, Volume 27, pages 65-67.

[103] The UK Gambling Commission's discussion of the single customer view can be found at https://www.gamblingcommission.gov.uk/licensees-and-businesses/guide/page/single-consumer-view

[104] The story goes that over dinner in September 1974 with Wall Street Journal editor Jude Wanniski and Nixon administration officials Dick Cheney and Donald Rumsfeld (whatever happened to those guys ...) economist Arthur Laffer sketched out the curve on a napkin.

[105] See www.karlwhelan.com/Papers/BettingTax.pdf

[106] https://www.gamblingcommission.gov.uk/news/article/tgp-europe-leaves-gb-market-following-commission-investigation

[107] See this article by Phillipe Auclair for details. https://josimarfootball.com/2026/01/13/same-old-same-old/

[108] https://www.lexology.com/library/detail.aspx?g=2d478285-1eb5-4806-bcca-9eddbb84f70f

www.ingramcontent.com/pod-product-compliance
Lightning Source LLC
LaVergne TN
LVHW022024051126
851858LV00003B/34